Rediscovering America

Exploring the Small Towns of

Virginia
& Maryland

Mary & Bill Burnham

HUNTER

HUNTER PUBLISHING, INC.
130 Campus Drive
Edison, NJ 08818-7816
☎ 732-225-1900 / 800-255-0343 / fax 732-417-1744
www.hunterpublishing.com
E-mail: comments@hunterpublishing.com

IN CANADA:
Ulysses Travel Publications
4176 Saint-Denis, Montréal, Québec
Canada H2W 2M5
☎ 514-843-9882 ext. 2232 / fax 514-843-9448

IN THE UNITED KINGDOM:
Windsor Books International
The Boundary, Wheatley Road, Garsington
Oxford, OX44 9EJ England
☎ 01865-361122 / fax 01865-361133

ISBN 1-58843-319-6
© 2003 Mary & Bill Burnham

Cover: *Fifes and Drums at Yorktown, Virginia*,
Courtesy of the York County Public Information Office
Back cover: *Street Scene in Little Washington, Virginia*;
photo by Mary Burnham
Maps by Lissa K. Dailey, © 2003 Hunter Publishing, Inc.
Index by Nancy Wolff

Acknowledgments

We'd like to thank our publisher, Michael Hunter, for the opportunity to write this book, and for giving us carte blanche to present it in our own style and voice. Thanks also to our editor, Lissa Dailey, for her attention to detail on all aspects of this book.

We thank our parents for all their support. Special thanks to Mary's mom, Fran Kubick, for driving us around the Eastern Shore, showing us her favorite places.

There are numerous people in every small town we visited who provided everything from lodging to historical insight to the latest local gossip. To every tourism director, innkeeper, historian, shop owner — even the proverbial man or woman on the street — who aided our discoveries, thank you for sharing what you love best about your small towns.

To everyone who purchases this book – we thank you, most of all!

Happy trails,

Mary and Bill Burnham
Gloucester, Virginia

About the Authors

Bill and Mary Burnham, of Goucester, Virginia, met as small-town newspaper reporters a decade ago. Since then they've blended their love of the outdoors and travel with their writing and photography skills into a dual freelance career. They contribute to several regional and national magazines and newspapers, and tour the Commonwealth giving travel-related outdoor talks and slide shows. Other books by the Burnhams include *The Virginia Handbook, 2nd Edition* (with Blair Howard), by Hunter Publishing, and *Hike America Virginia*, The Globe Pequot Press.

We welcome your comments, suggestions and even corrections. If we left out your absolute favorite town, restaurant or inn, please contact us, and we may include it in a future edition. Send e-mail to comments@hunterpublishing.com, or visit our Web page, www.BurnhamInk.com, where you can find out where our writing adventures are taking us next!

Dedication

In memory of Ellsworth Buck, who gave his granddaughter a love of writing, photography and travel.

Contents

Contents

MAPS

Introduction

What is it about small towns? Do they remind us of where we grew up, or perhaps where we wish we had? Bill and I both grew up in small towns. We met in a small town, we now live in one in Virginia, and we've spent most of our 10 years together exploring places where we can avoid crowds. Our home in Gloucester, Virginia, is a place where people wave as they pass one another on back roads. The weekly newspaper might have a photograph of a local kid with the big fish he caught, or a farewell letter to the friendly postmaster.

Our town is just one example of the many where the values that shape us as individuals and a nation are on daily display. The hardware store and bookstore may still be locally owned; the library has a book sale on the porch (with payment on the honor system); the pharmacy may still have a soda fountain. You may still be able buy groceries, shoes, office supplies and even furniture on Main Street, without patronizing the new, nationally owned "big box" stores. People in small towns appreciate their roots. Old buildings are restored and historic sites preserved as museums or visitors centers. Cottage industries in pottery, quilting, woodworking or artistry support a local populace and attract visitors.

In writing this book, we carefully selected and visited each town for you, the reader. We sought out people, places, and history that shape a unique character. There are fishing villages where most people still derive their livelihood from the waters of the Atlantic and Chesapeake Bay, old railroad towns, college towns alive with music and art scenes, and crossroads rich with Colonial and Civil War history. Of the nearly 60 towns included in this book, most are within a few hours' drive of the metropolitan areas of Baltimore, Washington DC, Richmond or Hampton Roads.

While most towns we've included in the book have populations of fewer than 25,000 people (most far less), we made sure the amenities required by urban or sophisticated travelers were available. Each town typically has at least one quaint bed & breakfast or historic inn. Since we like to travel with our dog, we tried to include at least one pet-friendly lodging for each area as well. There is a good selection of locally owned and regionally influenced restaurants, and enough activities to satisfy the on-the-go traveler for a weekend or longer. Interesting local customs and correct pronunciation of unusual place names are also included.

Also included are some of the best outdoor recreation opportunities available just minutes outside the town centers. We gladly accept the label of "outdoor nuts." We love hiking and camping in the mountains of the mid-Atlantic region, walking along unspoiled beaches, or paddling ocean, bay and rivers, and photographing everything from breathtaking panoramas to tiny wildflowers.

These getaways are designed for the time-stressed traveler, the individual, couple or family that has only a weekend to spare, without traveling too far from home. Whether discovering a town for the first time, or rediscovering a much-visited one, we hope these pages will help take you far away from your regular routine in just a few hours.

Virginia

In 2007, the Commonwealth of Virginia will commemorate the 400th anniversary of America's first permanent English settlement. Virginia arguably has more Colonial and Civil War history to share than any other state. There is natural beauty as well, along sparkling white sand beaches, the rich waters of the Chesapeake Bay, or the spectacular mountain scenery of the Blue Ridge and the Appalachians. Virginia's small towns combine the best of both history and natural beauty, changing with the times, but retaining their own authentic and special quality.

For general travel information, contact the **Virginia Tourism Corporation**, ☎ 800-VISIT-VA, www.virginia.org, which also has a toll-free bed & breakfast reservation line: ☎ 800-934-9184. Staffed welcome centers are located where all major roads enter the state, and are open daily, 8:30am-5pm.

Maryland

George Calvert, the first Lord Baltimore, won Maryland in a game of cards with King Charles I in 1632. The Potomac River as its southern border gave the state its unique shape and a prosperous seafood industry. Its decidedly Catholic heritage, as opposed to Protestant Virginia, is only the tip of how these neighbor states differ. There is character packed into the old fishing and farming towns of the Eastern Shore, or the railroad and logging towns of the mountain regions. Fast-changing urban regions around Baltimore and bordering the nation's capital seem to melt away as the countryside moves toward the lowlands of the Chesapeake Bay.

For more information, contact the **Maryland Office of Tourism Development**, ☎ 877-333-4455, www.mdisfun.org.

Maryland's commercial airport is **Baltimore/Washington International** (BWI), ☎ 410-859-7111, www.bwiairport.com.

Accommodations

Throughout the book we have listed accommodations that we thought were comfortable, noteworthy, or a good value. To assist you in planning your trip, we have shown price ranges according to the following key. Rates are for one night, based on double occupancy.

$.	Under $75
$$	$76-$125
$$$	$126-$175
$$$$.	Over $176

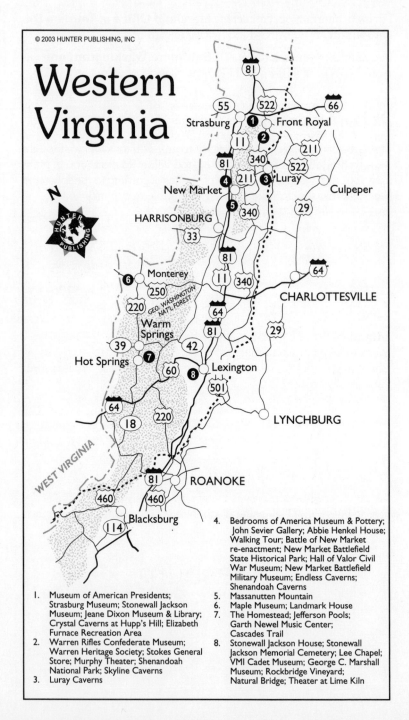

© 2003 HUNTER PUBLISHING, INC

Western Virginia

N
HUNTER PUBLISHING

Strasburg
Front Royal
New Market
HARRISONBURG
Monterey
GEO. WASHINGTON NAT'L FOREST
Warm Springs
Hot Springs
Lexington
Luray
Culpeper
CHARLOTTESVILLE
LYNCHBURG
ROANOKE
Blacksburg
WEST VIRGINIA

1. Museum of American Presidents; Strasburg Museum; Stonewall Jackson Museum; Jeane Dixon Museum & Library; Crystal Caverns at Hupp's Hill; Elizabeth Furnace Recreation Area
2. Warren Rifles Confederate Museum; Warren Heritage Society; Stokes General Store; Murphy Theater; Shenandoah National Park; Skyline Caverns
3. Luray Caverns

4. Bedrooms of America Museum & Pottery; John Sevier Gallery; Abbie Henkel House; Walking Tour; Battle of New Market re-enactment; New Market Battlefield State Historical Park; Hall of Valor Civil War Museum; New Market Battlefield Military Museum; Endless Caverns; Shenandoah Caverns
5. Massanutten Mountain
6. Maple Museum; Landmark House
7. The Homestead; Jefferson Pools; Garth Newel Music Center; Cascades Trail
8. Stonewall Jackson House; Stonewall Jackson Memorial Cemetery; Lee Chapel; VMI Cadet Museum; George C. Marshall Museum; Rockbridge Vineyard; Natural Bridge; Theater at Lime Kiln

Western Virginia

Mineral springs and cooler climes have drawn vacationers to the resorts of the Shenandoah Valley and Blue Ridge for more than a century. Civil War campaigns raged up and down the valley, leaving nearly every small town with a tale to tell and a battlefield nearby. Today's visitors come searching for antique treasures, to explore deep caverns, and view the waterfalls and vistas of Shenandoah National Park.

THE TOWNS
❈ Strasburg
❈ Front Royal
❈ New Market
❈ Monterey
❈ Blue Grass
❈ Hot Springs & Warm Springs
❈ Lexington

Getting Here

Interstate 81 and the **Blue Ridge Parkway** run through the heart of Western Virginia along the Blue Ridge, providing easy access to the Shenandoah region. Travelers arriving by air generally use **Roanoke Regional Airport**, ☎ 540-362-1999.

Regional Information

Shenandoah Valley Visitors Center, I-81, Exit 264, New Market, ☎ 877-Visit-SV, www.shenandoah.org.

Western Highlands Travel Council, 241 W. Main Street, Covington, ☎ 540-962-2178, www.alleghanyhighlands.com.

Strasburg

Strolling down Holliday Street at twilight after a fine dinner at the Hotel Strasburg, I'm overcome by the scents of spring: fresh-cut grass, wisteria climbing a porch trellis, honeysuckle intruding into a hedge. In the approaching darkness, lights shine from inside Victorian-era houses. Cars start to leave the nearby high school as a ball game lets out.

Around Town

As with many small towns, walking is the best way to appreciate Strasburg. Only on foot can you discover the old-fashioned soda fountain at the pharmacy or the honor system book sale on the library's front porch. A common sight is a tractor trundling through the business district at about 15 mph. At **People's Drug Store** you browse a selection of the famous Strasburg pottery, then have a snow cone at the old-fashioned soda counter. At **Artz Hardware** you can send a telegram, ship your purchases home, get a hunting or fishing license and, of course, buy hardware.

Strasburg's self-guided walking tour has 34 stops noting sites of early potteries and the fascinating former uses of existing buildings. Where a Texaco Station now stands, a federal colonel returning from the Battle of Newmarket drew his revolver and committeed suicide. Union general Philip Sheridan left his linen sheets stamped "USA" when he stayed at the Massanutten Hotel (stop #10 on the tour). In time they were cut up and embroidered to make tablemats. Today the building houses the **Hi-Neighbor Restaurant**, a favorite lunch place with the locals. The town has a rare diversity of architectural styles and periods spanning two centuries. Several present-day buildings have clapboards over the original logs.

Strasburg History

German settlers first knew the settlement as Stony Lick, then Staufferstadt, and finally Strasburg, when it was established as a town in 1761. For the period of the French and Indian War, citizens of this frontier outpost suffered raids and death at the hands of French-allied Indians. Later, the countryside saw Confederates under command of Thomas J. "Stonewall" Jackson defeat Northern troops twice in 1862. From the top of Signal Knob, the striking mountain that rises steeply southeast of town, Jackson's famous mapmaker, Jedediah Hotchkiss, gained a bird's-eye view that aided his cartography. It's said he etched his initials in the rocks somewhere on the mountaintop.

First as a station on the Great Wagon Road, then as a railroad depot, Strasburg prospered as a center of trade, especially in the making of pottery. Production of folk pottery began in the 1760s and continues today in the form of the **Shenandoah Potters Guild**, whose members sell their work through local merchants. The nickname "Pot Town" began to stick after the Civil War due to the volume being produced. **The Bell Pottery company** (1833-1908) produced some of the most sought-after pottery in the country, which it still is today, with rare pieces bringing values in the five figures.

By 1900, Strasburg was served by two railroads and was a social hub for locals and travelers. It still is, for those lucky enough to get off I-81, which runs parallel to Route 11 (called King Street in town). Besides Pot Town, it's also known as the "Antiques Capital of Virginia," largely due to the **Great Strasburg Antiques Emporium**. With 1.4 acres of antiques and more than 100 dealers under one roof, it's one of Virginia's largest antiques stores (☎ 540-465-3711, 160 N. Massanutten Street, www.waysideofva.com/emporium/).

Western Virginia

★ LOCAL HISTORY

German was the predominant language in early Strasburg. From 1820 to the 1840s St. Paul's Lutheran Church had two congregations, one English-speaking and the other clinging to German. Several of the town's churches were used as hospitals during the Civil War; 137 unknown Confederate soldiers are buried behind the Presbyterian Church on High Street.

Attractions

The Museum of American Presidents displays Presidential memorabilia privately collected over a 60-year period. A children's area has hands-on activities, costumes to try on and toys. Leo Bernstein, a local entrepreneur and history buff, has collected autographs from half the signers of the Declaration of Independence and most of our presidents. Open daily, 10am-5pm, May-October; during the rest of the year, open Friday-Sunday, 10am-5pm. $3 adults; $2 children ages six and older and for seniors (130 N. Massanutten Street, ☎ 540-465-5999, www.waysideofva.com/presidents/).

The **Strasburg Museum** is housed in an 1891 pottery factory, which served as a train depot until 1970 when the museum was established. It displays the wares of potters, farmers, coopers, blacksmiths and some railroad, Indian and Civil War relics. Open May through October, daily, 10am-4pm (East King Street, ☎ 540-465-3175).

The **Stonewall Jackson Museum** at Hupp's Hill displays weapons, documents and uniforms from his 1862 Valley Campaign, a period in which his troops inflicted heavy casualties on Union forces despite being outnumbered. Within a few miles of Strasburg are Civil War battlefields at Cedar Creek, Toms Brook, Fisher's Hill and Hupp's Hill. Open daily, 10am-5pm; closed major holidays. Adults, $3; children ages six and over, $2 (Route 11, ☎ 540-465-5884, www.waysideofva.com/stonewalljackson).

> ★ DID YOU KNOW?
>
> Stonewall Jackson captured enemy train engines in Martinsburg, West Virginia, and pulled them by horse to return them to the rails in Strasburg. From there they were sent south for the Confederate cause.

The **Jeane Dixon Museum & Library** tells the story of the 20th-century psychic. Tours at 10am and 2pm, Friday-Sunday, May-October (132 N. Massanutten Street, ☎ 540-465-5884, www.waysideofva.com/jdm).

Crystal Caverns at Hupp's Hill, a half-mile north of Strasburg, is one of the oldest documented commercial caves in Virginia. Jeane Dixon, one-time psychic to US presidents, visited Crystal Caverns to meditate and rejuvenate her powers. Open daily, 10am-5pm. Admission $8 adults; $6 children and seniors; includes entrance to the Stonewall Jackson Museum (☎ 540-465-5884, www.waysideofva.com/crystalcaverns).

Recreation

Iron ore production was an early and successful industry throughout western Virginia thanks to ore deposits. Learn more about this at **Elizabeth Furnace Recreation Area**, which holds ruins of iron works that operated here until the Civil War, when Union forces destroyed them. It is now part of the **Lee Ranger District** of the George Washington National Forest (☎ 540-984-4101). Trails radiate from the campground (30 sites) and are popular with mountain bikers and hikers. The Pig Iron Trail is a short (.2 mile) interpretive trail that explains how the furnace produced pig iron (the term refers not to livestock, but to the molded ore ingots). The Charcoal Trail (.5 mile) explains how trees were burned to make charcoal fuel on which furnaces ran. Those with more time (and sturdy shoes) can take a 10.2-mile round-trip hike up the Signal Knob Trail. The steep, strenuous climb ends with a commanding view of Strasburg and the entire "lower valley."

Dining

At the **Hotel Strasburg,** choose your seat from an array of antique tables and chairs, set with vintage china. Virginia products like ham and peanuts are used in dishes, and Virginia wines from local wineries are served with dinner. Serves lunch and dinner daily, breakfast on Saturday and brunch Sunday. The Depot Lounge, a pub decorated with railroad memorabilia, Tiffany-style lamps and stained-glass windows, serves lighter fare (213 S. Holliday Street, ☎ 800-348-8327, www.shenandoah.org/thehotel).

There are several restaurants on the main drag, King Street, including **Sharon's Deli** for a quick bite (☎ 540-465-4900), and **Cristina's Mexican Restaurant,** owned by Mexicans who serve authentic cuisine from their home country (☎ 540-465-5300). Also on King Street are the **Hi-Neighbor Restaurant,** locally famous for its country cooking menu items like scrapple and puddin' meat, serving breakfast and lunch daily, with dinner Monday-Friday (☎ 540-465-9987), and **The Hungry Dog Café,** serving fabulous home-cooked BBQ and homemade cole slaw. They serve lunch and dinner daily, and Saturday nights feature live music (☎ 540-465-5500).

The Old Mill Restaurant offers casual, fine dining in the wonderful atmosphere of a renovated mill on Route 11. It's open for dinner Friday through Sunday only (☎ 540-465-5590).

The Daily Grind is a coffee shop that does light breakfasts and lunches; their homemade cheesecake melts in your mouth. Open 7am to 8pm daily (160 North Massanutten Street, ☎ 540-465-8078).

On Shopping Center Road, there's **Ciro's Pizza** (☎ 540-465-5125), and **Great Wall** Chinese restaurant (☎ 540-465-8336). **Fox's Pizza & Chicken** is at 289 N. Massanutten Street (☎ 540-465-3251).

Western Virginia

Lodging

 Hotel Strasburg is an 1890 Victorian hotel within walking distance of everything in town. The former hospital is now outfitted as a Victorian hotel with all the amenities: restaurant, Victorian pub, and comfortable beds piled high with quilts. Some have bathrooms with deep claw-foot tubs; others with whirlpool jetted baths. The 29 rooms, dining rooms, lobby and Victorian pub are all furnished with antiques, many from the Strasburg Emporium and for sale. No extra charge for pets, but please call ahead (213 S. Holliday Street, ☎ 800-348-8327, www.shenandoah.org/thehotel, $$).

The Hyde Away Bed & Breakfast is a remodeled Victorian with wicker chairs on the front porch. Guests are greeted with English Tea in the parlor and fresh flowers in their rooms. In the morning, coffee and tea are served upstairs before a full breakfast in the dining room. The hosts grew up in the hospitality business: Maggie Hyde was raised in her father's hotel in Australia, and John Hyde in his family's famous Purefoy Hotel in Talladega, Alabama (362 W. King St., ☎ 540-465-8680, www.HydeAwayBandB.com, $$).

Out on Old Valley Pike are the **Budget Inn**, which takes pets (☎ 540-465-5298, $); and **Valley View Motel** (☎ 540-465-8510, $).

Information

Strasburg Chamber of Commerce, ☎ 540-465-3187, www.strasburgva.com.

Event

Mayfest, held the second weekend in May, brings crafters and a parade to the streets of Strasburg. For information, contact the chamber of commerce, ☎ 540-465-3187, www.strasburgva.com.

Front Royal

Our friend's grandfather moved his family to Front Royal from Philadelphia more than 50 years ago. Now 92 years old, he doesn't have time to explain all the reasons why he loves it so, except that "it's God's country," as anyone with two eyes can plainly see for themselves.

Surrounded by the Massanutten range and the Blue Ridge, Front Royal is the northern entranceway for Skyline Drive and Shenandoah National Park. It began as a frontier settlement at the crossing of trails, like many old Virginia towns. In this case, trails from Manassas and Chester Gaps met at the foot of the Blue Ridge near the mouth of Happy Creek, then continued on as one for half a mile, giving Front Royal a distinctive Y shape.

The city is still a major crossroads, now of modern motor trails, interstates 81 and 66. From Washington DC it's a scant 40 minutes on I-66, the fast lane to God's country.

In the beginning, many referred to Front Royal as Helltown, for all the raucous doings a trail town can muster, but others, probably the more devout, called it Lehewtown, in honor of an early French Huguenot settler. The present name came about because of a huge oak – the royal tree of England – at the joining of Chester and Main Streets today. During colonial times the militia-in-training were told to "front the royal oak," meaning salute the tree. Hence, the town's name, as well as Royal Oak Tavern, Royal Oak Bookshop, Royal Oak Computers... you get the gist.

Around Town

The first railroad into the Shenandoah Valley made its grand entrance by Manassas Gap and Front Royal on Oct. 10, 1854. Even though passenger service ended in 1946, the railroad legacy is clearly visible in the form of the historic train station at 414 E. Main Street. Restored in the 1980s, it now houses the **Front Royal Visitors Center** (☎ 800-338-2576, www.front-royal.va.us). Next to it is a caboose donated by the Norfolk and Southern Railway Company that rests on some original tracks.

The train station is the starting and ending point for a self-guided walking tour. There's plenty of parking adjacent at the Village Commons (you can't miss the gazebo), which is where the Royal Oak stood.

The one-mile tour has 34 stops, primarily on Chester and Main streets. Remember that Y shape of the original settlement? This tour more or less outlines it, with Main Street approximately where the trail to Manassas Gap was, and Chester Street being the original road linking the Shenandoah Valley over the Blue Ridge via Chester Gap. Named for Thomas Chester, the early entrepreneur who started a ferry across the Shenandoah River in 1736, the street became home to the leading families in the area and has 17 historic buildings remaining. One is the **Chester House Bed & Breakfast** (stop #10, see page 14). Stop #14 is **Cozy Corner** (64 Chester Street), the Victorian home the Buck family built when they were forced to sell their ancestral home, Bel Air. Lucy Rebecca Buck published a journal of Civil War life in Front Royal: *Sad Earth, Sweet Heaven.*

The **Warren Rifles Confederate Museum** houses Stonewall Jackson's signal cannon and the Union flag surrendered to him after the Battle of Front Royal. The battle took place on May 23, 1862 at the beginning of Stonewall Jackson's famous Valley Campaign. The museum is open April 15-October 31 (95 Chester S., ☎ 540-636-6982).

The **Warren Heritage Society** inside Ivy Lodge contains exhibits on local history. Next door is the **Cottage of Belle Boyd**, the Southern Teenage Spy, who carried information about the Union troops from Front Royal to Stonewall Jackson, which helped Jackson win the Battle of Front Royal (101 Chester Street, ☎ 540-636-1446). To learn more about the battle, check out the self-guided driving tour of the Battle of Front Royal.

Main Street is a quaint historic district with a healthy row of shops – antiques, furniture and clothing stores, restaurants and coffee shops. **Stokes General Store** (☎ 540-635-4437) has supplied Front Royal shoppers with shoes, cookware, clothing, leather chaps and cheese since 1944. Their motto: "If you need it, we have it." After a day of shopping you might need some fresh air and exercise. The **Happy Creek Trail** begins right outside the store and follows the stream for a quarter-mile.

A testament to Main Street adaptability is the **Murphy Theater**, 131 E. Main, built first as the Methodist Church, then serving successively as Colonel Murphy's Vaudeville Theatre, a silent movie house, a candy store, fruit stand, post office, clothing store, and a computer center.

There seems to be a thing about "doggies in the window" in Front Royal. At least two shops – **Grandma Hazel's Attic** and **Goldsmith Jewelers** – have pet dogs that sit in the windows and people-watch. At Grandma Hazel's, the small dog has his own canopy bed set up in the window. There's even a furniture store with a couple of wooden dogs propped in the window.

Another Main Street curiosity is the **"Not So National Zoo and Aquarium"** (stop #34 in the brochure). Local artist Pat Windrow has painted zoo and barn murals on the sides of buildings leading to her **Windrow Gallery and Murals**. Her whimsical scenes make it look as if there's a second street running alongside, and as though elephants and horses are peering out of doorways. You can see more of her work inside the Main Street Mill restaurant.

 TIP

Don't stretch out Front Royal to anything as pretentious as "Roy-ale." In fact, true locals pronounce it "Front Rawl," and Warren County as "Worn County."

Recreation

Front Royal is known as the **Canoe Capital of Virginia**, thanks to the South Fork Shenandoah River, a wide, steady-flowing river with some Class II whitewater. Several outfitters offer canoe and tubing trips: **Downriver Canoe Company** (☎ 800-338-1963, www.downriver.com); **Front Royal Canoe** (☎ 800-270-8808, www.frontroyalcanoe.com); and **Shenandoah River Trips** (☎ 800-RAPIDS-1, www.shenandoah.cc).

Front Royal Canoe also offers guided **horseback rides** April through October, as does **Highlander Horses** (☎ 540-636-4523 www.highlanderhorses.com) and **Pandhandle Trail Rides** (☎ 540-635-6294).

The 195,000-acre **Shenandoah National Park** (☎ 540-999-3500, www.nps.gov/shen) attracts millions of visitors with its magical Skyline Drive and backcountry wilderness. Three lodges in the park offer food and one, Skyland, has accommodations. Hikes range from short jaunts past waterfalls and lookouts, to long backpacking trips, including the Appalachian Trail. **Skyline Drive** runs 100 miles through the park and along the Blue Ridge Mountains, with Front Royal its northern terminus.

The **George Washington National Forest** is also convenient to Front Royal, with trails running along the Massanutten Range (☎ 540-984-4101). **Guest Shenandoah River State Park** (☎ 540-622-6840) has 1,600 acres along five miles of the South Fork Shenandoah River.

Two miles south of Front Royal is **Skyline Caverns** (☎ 800-296-4545, www.skylinecaverns.com). You've certainly heard of stalagtites and stalagmites (quick – which grow up and which grow down?), but anthodites? This is one of the only places in the world you can see these "orchids of the mineral kingdom." Three underground streams flow through the caverns and Rainbow Falls plunge 37 feet. Open year-round. Open 9am-6:30pm in summer; closes earlier the rest of the year. Adults, $12; children seven-13, $6.

Dining

Locals remember when the **Royal Oak Tavern** was a Golden Corral with an all-you-can-eat buffet. Today, it's whitewashed and clean-looking inside and out. It has an extensive surf-and-turf menu, as well as burgers and sandwiches for lunch or late-night munching. The kitchen is open until midnight. There's a separate smoking area and a bar (101 West 14th Street, ☎ 540-551-9953, www.jesara.com).

Jalisco Authentic Mexican Restaurant serves some of the best authentic Mexican food in Virginia (1303 N. Royal Avenue, ☎ 540-635-7348); and locals swear **Melting Pot Pizza** has the best thin-crust pie and homemade onion rings. It must be good – it's been in business for 30 years (138 West 14th Street, ☎ 540-636-6146).

By day the **Main Street Mill** serves up pasta, steak and seafood in an atmosphere with chestnut beams and hand-painted murals. By night, the "Feed Mill" is a favorite local nightspot, with bands playing on the second floor of the 19th-century mill (500 East Main Street, ☎ 540-636-3123).

Stadt Kaffee & Restaurant is a good German restaurant in the historic downtown (304-A East Main Street, ☎ 540-635-8300).

Lodging

The **Chester House Bed & Breakfast** is an Italian Renaissance estate on two acres in the historic district. Once inside the elaborate gardens, you'd never know Main Street was only a block away (43 Chester Street, ☎ 800-621-0441, www.chesterhouse.com, $$).

Killahevlin is an historic Edwardian Mansion built by an Irish immigrant, William Edward Carson, who came in 1885 at the age of 15. As the first chairman of the Virginia Conservation and Development Commission, Carson is credited with the creation of Skyline Drive, the development of Jamestown, Williamsburg and Yorktown Colonial National Monument, as well as historical markers placed throughout the state. He sited his mansion on one of the highest spots in the area, and named it for Killyhevlin in Northern Ireland. It's now a bed & breakfast with six guest rooms (four with working fireplaces) private baths, antique furnishings and mountain views. Innkeeper Susan O'Kelly has restored the mansion in keeping with Irish influences, right down to the pub, where the Irish beer on tap flows freely for guests while they're playing a game of cribbage or backgammon. Outdoors are two gazebos, a koi fish pond, boxwood gardens, and the Tower House, a renovated water tower that once collected rainwater and now houses two guest suites (☎ 800-847-6132, www.vairish.com, $$$).

The **Lackawanna Bed & Breakfast** is an 1869 house with a front porch overlooking the Shenandoah River. There's an in-ground pool and canoeing on the river. Children ages 10 and older only (☎ 877-222-7495, www.lackawannabb.com, $$).

The **Mountainside Cottage at Skyline Drive** is a knotty pine cabin turned into a comfy guest cottage by owners Diane and Cecil Keen. Two bedrooms with feather beds, down comforters and terry robes, a modern kitchen, fireplace with all the wood you need, front and back porches for mountain views. Cable TV, VCR and stereo. Well-behaved dogs are welcome, with a $25 non-refundable cleaning fee (www.mountainsidecottage.com, ☎ 540-622-6221, $$$).

Information

The **Front Royal/Warren County Chamber of Commerce and Visitor Center** are at 414 E. Main Street, inside a restored train station. Open daily, 9am-5pm, ☎ 800-338-2576, www.frontroyalchamber.com.

Events

Main Street is the site of a variety of festivities:

The **Virginia Wine & Craft Festival** (☎ 540-635-3185), the third Saturday in May, features samplings of Virginia wines and craft vendors; the **Warren County Fair** (☎ 540-635-5827) happens during the first week in August; **Octoberfest** (☎ 540-635-3185) is held the fourth Saturday in September, with a chili cookoff and art show.

The **Festival of Leaves** (☎ 540-636-1446) is the second weekend in October and features a parade and street festival; and the **Community Christmas Parade** (☎ 540-636-3566) is the first Saturday in

December. Summer brings **Gazebo Gatherings** on Friday evenings, with free, live music ranging from classical to county.

> ⭐ LOCAL HISTORY
>
> The Mosby-Sheridan feud originated and reached its climax here in Front Royal with the execution of a half-dozen Mosby's Rangers who were captured in battle. They were paraded through the streets, then hanged atop a hill north of town. A monument to them stands at the entrance to Prospect Hill Cemetery, where 276 Confederate soldiers, representing each of the 13 southern states, are buried.

New Market

Around Town

A single corner in New Market neatly sums up this town's past. The intersection of Congress Street (Route 11) and Old Cross Road marks where long ago two major Indian trails crossed. As German and Scotch-Irish poured down the Great Wagon Road, the town acquired the name Cross Roads. On the southeast corner, Stonewall Jackson sat on his horse and reviewed 17,000 of his troops as they made the turn onto what was then the east-west Luray Road in 1862. There's a plaque referencing the event on the side of a building that was built by John Strayer as a store, then later became the Lee Jackson Hotel. In 1864, rebel General Jubal Early used it as his headquarters.

Today, the old building is home to **Bedrooms of America Museum and Pottery** (☎ 540-740-3512), self-proclaimed alternately as "Virginia's Most Unusual Attraction" and "America's Most Unique Museum." (Having once visited the Museum of Obsolete Medical Devices in St. Paul, Minn., we're guessing they might have competition for the title.) The street-level floor is a jumble of antiques, baskets, pottery and knick-knacks, as well as an impressive antique doll collection. Upstairs (you're asked to pay $2 to go up) is Bedrooms of America, a truly unique concept in themed museums. Travel through time via eleven furnished bedrooms representing every period of American décor, from William & Mary (1650) to Art Deco (1930).

Directly across Congress Street is a log cabin (yes, a log cabin in the middle of downtown), housing the **John Sevier Gallery** (☎ 540-740-3911). John Sevier, the founder of New Market, had a trading post here about 200 years ago. The logs are purportedly from that original building, and were used to reconstruct the current 1920s structure. Maybe New Market got too busy for Sevier. He stayed only five years, then went west to settle in Tennessee and became its first governor, serving six terms.

The current occupant of Sevier's old post is Judy DeLaughter, who bought it about 12 years ago. She says the local paper was once put together here, and at another time it served as the Greyhound bus station. She's been in New Market a little over 25 years, but still claims to be a newcomer from Maryland. She's a painter who came for the peace and quiet. Her gallery sells art, crafts and books by local artists.

Across the street again is the F&M Bank. But don't let looks deceive: This commercial building is believed to be the oldest structure in town. The limestone and brick house, known by historians-in-the-know as the **Abbie Henkel House**, pre-dates the Revolution. Abbie Henkel didn't build it, nor was she an original occupant. She was simply the most memorable resident over the years, a pianist who gave lessons from her home for decades.

Lastly, on the northeast corner, is a gas station. Not so exciting, unless you've picked up the **Town of New Market Walking Tour** brochure and learned that there was an old house here, moved one lot east in 1928 to make room for a filling station to serve the new mode of transportation in the Shenandoah Valley. The circa-1806 house still stands with an original main section made of logs. It's been used as a Singer sewing machine shop, a tailor and the post office.

The pace of New Market is laid-back and casual. The parking meters, which still accepted pennies, were apparently not pulling their weight, and were removed a few years back to allow for free two-hour street parking. When the owner of **Pack Rat Willy's Antiques** goes out for a bite, he puts up a sign: "National Pack Rat Holiday – had to get some cheese."

Things speed up in May for the re-enactment of the **Battle of New Market**, one of the last Confederate victories in the Shenandoah Valley. The event draws 3,000 re-enactors and up to 8,000 spectators on the third weekend in May. It's New Market's largest event by far.

Western Virginia

The May 15, 1864 battle was actually fought in the streets of New Market, as well as west and north of town on the Bushong Farm, preserved today as **New Market Battlefield State Historical Park**. The battle is best known for the participation of 257 teenage cadets from the Virginia Military Institute in Lexington. Their efforts, with the loss of 10 of their ranks, helped achieve the Confederate goal of delaying the North's march on Richmond. In 1970, VMI constructed the **Hall of Valor Civil War Museum** on the battlefield grounds to memorialize their contribution. The original Bushong farmstead portrays 19th-century farm life, one violently disrupted by the war, as the orchards were turned into a battlefield and the house into a hospital. Now quiet paths lead to the "Field of Lost Shoes" and a stunning bluff overlooking the Shenandoah River. It's open daily, year-round. The Hall of Valor houses a visitor center and museum and shows two short films on the valley campaign and the cadets. A walking tour brochure of a mile-long loop trail is available (☎ 540-740-3101, www.vmi.edu/museum/nm).

★ DID YOU KNOW?

The name New Market comes from the English racetrack of the same name. In the early days of the Virginia town there was a racetrack nearby.

Attractions

A private museum, the **New Market Battlefield Military Museum,** opened in the 1980s, a white-columned replica of Robert E. Lee's Arlington House. It houses an impressive collection of thousands of items from all American wars (☎ 540-740-8065).

Of all the commercial caves in the Shenandoah region, **Endless Caverns** gives the most "natural" experience, with formations and passageways lighted only with white light. Tours last an hour and 15 minutes, and are given year-round (☎ 540-896-2283, www.endlesscaverns.com).

Dining

There's plenty of good, Southern, home-style cooking in New Market: **Battlefield Family Restaurant**, 9403 Congress Street (☎ 540-740-3664), **Lottie Kelso's**, 9403 Congress Street (☎ 540-740-3664),

New Market Café, 9478 Congress Street (☎ 540-743-8433), and **Southern Kitchen,** 9579 Congress Street (☎ 540-740-3514).

For historic atmosphere, **The Valley Inn** serves lunch Wednesday through Saturday in an 1840s Italianate Victorian house decorated with antiques and collectibles. There are three dining rooms and the fare is traditional Southern cooking, most notably their homemade chicken salad, soups and Smithfield ham. Open noon to 2:30pm (9400 Congress Street, ☎ 540-740-8900).

See also *Shenvalee Golf Resort,* below.

Lodging

The **Shenvalee Golf Resort** sits on land with a fascinating history. It was once part of the 1749 plantation of Valentine Sevier (father of New Market founder John Sevier), and ground that was part of the Civil War Battle of New Market. The nine-hole golf course opened in 1927, built by hand labor and the first one in the Shenandoah Valley. During WW II the US State Department took over the resort to hold Italian diplomatic prisoners. Today there's a 27-hole PGA course, with a lodge and a restaurant known for its Sunday buffets that serves breakfast, lunch and dinner daily (☎ 540-740-3181, www.shenvalee.com, $).

Cross Roads Inn B&B on Route 211 is a white clapboard Victorian inn with a beautiful view of Massanutten. It's operated by an Austrian couple who serve homemade apple strudel and mulled wine or Austrian coffee in the afternoon. Six guest rooms, each with a private bath, are furnished with antiques and down comforters on canopy beds. Children welcome, but no pets. The innkeeper, Roland Freisitzer, is a native Austrian from Salzburg. He and his American wife, Mary-Lloyd, lead seven-day Austrian ski tours (☎ 888-740-4157 or 540-740-4157, www.crossroadsinnva.com, $$).

The **Red Shutter Farmhouse B&B** sits on 20 acres off Rt. 793 near Endless Caverns (☎ 540-740-4281, $).

 The nearby **Budget Inn** (☎ 540-740-3105, $) and **Days Inn** (☎ 540-740-4100, $) both accept pets.

Information

New Market Area Chamber of Commerce, ☎ 877-740-3212.

Town of New Market, ☎ 540-740-3432, www.newmarketvirginia.com.

Events

The **New Market Battlefield Re-enactment** is held in mid-May (☎ 540-740-3101), and **Heritage Days** are the fourth weekend in October (☎ 540-740-3212).

SIDE TRIP

Massanutten Mountain

Like many Indian terms, "Massanutten" as it's used today has little in common with its original meaning. Our name for a 30-mile mountain range that crops up dramatically from the lower Shenandoah Valley meant, to Indians, "basket" or "potato ground" (proof positive that we can't be sure of the original meaning of Indian words!). Be that as it may, this long range stretches from Harrisonburg to Strasburg. Paralleling to the east of the valley's major north-south routes, it rarely rises to any significant peak and is broken only now and again by gaps.

One such passage, east of Edinburg, leads into Fort Valley, a depression in the mountain range through which Passage Creek flows north into the Shenandoah River. Here, the mountains rise steeply from either side to form an isolated spot of few inhabitants, refreshingly free of strip malls, billboards and neon signs. George Washington surveyed this valley for Lord Fairfax, making it one of the few spots in Virginia where a hiker can literally walk the path of our first commander-in-chief and president.

Whereas Shenandoah National Park, which lies due east of Massanutten, gets the car traveler and tourist, Massanutten Mountain gets those hungry for human-powered recreation. There is a 70-mile trail that loops around the east and west ridges – the "eye" of this sewing-needle-shaped range. The ridge top trail leads to more remote paths down either side of the mountain, which are popular with hikers. Near Harrisonburg, the Massanutten Resort operates in four seasons with skiing in winter.

The place for information about outdoor fun in-and-around Massanutten is the national forest visitors center in New Market Gap, a few miles east of New Market on US 211. Besides a complete natural history, it offers short interpretive trails, like the Massanutten Storybook Trail, which explains the mountain's geologic history. The .2-mile Discovery Trail is wheelchair-accessible, and the Lion's Tale National Recreation Trail was designed for visually impaired.

Camp Roosevelt is a campground north of New Market gap that dates to the creation of the Civilian Conservation Corps. It was the first CCC camp in America, opened in 1933 during the Great Depression. For a decade thereafter, unemployed men planted trees, built fire towers and improved the surrounding national forest. An easy 3.4-mile hike leads from Camp Roosevelt up Massanutten's east ridge to end at Kennedy Fire Tower, an impressive structure made of limestone blocks quarried by the CCC. In the early days of the national forest, fire towers and the local residents who manned them were critical to fire suppression efforts. Rivalries developed between different groups of wardens, ultimately to be settled in grand games of tug-of-war at the Shenandoah County Fair.

Western Virginia

Monterey

If we added up receipts from gas pumped at the town station in Monterey over the years, it would probably be enough to buy a good used car. You see, the town's main strip is US 250, the only road from Staunton over the Allegheny Mountains into West Virginia, a trip we've taken quite often. And there aren't a lot of places to get gas along the way. It's a twisting road, full of switchbacks and hairpin turns, with few flat places to plant a town. Yet here sits Monterey, nicknamed "Little Switzerland," where it's said sheep outnumber people (who's counting, we wonder?) and some locals still come to town by horse-and-buggy.

Around Town

This tiny community of around 200 people, the county seat of Highland County, has the highest mean elevation of any east of the Mississippi. Not surprising, it is also one of the very few places in Virginia that produces maple syrup. Western Virginia is the southernmost spot in the US with the right climate for syrup production.

During the second and third weeks in March, freezing nighttime temperatures and warm, sunny days spur county sugar camps to peak performance. Friends and family pitch in to help farmers tap trees and boil watery sap until it is reduced to syrup. The **Highland Maple Festival** follows in March, a time when tours of sugar camps shows this process in full swing. Methods span the generations, from traditional bucket and iron kettle operations that utilize antique tools to modern methods of vacuum pumps, miles of plastic tubing, reverse osmosis and evaporators. A visit to the open-air **Maple Museum** will put all this in perspective. Indians used neither iron nor plastic. Rather, they carved a sharp-tipped piece of wood and pierced the tree. Sap that dripped from the tree wound was collected for boiling over a nearby fire.

Be sure to sample the sweet stuff on some buckwheat pancakes at an area restaurant or the all-you-can-eat community breakfast at the school. Evening festivities include a Maple Queen Ball, a Maple Hoedown and a Sugar Shake-up Dance.

If plans call for staying in Monterey during the Maple Festival, make reservations a year in advance. **The Highland Inn** starts taking reservations on April 1 for the *following* March and, by day's end, is pretty well booked solid. It's the same story for other inns and bed and breakfasts around town. Failing this, don't despair. Staunton is a good-sized city within an hour's drive, with plenty of commercial hotels.

Despite its size, as a stop on the US 250 thoroughfare, Monterey is savvy to the benefits of through-traffic and tourism. The main street is lined with antique, arts and crafts shops, country stores, B&Bs and home-style restaurants.

Originally called Bell's Place in the late 1700s, Monterey was just a small settlement of cabins named for James Bell, owner of the Landmark House, which housed the most popular landmark in any pioneer town – the tavern. Built in 1790, the **Landmark House** is still standing on Main Street, across from the courthouse, and is believed to be the oldest remaining building in town. In it, in 1847, a group of justices organized Highland County, designating 450 acres for the county seat of Highland. In 1848 they changed the name to Monterey in honor of newly elected President Zachary Taylor's previous victory at the Battle of Monterrey in Mexico. Today, the original logs are visible and inside, the SPCA runs a shop to benefit stray animals.

A walking tour brochure called *A Walk Around Monterey, Virginia* gives great tidbits about the town's buildings, many of which are open to the public as shops. Local lore includes a haunted house and a wall every child in town has learned to balance on for the last 100 years. The brochure is available at most shops in town, at The Highland Inn, or at the Chamber of Commerce on Spruce Street.

Pop into the **Corner Room** (☎ 540-468-2161), a shop located inside the Campbell House on Main Street, not only to browse the antiques and gifts, but also to look for the framed windowpanes bearing the etched names of two soldiers wounded in the Battle of McDowell. The 1852 building was used as a Civil War hospital. Look carefully at the Confederate monument in the court square. It differs from others in Virginia in that the soldier shades his eyes with one hand and grips his gun with the other.

You might catch sight of **Carl Hiner** (☎ 540-468-2957) running errands from his horse and buggy. He's turned his hobby into a business, giving rides to visitors and transporting bridal couples to their nuptials.

Recreation

Highland County has been called the "trout capital of the southeast." **Rainbow Springs Retreat** (☎ 804-353-1112), four miles north of Monterey on Route 220, has six stocked ponds and a stream where you can try your hand at fly-fishing for catch-and-release brown, rainbow and native brook trout. There's a lodge and guided trips available. At **Virginia Trout Company** you can fish for your dinner or buy trout to go. Located on Route 220, five miles north of Monterey (☎ 540-468-2280).

Highland Adventure rents mountain bikes and provides shuttle, mapping and guide services for caving, rock climbing, mountain biking and camping (☎ 540-468-2722).

Monterey is central to **Ramseys Draft Wilderness** and **Laurel Fork Special Management Area**. These units of the **George Washington National Forest** receive heightened protection for the stands of old growth hemlock and red spruce trees. Ramseys Draft covers rugged Virginia terrain and is not suitable for beginner hikers. Laurel Fork has a more developed and maintained trail network, but take caution in spring when the water level on this tributary of the Potomac River rises. Steel cables stretch from shore-to-shore, a testament to the aid hikers need in crossing at high water. For information about Ramseys Draft, call ☎ 540-885-8028. Those wishing to hike Laurel Fork should call ☎ 540-838-2521.

Western Virginia

Dining

Two inns in town also serve meals to the public: **The Highland Inn** (☎ 540-468-2143) serves dinner Wednesday through Saturday and Sunday brunch, and the **Mountain Laurel Inn** (☎ 540-468-3401) serves soup and sandwiches for lunch.

You can't miss the **Maple Restaurant** on Spruce Street. There's a big fish on the roof, no doubt because rainbow trout from the hatchery up the road is one of the house specialties. Dinners are usually less than $10 and come with two vegetables and homemade bread. They also serve country ham and homemade baked goodies. This is country food, inexpensive, where it's been served for more than 35 years (☎ 540-468-2684).

Lodging

For such a small town, Monterey has quite a number of Victorian B&Bs and inns, sporting goodies like gingerbread trim, wrought-iron fencing, and rocking-chair porches.

Perhaps the most conspicuous B&B is **The Highland Inn** on Main Street, with its double-decker front porches. What's amazing is that it survived the fires and dilapidation most wood-frame hotels have succumbed to. Originally called Hotel Monterey when built in 1904, it had a picket fence to keep the sheep off the lawn. Guests included Harvey Firestone, Henry Ford and Gen. Erwin Rommel, Germany's WWII "desert fox," who spent three months here in the late 1930s studying the battle tactics of Confederate Gen. Stonewall Jackson. It has 17 guest rooms, several suites with sitting areas, a dining room and tavern. It may be an old hotel, but rooms have private baths and cable TV (☎ 888-466-4682 or 540-468-2143, $).

★ GHOST STORY

The resident ghost at The Highland Inn is a friendly, if sad one. Emily, the wife of the inn-keeper when the hotel took boarders, had an affair with one of the residents. When her husband found out, he shot her. Consequently the towns-people hanged him outside of town. Whether it's true or not, it makes a great story.

Cherry Hill B&B on Mill Alley one block off Main Street, overlooks the town (☎ 540-468-1900, $$).

The **Mountain Laurel Inn** was built in 1900 as the Arbogast House. It has five guest rooms, a guest parlor with fireplace and an antique grand piano (☎ 800-510-0180, www.va-bedandbreakfast.com, $$).

Trimble Acres Bed & Breakfast is another Victorian surrounded by a wrought-iron fence on Spruce Street (☎ 540-468-1524, $$).

The innkeeper at the **Selby Inn** on Main Street conducts tours of Civil War sites in the area and displays his collection of "Goofus Glass," an early 1900s pressed glass. The inn is furnished with period pieces, and has gardens and a stream in the backyard (☎ 540-468-3234, www. highlandcounty.org/selbyinn, $$).

For a different experience, **Bobbie's Bed & Breakfast** is part of a working sheep and cattle farm. It's a half-mile west of Monterey on US 250 (☎ 540-468-2308, $).

Information

Highland County Chamber of Commerce, Highland Center, Spruce Street, ☎ 540-468-2550, www.highlandcounty.org. The office is open Monday-Friday, 10am-5pm, but there's a brochure rack outside if you visit when the office is closed.

Events

In addition to the **Highland Maple Festival** the second and third weekends in March, the **Mountain Mama Road Bike Challenge** and the **County Fair** are in August, **Hands & Harvest Fall Foliage Festival** is in mid-October, and **Wintertide** is the first weekend in December. Two events alternate years: the **House & Garden Weekend** is held on "even" years in mid-July, and the **McDowell Battlefield Days** are held in May on "odd" years at the site of one of Stonewall Jackson's victories in the Valley Campaign of 1862 (☎ 540-468-2550, www.highlandcounty.org).

Blue Grass

I'm guessing a lot of people have a moment where, after they discover some small town somewhere, they fantasize about chucking it all and moving there to raise sheep and grow herbs. For Bill, it's Troutdale, Virginia, where author Sherwood Anderson retired. For me, it's Blue Grass.

We found it purely by accident, driving in from the backside while "bushwhacking" off the mountain from Laurel Fork Wilderness after a weekend of hiking. We were trying to avoid driving the long way back home – the main route had us going west into West Virginia, around, then finally east on Route 250. With trusty gazetteer in hand, we had spied a back roadway off the mountain, although it meant taking some dotted lines. (You can do this sort of thing only with a four-wheel-drive vehicle.)

As we drove down into the valley, blue with typical Virginia August haze, it seemed as if God himself had planted it there. After the rugged terrain of Laurel Fork, the valley was like an oasis, soothing to the eyes, the mind, and even the sore muscles. Rolling pastures were dotted with black cows and bounded by split rail fencing. It may have been the hunger and fatigue, but I felt we could just pull into any one of the dirt driveways and move in. A hay wagon filled with the whole family was pulled to the side of the road, the driver talking and laughing with someone who had pulled over in a pick-up.

Then a small white sign finally told us the name of this oasis: "Blue Grass." We blinked and almost missed it, but eventually we came to the "town," a row of white storefronts, perhaps a block long. I wolfed down a bag of chips and a cold Route 66 root beer from the **Country Convenience** store. Junk food never tastes so good as after a weekend of trail mix and exertion.

I found out later that Blue Grass was the shopping center of the county before WWII, with a jeweler, a cinema, and the largest mercantile in the county, where you could buy the latest in home appliances – washing machines and radios.

To get to Blue Grass, go north from Monterey on US 220 about six miles. The **Ginseng Mountain Store** on the way is a great stop, as is the **Virginia Trout Company**. Turn left on Route 642 and follow the South Branch of the Potomac for about 2½ miles to the village. There are no places to stay or eat in Blue Grass, which may be a good thing. Maybe it will remain just as it is until we can buy a farm and move in.

★ FILM CLIPS

The 1921 silent film *Tol'able David* was filmed in the Blue Grass Valley and is shown throughout Monterey's Maple Festival in March. The story features a mountain boy and his family tormented by vicious brothers who have invaded the small Virginia town. Shot on location and featuring the bucolic scenes of western Virginia, the film opened to rave reviews as a tragedy of "uncompromising power" (*Photoplay*, 1922). Much later, Leonard Maltin called it "beautifully crafted Americana, shot on location in Virginia." One modern-day viewer compared it to *Sling Blade* in portraying the slow, yet rich, nuances of small-town America. In case you're curious, the name of the film comes from the protagonist's mother: "David, you're not a man quite yet. You're only tol'able – just tol'able."

Western Virginia

Hot Springs & Warm Springs

Around Town

Hot Springs and Warm Springs rose to national prominence on the wellspring of warm water. As the county seat of Bath County, Warm Springs enjoyed its greatest popularity in the late 18th and early 19th century, when doctors postulated that water at body temperature had medicinal value. Travelers braved a bumpy carriage ride from East Coast cities like Washington DC to check in at Col. Fry's **Warm Springs Hotel**, a process that included a weigh-in. After a few weeks of touring area springs, guests weighed themselves before leaving.

Quite opposite of our modern tendency to bemoan weight gain while on holiday, these people strove to add extra pounds.

Two white octagonal structures on the southbound side of US 220 in Warm Springs are original bathhouses in which the elite of American history have dunked their derrieres, and visitors still do today. The men's house was built in 1761, and the women's in 1838. Thomas Jefferson spent three weeks here in 1818, bathing twice daily and declaring the baths "of the first merit." Today, the Jefferson Pools bear his name and are listed on the National Register of Historic places. The women's bathhouse has a ducking chair that enabled invalids to bathe in the 98-degree mineral water. Mrs. Robert E. Lee used it on her visits, hoping the waters would assuage her rheumatoid arthritis.

As time progressed, notions about body temperature springs being the most beneficial gave way to belief that hot springs were of highest value. Encouraged by published reports of one Dr. Thomas Goode, visitors came to regard the 105-degree springs five miles south as more beneficial. Not entirely unbiased, the good doctor also owned **The Homestead** resort at the appropriately named town of Hot Springs.

While Dr. Goode is credited with creating the first resort at Hot Springs, he wasn't the first to put up guests. Thomas Bullett, a member of the Virginia militia and co-patriot with George Washington, built the first Homestead in 1766. Washington visited here on his travels from Fort Dinwiddie, prior to his becoming our first chief executive. Since then, at least 14 US Presidents have visited the various incarnations of this resort. Their portraits hang in the President's Lounge, from Washington to Bill Clinton. Order a Manhattan or a martini and just soak in the ambience.

The Homestead built a reputation as the place where the wealthy wiled away the summer. Cities of the Tidewater region suffered from unbearable heat, poor sanitation, mosquitoes and epidemics of yellow fever. Those with the means to do so escaped this by spending summers in the mountains, where they "took the cure," drank fresh mountain spring water and soaked in the springs.

In the last two decades of the 1800s, J.P. Morgan became a shareholder in a company that operated The Homestead. Aided by his financing and resources of the C&O Railroad, whose president was also involved with The Homestead, a rail line was built from Covington to Hot Springs – but extended no farther. It proved the final straw for Warm Springs' biggest resort, which closed in the 1920s and was torn down.

The late 20th century brought a revival of small, exclusive inns at Warm Springs, and the restoration of The Homestead into a golf and spa resort that today ranks among the top family vacation spots in the nation. The Homestead's turn-around, completed in the last decade, comes compliments of its new owner, the Pinehurst Company. They also own resorts in the Carolinas, Texas, and Mexico.

In so many ways, the Homestead experience is beyond words, and only through first-hand experience can one fully appreciate the richness. The Great Hall, with vaulted ceilings and balconies at either end, recalls grand hotels in Europe. Tea is served every afternoon in the small alcoves that line the spacious corridor, which are in fact anterooms for more private spaces, set off the hall and furnished with couches, ornate tables and tall mirrors. A warren of hallways leads past reading libraries and gift shops to an indoor pool warmed by the natural springs. The recently refurbished spa area offers guests (and for a surcharge, visitors) mineral baths, Swedish massages, herbal wraps or salt scrubs. There's a fitness center, a salon, and a full-sized bowling alley.

Families are catered to in every way. KidsClub provides programs for ages three-12. There's a movie theater, four tennis courts, horseback riding and evening hayrides to a bonfire to cook s'mores. There are nine downhill ski runs, day and night skiing, a ski school, and an Olympic-size skating rink.

If your idea of a vacation involves more rest and relaxation than a buzz of activity, sit back and soak in the mountain scenery. Take a leisurely carriage ride or soak in the pool. My favorite spot at the Homestead is the sun-filled elevated walkway that leads from the hotel to the spa and pool building. The window seat along the full length has tempting pink-and-white striped cushions and cheery floral pillows. I could spend an entire afternoon there, staring at Sunset Hill and imagining that time when children ran up the steep incline, hoping to outpace their chaperones and steal a quiet moment watching the sun slip behind Virginia's seemingly endless Allegheny range. See pages 31 and 32 for contact information about the Homestead.

★ DID YOU KNOW?

There are no traffic lights in Bath County.

Attractions

Besides spa offerings at the resort, The Homestead owns and operates **Jefferson Pools** in Warm Springs. A one-hour soak in these historic baths costs $12, while a gift shop on-site sells spa products made from the pool's waters. Open mid-March through October, 10am-7pm, November and December, weather permitting (☎ 800-838-1766, www. thehomestead.com).

Garth Newel isn't a person (as we mistakenly thought). Rather, it's a Welsh term for "new home." **Garth Newel Music Center** is a 114-acre estate in Warm Springs where Saturday concerts are followed by four-course gourmet dinners, and accommodations in the Manor House are available on special Music Holiday Weekends. The concerts are performed in a converted horseshow ring, which has great acoustics (☎ 877-558-1689, www.garthnewel.org).

Recreation

Even as age-old traditions like formal dining and dancing are maintained, the Homestead courts a new breed of traveler who may not want to wear a coat and tie to dinner, or even play golf. The resort-owned **Allegheny Outfitters** offers fly-fishing instruction and guides (April through mid-August), as well as daily guided hikes on Homestead-owned trails, mountain bike tours, caving excursions, and canoe and kayak trips on the Jackson River or Lake Moomaw (☎ 540-839-7760, www.thehomestead.com).

Of the 100 miles of trails on Homestead property, the **Cascades Trail** is our favorite. It follows alongside Cascades Creek for 1.5 miles, a stretch that includes 13 waterfalls, several with bridges spanning them for a bird's-eye view. Access to the trail is by a Homestead guide only, and a fee is charged. It's highly recommended, in part for the local guides, who unload a wealth of information about the flora and fauna along the trail, from beaver activity, to why the hemlock trees are dying, to what plants are edible (the wild watercress is delicious, and the Homestead uses it abundantly in its menus). Spring brings a profusion of wildflowers – trout lily, trillium, jack-in-the-pulpit, and pink and yellow Lady's Slippers. There are also three self-guided, well-groomed trails, ranging in difficulty from moderate to strenuous.

There are extensive national forestlands around Warm Springs Valley. The **Warm Springs Ranger District** (☎ 540-839-2521) covers portions of two national forests (the George Washington and Jefferson), as well as the Bolar Mountain and Bolar Flat Recreation Areas, Lake Moomaw, the Jackson River, and myriad streams and hiking trails. Camping, hiking, boating, swimming, fishing and hunting are some of the recreational opportunities. There's even a restored B&B – **Hidden Valley Bed & Breakfast**, on the Jackson River, is housed in the 1851 Warwick Mansion (Hidden Valley Road, Warm Springs, ☎ 540-839-3178, $$).

★ FILM CLIPS

Much of the Civil War-era film *Sommersby*, starring Richard Gere and Jodie Foster, was filmed in 1992 at Warwick Mansion.

Dining

Hot Springs

Choices for dining at **The Homestead** include the formal **Dining Room** (jacket and tie required in the evening), the **Casino Club Restaurant** with patio dining, the **1766 Grille**, the **Players Pub**, and **Sam Snead's Tavern**, which is located in downtown Hot Springs. There are also restaurants at the **Cascades** and **Lower Cascades** golf courses, and in the **Mountain Lodge** at the ski mountain. Even if you balk at the evening coat-and-tie requirement in the Dining Room, the breakfast buffet is to die for and requires only "resort attire." They serve the biggest raspberries and blackberries we've ever seen. For all Homestead restaurants, call ahead for reservations and dress codes (Route 220, ☎ 540-839-7989).

Elliott's in Hot Springs is open for lunch and dinner Monday-Saturday, serving eclectic fare, like horseradish potatoes and grilled salmon over bowtie pasta (3 Main Street, ☎ 540-839-3663). **The Village Roost** is a local hang-out known for great burgers. Open 9am to 3:45pm Monday-Saturday (Main Street, ☎ 540-839-2142). Two moderately priced American-style restaurants are operated by two sisters and their husbands, at either end of town: **Valley View Restaurant** is a mile north of Hot Springs on Route 220 (☎ 540-839-8964), and the **Country Café** is one mile south (☎ 540-839-2111).

There are several places on Main Street in Hot Springs to get a quick bite if you're on the go. **Duck In Deli & Market** has the only fast-food franchise in the entire county, a Subway take-out counter (☎ 540-839-3000). The **Homestead Market** sells wine, beer, imported cheeses, pizza to order, and take-out sandwiches that are to-die-for, like stir-fry chicken on a croissant, as well as Virginia-made products like Route 11 Chips and Route 66 Root Beer (☎ 800-838-1766). **McAllister's One Stop Market** has carryout only, things like taco salads, potpies and ice cream cones (☎ 540-839-2242).

Warm Springs

The Waterwheel Restaurant at Gristmill Square combines a rustic, Colonial atmosphere with a great wine cellar stashed in the workings of the old mill. There's been a mill here since 1771, and the current one operated until 1971. Open for dinner only, nightly; closed Tuesdays in the winter (Route 619, Warm Springs, ☎ 540-839-2231, www.gristmillsquare.com).

John's Steakhouse serves steaks, of course, but also seafood, poultry and native Allegheny Mountain Trout. Open daily for dinner only, with dining inside and out. Located one mile south of Warm Springs, next to the high school (Charger Lane, ☎ 540-839-2333).

Just across the road from the high school, all the menu items at **The Varsity** are named for things to do with the school. The fresh deli sandwiches are served on homemade bread, and they make at least one soup each day. Eat inside or out on the porch. Open daily, 7am to 10pm (☎ 540-839-4000).

For carryout, there's **The Fast Break**, serving sausage biscuits for breakfast and pizza for lunch (☎ 540-839-2942).

Lodging

The Homestead has 518 rooms, including 81 suites, all with terry cloth robes, mini-bars, two-line speakerphones with voice mail and data port, TV and VCR with movies on demand. Amenities include golf, fitness center, indoor pool, spa, skiing, hiking, bowling, valet parking, shuttle service, and nightly movies in the turn-of-the-century theatre. Accommodations range from cozy standard rooms to luxurious and spacious suites with fireplaces and balconies. Rates are per person, with some plans that include dinner, breakfast and afternoon tea. Off-season and weekday rates are available (Route 220, ☎ 800-838-1766 or 540-839-1766, www.thehomestead.com, $$$$).

TIP

On the Homestead grounds is the Shrine of the Sacred Heart Catholic church. Mass is held at 5pm on Saturday and at 9am Sunday.

If a quiet country cottage is more your speed, **Hickory Cottage** is two miles north of Hot Springs in a secluded, wooded setting, sleeping up to eight people (☎ 540-839-2645, $$). **King's Victorian Inn** offers rooms in the main 1899 house, as well as two cottages. Inside are antiques and Oriental carpets, outside, rockers sit on a verandah that wraps around the house. Full breakfast is served in the formal dining room (☎ 540-839-3134, $$).

 The Anderson Cottage Bed & Breakfast is in the part of Warm Springs known as Germantown until World War I. The original four rooms made of logs were an 18th-century tavern. Additions were made over the years, and the building has served as a doctor's residence, girls' school, inn and family vacation home. It's been in the same family since the 1870s, and the library has several thousand books. The separate 1820 brick kitchen is now a guest cottage, where *pets* can stay, no extra charge (Old Germantown Road, ☎ 540-839-2975, $$).

The **Inn at Grist Mill Square** in Warm Springs is a quaint complex of restored buildings centered around the 1900 mill, which is now a restaurant. The inn has 17 guest rooms and suites, all with private baths, cable TV, refrigerators, and private phone lines. Continental breakfast is served in your room, and an option is a package plan that includes a five-course dinner. There's an outdoor pool and tennis courts. The inn was created in 1972, using five 19th-century buildings, including an old blacksmith shop, a hardware store and two homes, one belonging to the miller. Today the buildings house the **Warm Spirit Spa** (☎ 540-839-6600, $$) and the **Country Store**, in addition to guest rooms (Route 619, ☎ 540-839-2231, www.gristmillsquare.com, $$).

Meadow Lane Lodge sits on 1,600 acres of forest, meadows and streams, with fly-fishing, 20 miles of hiking and mountain biking trails. A reading room is located in a former slave cabin that was once a part of Fort Dinwiddie in 1805. The barns and lodge were built in 1920 by Allan Hirsh, whose descendants still operate the inn's 14 guest rooms, suites and cottages. Some have fireplaces and porches, and all have private baths. A full country breakfast is served. The Lodge also owns the **Francisco Cottage** in the village. **Horses** can be boarded for

$20/night (Route 1, ☎ 540-839-5959, www.meadowlanelodge.com, $$).

 In Hot Springs, the **Vine Cottage Inn** is a casual country house, open since 1905, that takes pets in certain rooms for a $15 charge. Private baths, breakfast, and dinner by pre-arrangement. Located on Route 220, one block south of the Homestead (☎ 800-410-9755, www.vinecottageinn.com, $$).

Bonnie Brae Guest Cottage B&B is two miles south of Hot Springs on a private road, accommodating up to four people and pets at no extra charge (☎ 540-839-6466, $$).

 In Warm Springs, **Three Hills** is an Italianate mansion built by Mary Johnston, a novelist and feminist in the early 20th century. It's now a B&B with a coffee shop and several two-room suites. Pets are accepted for a $5 charge (☎ 888-23HILLS, www.3hills.com, $$).

The wrap-around porches of **Warm Springs Inn** overlook the Jefferson Baths across Route 220. A portion of the house is the 1803 Bath County courthouse and the old jail. Private baths, air conditioning, phones and cable TV. Breakfast and dinner are served in the **Courtroom Restaurant** (open only in the summer season), cocktails are served in the lounge, and picnic lunches can be ordered. Pets are welcome for a $10 fee (☎ 540-839-5351, $). **RoseLoe Motel**, one mile south of Warm Springs, takes small pets with a $10 charge per stay. Some rooms have kitchenettes (☎ 540-839-5373, $).

★ PET BOARDING

Philpot's Pampered Pooches is located in Carloover, Virginia, five miles south of The Homestead resort. The owners maintain an "open-door policy," meaning you can visit and walk Fido any time. It's open daily, but requires advance notice for pick-up and drop-off. (Our very own pampered pooch, Sasha, stayed there and she highly recommends the "treats.") Carloover Lane, ☎ 540-839-2727.

Information

Bath County Chamber of Commerce Visitor Center, Route 220 South (one mile south of Hot Springs), ☎ 800-628-8092. Open seven days, generally 9am-4pm; closed major holidays. Handicapped-accessible. Mailing address, PO Box 718, Hot Springs 24445.

Bath County Historical Society, ☎ 540-839-2543.

Bath County's official Web site is **www.bathcountyva.org**.

Lexington

Around Town

Steeped in Civil War history, the home of the esteemed Virginia Military Institute, and the final resting place of Confederate generals Robert E. Lee and Stonewall Jackson, Lexington nonetheless has a sense of fun and humor about itself.

A deceivingly official-looking plaque on a building next to the Stonewall Jackson House reads: "National Un-Historical Marker: On this spot on Feb. 29, 1776, absolutely nothing happened." Inside the Alexander-Withrow House (circa 1789) is the playfully named "Artists in Cahoots," a coop for local artists. A whimsical toy store window warns patrons to "Be Prepared to Smile." A tongue-in-cheek ghost tour includes a visit to Stonewall Jackson's grave.

Lexington has an astounding number of preserved buildings housing restaurants, shops, art galleries and lodging. Pick up a walking tour brochure of the compact historic district at the visitor center and check out the historical displays while you're there. A blackboard tells the day's events, and a friendly greeter points out the best routes on the map and will even advise you on a restaurant meeting your epicurean tastes. The walking tour includes the campuses of VMI and Washington and Lee University. A separate brochure highlights the half-dozen art galleries within walking distance.

At the **Stonewall Jackson House**, we found the restored garden most interesting. Markers tell you what plants you're looking at, including many popular in centuries past but virtually unknown today: for example, "salsify" is a Roman root vegetable brought to the colonies in the 1700s. Inside the house, furnished with many of Jackson's possessions, guided tours are on the hour and half-hour, Monday-Saturday, 9am-5pm, and Sunday, 1-5pm. Admission is $5 (8 E. Washington Street, ☎ 540-463-2552, www.stonewalljackson.org).

Jackson and his family are buried in the **Stonewall Jackson Memorial Cemetery** on South Main Street, along with more than 100 Confederate dead.

★ DID YOU KNOW?

"Stonewall" Jackson's given name was Thomas Jonathan Jackson. The nickname was earned for his unrelenting stand during the Battle of First Manassas. For 10 years before the Civil War he was a professor of Natural Philosophy at VMI. His home in Lexington is the only one he ever owned.

The **Lee Chapel,** on the Washington and Lee University campus, is imposing in its solemnity – men are asked to remove their hats upon entering. Silence prevails as visitors walk by the white marble sculpture of Recumbent Lee and the family crypt. Lee was president of Washington College and built this chapel. A wall plaque indicates where he sat during services. What we found perplexing were the number of plaques – three at least – memorializing men who drowned in the North River. Open April-October, Monday-Saturday, 9am-5pm, and Sunday, 1-5pm. Closes at 4pm the rest of the year. Free admission (☎ 540-463-8768, http://leechapel.wlu.edu).

On the VMI campus, there's the **VMI Cadet Museum,** open daily, 9am-5pm, with free admission (☎ 540-464-7334, www.vmi.edu/museum), and the **George C. Marshall Museum,** open daily, 9am-5pm, also free (☎ 540-463-7103).

★ LOCAL HISTORY

The dying wish of VMI professor Matthew Fontaine Maury was to be carried after his death through Goshen Pass when the rhododendrons were in bloom. He considered it the loveliest spot in all of Virginia. VMI cadets granted his wish in 1873.

It's not just military history that's preserved in Lexington. In 1999 a group of people nostalgic for drive-in theaters got together to save the 1950s **Hull's Drive-In** on Route 11, four miles north of Lexington. They formed a non-profit and called themselves Hull's Angels. Double features are shown on the giant, 50-foot tall screen, Friday, Saturday and Sunday nights, April through October (☎ 540-463-2621, www.hulls-drivein.com).

Outdoors

Ask for the excellent brochure *Rockbridge Outdoors*, available from the visitor center.

Within an hour of Lexington are dozens of hiking trails. Some of the many areas where you can enjoy the outdoors are: **Apple Orchard Falls**, **Crabtree Falls**, **Mount Pleasant National Scenic Area**, **Panther Falls Trail**, **St. Mary's Wilderness**, and of course, the **Blue Ridge Parkway**.

Take a road-trip to **Rockbridge Vineyard** (see page 41) for a tour and tasting, **Goshen Pass**, a mountain gorge 12 miles away where you can swim, canoe, fish and hike, or **Natural Bridge**, 14 miles south of Lexington. **The Drama of Creation** sound and light show is held at Natural Bridge each evening at dusk from April through October. The charge is $10 for adults, $5 for children (☎ 540-291-2121).

Dining

In the downtown district, **19 West** serves eclectic contemporary cuisine, at – you guessed it – 19 West Washington Street (☎ 540-464-1919). **Healthy Foods Market Soup and Juice Bar** is a healthy place for a quick bite (110 W. Washington Street, ☎ 540-463-6954).

Il Palazzo serves traditional Italian fare at 24 N. Main Street (☎ 540-464-5800, http://webfeat-inc.com/ilpalazzo), and **The Wilson-Walker House** serves gourmet American food accompanied by a full Virginia wine list in an 1820s townhouse (30 N. Main Street, ☎ 540-463-3020, www.wilsonwalker.com).

For between-meal treats: **Sweet Things Ice Cream Shoppe** (106 W. Washington Street), and **Lexington Coffee Roasting Co** (9 W. Washington Street).

TIP

Stop by or contact the Visitor Center for a copy of their *Dining & Lodging Guide*; ☎ 877-453-9822, www.lexingtonvirginia.com.

Lodging

The inns, B&Bs, cottages, cabins, and chain motels in the Lexington area are too numerous to mention here. Below are a few in the immediate historic district.

Historic Country Inns operates three lodgings in Lexington. Downtown, the **McCampbell Inn** is an historic hotel and **The Alexander-Withrow House** is a Georgian 1789 residence. For country atmosphere, the **Maple House** outside of town is on an 1850 plantation with swimming pool, tennis, walking trails and a stocked fishing pond. Guests at the downtown inns can use the Maple House's facilities (☎ 877-463-2044, www.lexingtonhistoricinns.com, $).

Sheridan Livery Inn was opened in 1887 by Irish immigrant John Sheridan. It reopened more than a century later, completely renovated with 12 rooms including three suites, some with balconies overlooking Main Street. There's an indoor restaurant and outdoor café (35 N. Main Street, ☎ 540-464-1887, www.webfeat-inc.com/sheridanlivery, $).

Llewellyn Lodge is a bed & breakfast specializing in outdoor adventures, offering guided fly-fishing trips and information on hiking trails. The innkeepers can arrange golfing, canoeing, kayaking, horseback riding and cycling trips (603 South Main Street, ☎ 800-882-1145, www.LLodge.com, $).

 An amazing number of chain motels around the city take pets, including **Best Western** Inn at Hunt Ridge (☎ 540-464-1500, $); **Comfort Inn-Virginia Horse Center** (☎ 540-463-7311, $); **Econo Lodge** (☎ 540-463-7371, $); **Holiday Inn Express** (☎ 540-463-7351, $); and **Ramada Inn Lexington** (☎ 540-463-6400, $).

Information

Lexington Visitor Center, ☎ 877-453-9822, www.lexingtonvirginia.com, 106 E. Washington Street. Open daily, 9am-5pm; in June and August, hours are 8:30am-6pm.

★ LOCAL HISTORY

Cyrus Hall McCormick (1809-1884) was a native of Rockbridge County who liberated agriculture through the invention of the mechanical reaper. He was a benefactor of Washington and Lee College where an impressive statue of him can be seen near Lee Chapel).

Events

Washington and Lee's famous **Mock Convention**, a raucous parade and a convention that has predicted the presidential nominees since 1908, is held in March in election years (☎ 540-463-8460).

The **Virginia Horse Festival** is the third weekend in April at the Virginia Horse Center on Route 39 (☎ 540-463-2194).

Trip Journal

Oh, Shenandoah

10 days in the Shenandoah Valley

A serious tour of the Shenandoah Valley can begin only by hopping off busy I-81 and driving local roads. Virginia's mountain scenery frames both long, straight highways and narrow mountain roads. Sheep and cows graze in neatly fenced farms and pastures, all with the backdrop of the Blue Ridge or Massanutten mountains.

Shenandoah is an outdoor playground with nearly inexhaustible options for fishermen, hikers, paddlers and spelunkers. Down the center of the Valley, small towns hum with local trade and out-of-towners in search of a festival, a Civil War

Western Virginia

battlefield, antiques or local art. Chain hotels are convenient to the interstate, but nicer quarters can be had in fine period homes renovated into bed & breakfasts. Restaurants serve up tasty local dishes and show a flair for haute cuisine. And for those who like their recreation in one spot, Shenandoah's four-season resorts – Bryce, Massanutten, Wintergreen and the Homestead – offer golfing, skiing and much more. For complete information, call **The Shenandoah Valley Travel Association**, ☎ 877-VISIT-SV, or visit their Web site, www. shenandoah.org.

DAY 1: TRAVEL

The **Blue Ridge Parkway** spans 470 miles of mountaintop from Virginia's Shenandoah National Park to Tennessee's Great Smoky Mountains. From Roanoke north to Buena Vista, it passes the Peaks of Otter, a mountain so steep Virginia settlers long considered it the state's highest peak. That is, until geologists actually measured Mount Rogers and declared it the tallest peak at 5,791 feet.

Pull into **Lexington** at the end of the day, where **Llewellyn Lodge** specializes in outdoor adventure. Innkeepers Ellen and John Roberts will hook you up with the best places to hike, fish, bike, ride horseback or play golf (603 South Main Street, Lexington, ☎ 800-882-1145, www.LLodge.com, $).

DAY 2: LEXINGTON

For breakfast, Ellen at Llewellyn Lodge serves up blue-ribbon omelets, waffles smothered in Virginia maple syrup, and John's Killer Hot Chocolate. All of it, great fuel for a busy day outdoors. John leads fly-fishing trips on Buffalo Creek, just eight minutes away. Beginners get personal "frustration-free" instruction in the fine art of casting. John brings lunch along.

Dinner can be early at **The Palms**, a former ice cream parlor that has hosted celebs such as Jodie Foster and Oliver North. The Shenandoah Valley Salad is topped with chicken, bacon and blue cheese (101 W. Nelson Street, ☎ 540-463-7911).

Bring along a sweater for an evening at the **Theater at Lime Kiln**. Plays run Tuesday through Saturday at 8pm. Typical productions feature plays set in Virginia, with some Shakespeare thrown in. An eclectic music lineup on Sundays might feature Celtic alt-rockers Carbon Leaf or bluegrass legend

Ralph Stanley (14 S. Randolph Street, ☎ 540-463-3074, www. theateratlimekiln.com).

DAY 3: TRAVEL

Before saying farewell to the Llewellyn Lodge, pick up John's "Top 20 Hikes & Trail Guide," then head for **Goshen Pass** and an easy three-mile hike. When rhododendrons bloom in June, this mountain gorge is one of the prettiest spots in Virginia. VMI professor Matthew Fontaine Maury thought so. Back in 1873 his dying wish was that his body be carried through the pass by VMI cadets, which they did.

Have a picnic lunch at the wayside park at Goshen Pass, then head on to Raphine for a tour and tasting at **Rockbridge Vineyard** (☎ 888-511-WINE), located in a renovated dairy.

Arrive in **Staunton**, the Shenandoah Valley's oldest city, in time to check in at a bed & breakfast or inn within walking distance of the historic downtown. Two inns worth noting are the five restored homes of the **Frederick House** (28 N. New Street, ☎ 540-885-4220, www.frederickhouse.com), and the **Victorian Belle Grae Inn** (515 W. Frederick Street, ☎ 540-886-5151, www.bellegrae.com).

DAY 4: STAUNTON

It's a full day of country music at the **Statler Brothers Complex** (☎ 540-885-7297), pioneer history at **The Frontier Culture Museum's** re-created villages (☎ 540-332-7850), and browsing among the 60-plus shops in Staunton. Good luck choosing a place for lunch – downtown has more than 20 restaurants.

DAY 5: SHENANDOAH NATIONAL PARK

From Staunton, head east through Waynesboro and climb Afton Mountain to reach **Shenandoah National Park**. Skyline Drive runs north the entire length of the park with numerous overlooks the Valley to the west ($10 entrance fee, ☎ 540-999-3500, www.nps.gov/shen).

Lunch at one of the park's lodges, **Skyland** (mile 41.7), which is on the highest point of Skyline Drive at 3,680 feet. The views of the Shenandoah Valley are even more spectacular after a short 1.6-mile hike up to **Stony Man Peak**, the second highest in the park. One day doesn't do this park justice, so plan on returning for a camping trip, a hike to one of the many waterfalls and a stay in one of the lodges. There's still the rest of Skyline Drive to travel, its heart-pounding twists and turns with pull-outs at breathtaking vistas.

Arrive in **Front Royal** tired and hungry. For lodging, go rustic at **Mountainside Cottage**, just below Skyline Drive (www.mountainsidecottage.com, ☎ 540-622-6221, $$$), or live it up at **Killahevlin Bed & Breakfast**, an Edwardian Mansion turned B&B (1401 North Royal Avenue, ☎ 800-847-6132, www.vairish.com, $$$).

★ SAY WHAT?

If you ask for directions in the Shenandoah Valley, chances are good the advice will sound odd – if not flat-out wrongheaded. Be patient. Valley residents have a peculiar sense of direction. For example, southbound travelers are said to be traveling "up the valley." Conversely, northbound travelers are headed "down the valley." The rationale is tied to the Shenandoah River, which flows north. To follow it downstream (north) is to travel "down the valley." If it gets confusing, remember the "lower Valley" is its northernmost reach. And to get there, you have to head "down."

DAY 6: FRONT ROYAL

Pack a picnic basket for a day exploring more of Shenandoah National Park, the Massanutten Mountain range, Skyline Caverns, or a day on the river. The south fork of the Shenandoah has some of the best canoeing in the east, with a steady current and even a little exciting whitewater. Several outfitters in town arrange trips.

Be sure to get back in time to explore Main Street in Front Royal. It's a small, quaint historic district with a restored train depot serving as the visitor center, and a genuine general store. No froufrou crafty items are to be had in **Stokes General Store**, but you can get a wedge of Wisconsin cheddar cheese, some hip-waders, leather chaps or a cast iron pan, should the need arise.

It's been a long day, so just walk up the street for dinner – to either the **Main Street Mill**, a 19th-century feed mill that now rocks with live bands until the early morning hours, or the more sedate **Stadt Kaffee** German restaurant.

DAYS 7, 8 AND 9

From Front Royal, head west to **Strasburg**, a charming base for exploring Shenandoah County's Civil War battlefields, museums, wineries and antiques shops. If you've got the time, you could spend another few days or a week visiting the small towns on Route 11. Our favorites are **Middletown**, **Strasburg**, **Woodstock**, **Edinburg**, **Mt. Jackson**, and **New Market**.

DAY 10: WINCHESTER

Now it's to the lower Shenandoah Valley and the end of our tour – in Winchester. A pleasant, leisurely introduction to the city is the visitor center, located in an 1833 grist mill next to **Abram's Delight**, the oldest house in Winchester, which houses a museum. Just behind the visitor center is **Duncan Park**, where Wilsons Lake is stocked with trout. Take a stroll on the paved walkway that circles the lake, which is also stocked with geese and ducks (no feeding, please!).

Downtown, Winchester's 45-block historic district, known as **Old Town**, has more than 200 shops and restaurants. Loudoun Street is a brick-paved pedestrian mall with benches, shops and outdoor dining at several taverns and cafés. It's the nucleus for summer festivals, concerts and events. Country singing legend **Patsy Cline** was born in Winchester. She worked as a "soda-jerk" at Gaunt's Drug Store, started her career on the local radio station, and was buried in Shenandoah Memorial Cemetery after her brief 31 years ended in a plane crash. Do try to eat at **Café Sofia**, the only Bulgarian restaurant in the Shenandoah Valley (and maybe Virginia, for that matter). It's open for lunch, Tuesday-Friday, and dinner, Tuesday-Saturday (2900 Valley Avenue, ☎ 540-667-2950).

Western Virginia

Caverns

Starting in the late 19th century and lasting until the Great Crash of 1929, entrepreneurs built the Shenandoah Valley into a major tourist draw for city residents. Few were as successful as those who made commercial enterprises out of massive caverns by charging admission and guiding curious visitors into the depths of the Blue Ridge Mountains.

The many billboards directing visitors to their entrances may be a little cheesy, but there's no denying the awesome geological events that created the many caverns. They started forming hundreds of millions of years ago as small cracks in limestone rock. Limestone is soft and easily eroded by water that contains naturally occurring acids. The massive rooms that have resulted are, in at least one instance, big enough to hold a 40-story building.

Luray Caverns, Luray

Claim to fame: The "stalacpipe" organ covers 3½ acres and has been called the largest natural instrument in the world.

★ MUSICAL STALACTITES

In 1954, scientist and mathematician Leland Sprinkle searched the caverns, selecting stalactites to match the musical scale, then wired them to electronic rubber mallets. It took three years to construct the organ. Tunes can be played automatically like a music box, or manually (*Oh, Shenandoah* is a favorite).

How it got there: Stalactites form when water droplets seeping through the ceiling of a cave leave tiny deposits of calcite (the crystalline form of limestone). Over the years the stalactites (and corresponding stalagmites on the ground, growing up) get impressively huge. Luray Caverns has a 170-ton fallen stalactite the size of a school bus.

Luray Caverns is open every day of the year. From mid-June through Labor Day, hours are 9am-7pm; it closes earlier the rest of the year. $16 adults; $14 seniors; $7 children ages seven-13 (☎ 540-743-6551, www.luraycaverns.com).

Endless Caverns, New Market

Claim to fame: Possibly the largest billboard in the eastern US, visible for miles. Why? The name of the caverns with the "Hollywood-type" signage comes from the fact that no one has ever reached the cavern's end. This is actually one of the more naturally displayed caverns, lit only by white light.

Open year-round; closed Christmas day. Hours from mid-June to Labor Day are 9am-7pm; earlier closing times the rest of the year. $12 adults; $6 children ages six-12 (☎ 540-896-2283, www.endlesscaverns.com).

Shenandoah Caverns, New Market

Claim to fame: The only caverns with an elevator.

How it got there: The elevator shaft was dug by hand in 1932, through 60 feet of limestone.

Open daily, year-round. From mid-June to Labor Day open 9am-6:15pm; closes earlier the rest of the year. $12.50 adults; $11 seniors; $6 children ages five-14 (☎ 540-477-3115 or 888-4-CAVERN, www.shenandoahcaverns.com).

Skyline Caverns, Front Royal

Claim to fame: The only cave in Virginia that has anthodites: delicate, spiny formations on the ceiling that somewhat resemble sea urchins.

How they got there: Still a mystery, but it's believed they grow about an inch every 7,000 years.

Open year-round. From mid-June to Labor Day hours are 9am-6:30pm; closes earlier the rest of the year (☎ 800-296-4545, www.skylinecaverns.com).

Crystal Caverns at Hupp's Hill, Strasburg

Claim to fame: One of the oldest documented caves in Virginia. Why? Although Native Americans probably used the caves for centuries, the first to document them were The Hupps, German emigrants who moved south through the Shenandoah Valley in the 1750s. They stored food in them, taking advantage of the constantly cool (54°) temperature.

Open daily, 10am-5pm. $8 adults, $6 children and seniors (☎ 540-465-8660, www.waysideofva.com/crystalcaverns).

Southwest Virginia

Resembling its closest neighbors, West Virginia and Kentucky, more than the rest of the Commonwealth, southwest Virginia to some degree really is about coal mining and bluegrass music, hollers and pick-up trucks. Yet its small towns are often centers of theater, art and music, surrounded by rugged mountains where you can hike for miles without seeing a soul. The people you do meet are among the friendliest anywhere.

THE TOWNS
▓ Blacksburg
▓ Catawba
▓ Marion
▓ Saltville
▓ Abingdon
▓ Damascus
▓ Big Stone Gap

Getting Here

Interstate 81 extends into southwest Virginia before heading south into Tennessee. To get to *far* southwest Virginia, **Route 58** is the main road.

Southwest Virginia is served by **Roanoke Regional Airport**, ☎ 540-362-1999.

Regional Information

Highlands Gateway Regional Visitor Center, 731 Factory Outlet Drive, Max Meadows, ☎ 800-446-9670, www.virginiablueridge.org.

Heart of Appalachia Tourism Authority, Big Stone Gap, ☎ 888-798-2386, www.heartofappalachia.com.

The **Virginia Tourism Corporation** (☎ 800-VISIT-VA, www.virginia.org) runs Virginia Highway Welcome Centers on I-81 at the VA/TN state line; I-77 at the VA/NC line; and on I-77 south of the VA/WV border.

Southwest Virginia

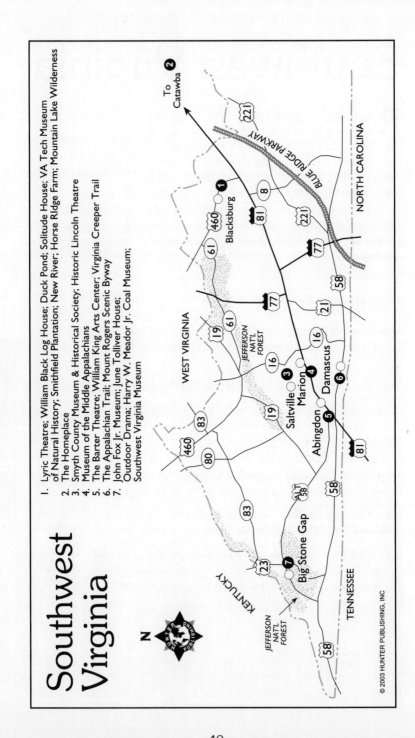

1. Lyric Theatre; William Black Log House; Duck Pond; Solitude House; VA Tech Museum of Natural History; Smithfield Plantation; New River; Horse Ridge Farm; Mountain Lake Wilderness
2. The Homeplace
3. Smyth County Museum & Historical Society; Historic Lincoln Theatre
4. Museum of the Middle Appalachians
5. The Barter Theatre; William King Arts Center; Virginia Creeper Trail
6. The Appalachian Trail; Mount Rogers Scenic Byway
7. John Fox Jr. Museum; June Tolliver House; Outdoor Drama; Harry W. Meador Jr. Coal Museum; Southwest Virginia Museum

© 2003 HUNTER PUBLISHING, INC

Blacksburg

Around Town

One accessory visitors to Blacksburg must pack, besides the requisite toothbrush, is a football schedule. Whether a fan or not, if the Virginia Tech Hokies are playing a home game during your stay, it may take tackling someone to get a room.

As is expected in a college town, a lion's share of businesses in Blacksburg cater to students, football fans, and visiting parents and alumni of Virginia Tech. This is the state's largest university (25,000 enrollment) and, while it swells the population to nearly 40,000 between September and May, Blacksburg manages to retain a small town atmosphere.

Taverns and music stores line Main Street closest to campus. An amusing array of shops capitalize on the university football team's nickname: Hokie Hair, Hokie House, and Hokie Sports, to name a few. You'll also find several art galleries, eclectic shops, the restored 1929 **Lyric Theatre** (135 College Avenue, ☎ 540-951-0604, www.thelyric.com) and interesting eateries in Blacksburg's thriving downtown.

The 16-block historic area was laid out on a grid in 1798 after William Black donated the land. A walking tour brochure details the buildings in the area bordered by Draper Road and Clay, Wharton and Jackson streets. Most of the churches and homes date to the mid-19th century. The oldest building on the tour is the **William Black Log House**, circa 1780s, at 141 Jackson Street. Today it houses the Downtown Merchants Association.

The Virginia Tech campus itself has several sites besides the football stadium to hold interest for visitors. The **Duck Pond** is a favored spot for picnicking and watching ducks and geese. Adjacent is the **Solitude House**, the oldest residence on campus, which sits on the site of the Draper Meadow Settlement and massacre of 1755. Shawnee Indians took Mary Draper Ingles captive and her 850-mile journey home is dramatized in a novel and in "The Long Way Home," an outdoor drama performed in Radford each summer (☎ 540-639-0679, www.thelongwayhome.org).

The **Virginia Tech Museum of Geological Sciences** exhibits minerals, fossils and a life-sized dinosaur model (☎ 540-231-3001), and the **Virginia Tech Museum of Natural History** showcases North American mammals (☎ 540-231-3001).

Adjacent to the campus, off Duck Pond Drive, is **Smithfield Plantation**, a 1772 Colonial house built by Col. William Preston. It's the birthplace of two Virginia Governors. Take the guided tour given every half-hour ($5 adults, $3 students, $2 children) and visit the Museum of Westward Expansion. Open April through the first weekend in December, Thursday-Sunday, 1-5pm (☎ 540-231-3947, http://civic.bev.net/smithfield).

> ★ TRAVEL TIP
>
> A new 460 Bypass completed in 2002 makes getting to Blacksburg from I-81 a lot easier and quicker.

Recreation

If not in town for something to do with Virginia Tech or football, most people visit Blacksburg as a convenient jumping-off place for outdoor recreation in Southwest Virginia.

There's tubing on the **New River**, horseback riding at **Horse Ridge Farm** (☎ 540-789-4731), and hiking to the **Cascades** or on the **Huckleberry Trail**, which runs six miles from Blacksburg to Christiansburg (☎ 800-288-4061). Bicyclists, walkers, runners, skaters and strollers are welcomed on this rail-to-trail.

Bring sturdy shoes for a hike up to the **Cascades** waterfall, a four-mile round-trip. This 68-foot waterfall forms on the Little Stony Creek as it flows through the Jefferson National Forest west of Blacksburg. There are bathrooms and a picnic area near the trailhead, and a parking fee is charged (☎ 540-552-4261).

The **Appalachian Trail** passes through **Mountain Lake Wilderness**, an 11,113-acre woodland that protects Virginia's only natural lake in the western part of the state. The **War Spur** and **Chestnut trails** form an easy day-hiking loop that passes a stirring rock overlook and old growth eastern hemlock trees (☎ 540-288-4061).

Dining

Check out the rooftop dining at **Boudreaux's Louisiana Kitchen**, a hip Cajun restaurant. On one warm March evening the outside tent-roofed lounge was already open. There's a long bar, restrooms and dining areas with tables overlooking Main Street for prime people watching. By graduation weekend, the entire roof comes off, exposing the bar to the open air. A little bit of Morgan's Landing in southwest Virginia. (We once had – and will never forget – a Thai dinner one hot summer night on a roof in Washington DC's Morgan's Landing neighborhood.) For $3.50 you take home the souvenir glass your drink comes in (205 North Main Street, ☎ 540-961-2330).

The Cellar Restaurant has a techno-industrial feel with stainless steel furniture and a concrete bar. The fare is inexpensive but creative, combining Greek and Italian favorites with new twists – i.e. Greek Spaghetti with flame-grilled breast of chicken – and many vegetarian choices (302 North Main Street, ☎ 540-953-0651).

Our Daily Bread Bakery and Café is a favorite lunch spot among locals. Started by a Virginia Tech graduate in 1980, the bakery has every kind of bread you can imagine, from lemon poppy seed to Portuguese sweet bread, as well as daily specials of unique sandwiches (chicken salad with artichokes one day, with grapes the next), homemade soups, organically grown coffee, and made-from-scratch cakes and pastries. About once a week they make what some have called the best Carolina barbecue in town. The daily menu is posted on their Web site Monday-Friday (keep an eye out for that barbecue!). Open Monday-Friday, 7am-6:30pm, and Saturday, 8am-5:30pm. Located in the Blacksburg Square Shopping Center (1329 S. Main Street, ☎ 540-953-2815, www.ourdailybreadbakery.com).

Any of the downtown Blacksburg restaurants can be hopping with college students at night, so if a quiet, adult dinner with candles and linens is what you're pining for, take a trip to Christiansburg to dine at the **Farmhouse Restaurant**. Built in the 1800s as part of the Ridinger Estate, the white clapboard farmhouse was transformed into a cozy, elegant restaurant in 1963. There's an old train caboose for a unique dining experience, a rustic lounge and a 250-seat banquet facility (285 Ridinger Street, Christiansburg, ☎ 540-382-3965, e-mail farmhous@ swva.net).

Southwest Virginia

Lodging

The **Clay Corner Inn** is a five-building B&B surrounding a heated pool. The rooms are themed: The Quilt Room has hand-embroidered pillows, the Sanibel Room features seashells and lace, and the Hokie Room is decked out in the team colors of orange and burgundy. The hospitality may be old-fashioned (ironed pillow cases), but the amenities are not – 59-channel cable TV, separate entrances, full kitchens and living areas in each guesthouse. You'll probably meet resident Labrador retrievers Kent and Solomon (who has authored his own book, *Solomon Says – Observations of an Innkeeper Dog*). The oldest building (1911) is the Huckleberry House, so-named because the Huckleberry Trail is just feet from the front door. You might run into one of the innkeepers walking Solomon and Kent on the trail. And, of course, pets are welcome (401 Clay Street SW, Blacksburg, ☎ 540-953-2604, www.claycorner.com, $$).

The **Best Western Red Lion Inn** may be a chain motel, but you'd hardly guess it, nor that you were right off I-460. The 13 acres of grounds have rolling lawns, trees, and even a stream with a little bridge over it. There's continental breakfast and dining in the Red Lion Restaurant. The décor and building design are German-influenced. The lobby has fireplaces, deep sofas and an "old world" atmosphere. Pets allowed with notice (900 Plantation Road, exit I-460 at Prices Ford Road, Blacksburg, ☎ 540-552-7770, $).

It's about 16 miles north of Blacksburg, but well worth the trip: **Mountain Lake Hotel** sits at the entrance to Mountain Lake Wilderness on its own 2,600 acres of mountain resort. There's hiking, mountain biking, boating, fishing, swimming, tennis, carriage and pony rides, and lawn games. The film *Dirty Dancing* was filmed in the elegant 150-year-old stone lodge. Open May through November (Pembroke, ☎ 800-828-0490 or 540-626-7121, www.mountainlakehotel.com, $$$$).

Information

Montgomery County Chamber of Commerce and Visitor Center, 1995 S. Main Street, ☎ 800-288-4061, www.montgomerycc.org.

The merchants of downtown Blacksburg have a Web site at **www.downtownblacksburg.com**.

Find information online at the Blacksburg Electronic Village, **www.bev.net**.

TIP

Don't even try visiting on Virginia Tech Parents Weekend (unless you're a parent, that is). It's the single busiest weekend, typically held in October, but all events are set after the football game schedule comes out in February. Check with the **Montgomery Chamber of Commerce** (☎ 800-288-4061, www.montgomerycc.org).

Side Trip

Catawba

Just seven miles off I-81 at Roanoke, about 20 miles northeast of Blacksburg, **The Homeplace** restaurant (☎ 540-384-7252) in Catawba seems worlds away from anywhere. At one table sit three high school couples, gowned girls on one side, tuxedoed boys on the other. At the next table, two unshaven, long-haired young men fresh off the Appalachian Trail shovel in one helping of food after another. They may be headed in opposite directions – the hikers to Maine and the high-schoolers to the Creek County High School prom – but for a few hours they share a dining room at The Homeplace, a local Catawba institution and, by word-of-mouth, a much-anticipated destination for hikers on the 2,167-mile AT that passes nearby. Hikers have been known to speed up their pace to make it by Sunday dinner.

The attraction – aside from a beautifully restored century-old house on just the prettiest spot in Catawba Valley, surrounded by mountains, rolling fields and manicured landscaping – is the food. The Homeplace serves up nothing more than the most delicious, down-home, all-you-can-eat, just-like-grandma-used-to-make meals. Outside, there are swings on the wraparound porch, a gazebo and a pond. For someone who's been on the trail since Georgia, reaching The Homeplace must be something akin to heaven on earth.

"Ever been here before?" asks the friendly waitress. We shake our heads. "Well, this is how it works. We bring everything family style – fried chicken, three vegetables and biscuits

Southwest Virginia

come with every meal – then we refill the dishes till you're just 'bout miserable. Then we top it off with peach cobbler."

There's no menu, the prices are not posted (it's only $11 per person), no alcohol, and only two main entrée choices: roast beef or Virginia ham. (On Thursdays there's pork barbeque.) They keep things simple. The Homeplace is open Thursday and Friday, 4-8pm; Saturday, 3:30-8pm; and Sunday, 11am-6pm.

Just as The Homeplace is the only place to eat in Catawba, there's only one place to stay: **CrossTrails Bed & Breakfast,** located on 15 acres where the AT and the TransAmerica Bicycle Trail cross. There are guest rooms in the main house and a loft in the carriage house, each with private bath, views of the mountains and air conditioning. Try cross-country skiing, fly-fishing, or just relax on the porch (☎ 800-841-8078, www.crosstrails. com, $$).

Marion

At the height of his popularity in 1925, world-famous writer Sherwood Anderson chose not New York, but one of the most obscure places in the country – Southwest Virginia – as his home. "I had grown tired of city life and wanted the quiet intimacy of life in a smaller place," he wrote in his autobiography.

The move to an old stone house beside a stream near Troutdale, Virginia, isn't all that astonishing, considering he was from a small town himself. His best-known work, the short-story collection *Winesburg, Ohio*, portrayed small-town life and people in all their strangeness and beauty.

What did astound the people of Smyth County was when Anderson bought Marion's two weekly newspapers and named himself editor. The writer who had rubbed elbows with the likes of Carl Sandburg and Theodore Dreiser covered school board meetings and barroom brawls. He frequented the Marion City Drug Store where he was known to throw back a beer with his local cronies.

In literature, Anderson is credited with breaking down the boundaries between fiction and autobiography, a style he applied in Marion's newspapers. Editor Anderson took on the persona of Buck Fever, a young mountain man who wrote with warmth and humor about the goings-on in the county. In his columns, Anderson championed causes like the Marion town band and better education for black children.

Even though he transferred editorship to his son in 1932 so he could travel and write more, Southwest Virginia always remained his home. He married a local woman, Eleanor Copenhaver, and when he died in the Panama Canal Zone on a friendship mission in 1941, she brought him home to be buried in Marion's Round Hill Cemetery.

The Andersons' home, **Ripshin**, is still owned by their nephew. The house is open to the public just one day a year – the second Saturday in September – as part of the annual short story contest in Sherwood Anderson's memory. Contact the Smyth County Chamber of Commerce for details: ☎ 276-783-3161.

★ DID YOU KNOW?

Marion is named for General Francis Marion, the "swamp fox" of the American Revolution, who was also the character Mel Gibson portrayed in the film *The Patriot*.

Around Town

In town, City Drug is no more, but Marion's Main Street is as alive as it was when Anderson worked there. And the Smyth County News is still published.

The entrepreneurial spirit thrives hand-in-hand with respect for historic preservation. The **Post Office Antique Mall** (☎ 276-782-9332) makes use of the town's restored post office. A busy lunch crowd frequents **Main Street Gifts & Eatery and Framing Unlimited,** run by three generations of local women. The women took over an old Piggly Wiggly store, an eyesore that had been empty for 30 years. Now the original hardwood floors, tin ceiling and brick walls have been revived for a delightful eatery and shop (212 E. Main Street, ☎ 276-783-9244).

A self-guided history walk takes in the **Smyth County Museum & Historical Society** (203 N. Church Street, ☎ 276-783-7286), the **Historic Lincoln Theatre**, the **Lincoln Inn**, and other sites.

Southwest Virginia

Dining

In addition to Main Street Gifts and Eatery (see previous page), Main Street dining includes the **New Pioneer** (☎ 276-781-1668) and **Preston's Place** (☎ 276-783-9528). Live country and rock bands now perform in the historic R.T. Greer & Company building, once a commercial business that dried herbs before shipping them to pharmaceutical houses throughout the country. It's now **Wright's Field Sports Café** (☎ 276-783-2233), which has preserved the weathered beams and exposed brick walls.

Outside town, the **Dip Dog Stand** is a local hang-out and landmark on Highway 11 West, famous for deep-fried hot dogs on a stick (☎ 276-783-2698), and the **Hungry Mother Restaurant** inside the state park offers dining with a great mountain lake view (☎ 276-781-7420).

Lodging

Marion has several chain and locally owned motels, and one B&B.

Best Western Marion accepts pets with a $20 deposit (1424 North Main Street, ☎ 276-783-3193, $), as does the **EconoLodge**, with a $25 deposit (1426 N. Main Street, ☎ 276-783-6031).

Windswept Bed & Breakfast (316 John Street, ☎ 276-782-0891 or 276-783-1853 after 4pm) is a country house near town (www.net-va.com/windswept, $).

There are two B&Bs in Troutdale, about 15 miles south of Marion on Route 16. **Tranquility Lodge** (1324 Ripshin Road, ☎ 276-677-3638, $) is a Christmas tree farm with its own hiking trails. The **Fox Hill Inn** (8568 Troutdale Highway, ☎ 800-874-3313, www.bbonline.com/va/foxhill, $$) is a secluded chalet-style inn surrounded by flower gardens and great views.

There's plenty of camping around Marion, at **Hungry Mother State Park** (☎ 276-781-7400 or 800-933-7275); the privately owned **Hun-**

gry Mother Campground (☎ 276-783-2046); **Interstate Campground** (☎ 276-646-8384); **Mt. Rogers National Recreation Area** (☎ 276-783-5196); **Houndshell Campground** (☎ 276-655-4639) in Troutdale; and **Tumbling Creek** in the Clinch Mountain Wildlife Area (☎ 276-944-4366 or 276-944-3434).

Information

Smyth County Chamber of Commerce, 124 W. Main Street, Marion, ☎ 276-783-3161, www.Smythchamber.org.

SIDE TRIP

Saltville

Salt does not enjoy the critical significance it once did. When you can buy a 26-ounce canister for less than a dollar and it lasts a few months, it is hard to appreciate what salt meant for people before refrigeration. In fact, in the 1800s, an army's success depended on salting meat to preserve it. And so it was that Union forces tried twice to capture the salt-mining operation in the town nicknamed "Salt Capital of the Confederacy."

Salt, deposited by an ancient inland sea, also preserves the town's ancient history. Remains of Ice Age mammals like wooly mammoths, mastodons and ground sloths, are uncovered during archeological digs, along with evidence of Native American habitation going back 11,000 years.

Much of this fascinating tale is told through exhibits at the **Museum of the Middle Appalachians** (☎ 276-496-3633, www.museum-mid-app.org, open Monday-Saturday, 10am-4pm, and Sunday, 1-4pm; $3 adults, $2 children ages six-12 and seniors). The week before Labor Day, there's a festival where the practice of salt-gathering is demonstrated, and a War Between the States battle re-enactment takes place.

While in Saltville, eat at the **Salt Box Café** (☎ 276-496-5999) on Main Street for hearty servings of hamburgers and fries, hickory-smoked barbecue and cornbread.

Southwest Virginia

 READING LIST

For a realistic story of growing up in Saltville, check out *Salt Mountain Girl* by Brenda Totten Blakey, who grew up in nearby Buckeye Hollow.

Abingdon

Around Town

After a week hiking in Virginia's Jefferson National Forest, we were overdue for showers, a good meal, a nice bottle of wine and a little culture. In such condition, Abingdon on a busy Saturday afternoon seemed to us like the mountain equivalent of Paris. Indeed, this small city of around 8,000 people reigns as the arts and cultural center of Southwest Virginia. A 20-block historic area of Victorian and Federal homes has dozens of antique and specialty shops, galleries, inns and restaurants. Add to this **the Barter Theatre** (Virginia's official state theater), the exclusive and expensive **Camberley's Martha Washington Inn**, a regional arts center, and the two-week **Virginia Highlands Festival**, and Abingdon stands out as a little nugget of sophistication in the middle of coal-mining country.

Chartered in 1778, Abingdon is the oldest town west of the Blue Ridge and the seat of Washington County. While the county was named for our first president, Abingdon was named in deference to his wife. Martha Washington's father was from Abingdon Parrish in England.

During the Great Depression, actor Robert Porterfield thought his hometown near the Tennessee border a good place to start a theater. He succeeded by offering employment to his out-of-work actor friends from New York City. The Barter Theatre's name comes from the practice of accepting produce as admission. In turn, the likes of Noel Coward, Tennessee Williams and Thornton Wilder received ham as royalties (vegetarian George Bernard Shaw got spinach instead). Today, it stages contemporary and classic plays alike, from Shakespeare to Shaw. Although they no longer take "ham for Hamlet," in 1965, one patron, Lady Bird Johnson, bartered a potted plant for a ticket. The season runs February through December (☎ 276-628-3991, www.BarterTheatre.com).

Delight is the best word to describe what awaits shoppers in Abingdon. The **Cave House Craft Shop**, an 1858 Victorian home, displays room after room of the wares of more than 150 members of the Holston Mountain Arts and Crafts Cooperative. Just as delightful is the story of how Cave House got its name. Apparently there's a cavernous limestone grotto beneath the house. Legend holds that Daniel Boone camped at the base of this hill on his first expedition to Kentucky in 1760. Wolves came out of the cave at night and attacked his dogs, so he named the area Wolf Hills (279 East Main Street, ☎ 276-628-7721).

William King Arts Center houses galleries and studios for painters, weavers, sculptors, dancers and potters and offers arts classes (415 Academy Drive, ☎ 276-628-5005).

Recreation

The towns of Abingdon and Damascus established the 34-mile **Virginia Creeper Trail**. Originally a Native American footpath, then a railroad bed, this hiking, biking and naturze trail gets its name from the early steam locomotives that struggled up the steep grades (the Virginia Creeper engine is on display at the Abingdon trailhead). The trail runs from Abingdon, through Damascus, to the North Carolina border, crossing Whitetop Station at an elevation of 3,576 feet. Daniel Boone used the path too, evidence by four documented campsites along the route. Bicycle rentals and shuttles are available from outfitters in both towns. Pick up a trail guide at the Abingdon Convention & Visitors Bureau, or at the trailhead.

Dining

The **Abingdon General Store & Gallery** is an art gallery, gift shop, bakery, gourmet deli, gardener's supply, general store, and an outdoor seasonal restaurant (301 East Main Street, ☎ 276-628-8382).

At the **Starving Artist Café**, sandwiches are named for famous artists, but art on the walls is by those lesser-known. The owner, once a starving artist himself, believes in promoting local artists who need to make a living doing something else – like restaurant work (134 Wall Street, ☎ 276-628-8445).

The Tavern is located in Abingdon's oldest building. Built in 1779, the likes of Henry Clay and King Louis Philippe have stayed under this roof. A later addition housed the first post office west of the Blue Ridge

Southwest Virginia

Mountains. Today's fare mixes Cajun dishes with meals reflecting the owner's German heritage. It features an extensive wine and imported beer list (222 East Main Street, ☎ 276-628-1118).

See the Dining Room at Camberley's Martha Washington Inn under *Lodging*, below.

Lodging

The B&Bs and inns in the Abingdon area are simply too numerous to list here. You'll have your choice of a stately home within walking distance of the historic district, a secluded cottage in the mountains, a country inn with a view of the river or grazing sheep. The **Abingdon Convention and Visitors Bureau** publishes a brochure listing more than a dozen of them. Call and request it at ☎ 800-435-3440, or visit www.abingdon.com/tourism/lodging.htm.

One establishment must be mentioned, however. The four-star historic **Camberley's Martha Washington Inn** is quite possibly the best place to rest your head in Southwest Virginia. The 1832 private mansion became the Martha Washington College for Women in 1860, and served as a Civil War hospital. Many believe it's haunted by several ghosts. While the Depression spawned the Barter Theatre across the street, hard times closed down the college and the mansion was used as a boarding house for actors. Today the hotel is graced with chandeliers, polished hardwood floors, elegant suites with fireplaces, period reproductions and fresh flower arrangements. The **Dining Room** is known for its Friday seafood buffet and Sunday champagne brunch. It's open to the public for breakfast, lunch and dinner daily. Reservations are recommended (150 W. Main Street, ☎ 800-555-8000, dining room 276-628-9151, www.marthawashingtoninn.com, $$$).

 The Empire Motel is an older motel, but has recently been renovated, and accepts pets with an $8 charge (887 Empire Drive, Exit 19 off I-81, ☎ 276-628-7131, $).

Information

Abingdon Convention & Visitors Bureau, 335 Cummings Street, ☎ 276-676-2282 or 800-435-3440, www.abingdon.com/tourism.

Event

Southwest Virginia's best-known arts event, the **Virginia Highlands Festival** runs for two weeks in August, drawing 200,000 people in celebration of the handmade arts. There are demonstrations and displays of crafts, writing, photography, music and dance, as well as hot air balloon rides, wine tastings, children's activities, and plenty of food (☎ 276-623-5266 or 800-435-3440, www.va-highlands-festival.org).

Damascus

"Trail Town USA"

B ordered by Virginia's finest mountain scenery and infused with the spirit of seekers and wanderers, Damascus is a picture-book town with a reputation that precedes itself. We first heard of its enchanting qualities while browsing Cave Spring House in Abingdon, where an artist painted a quick sketch for us of her hometown.

"I was hiking the Appalachian Trail up from Georgia," she said. "We'd been hiking up a steep ascent, then suddenly came out into a view of the valley below. I could see white houses with front porches and tree-lined streets. I decided right then that was where I wanted to live. I got off the trail, and went no farther. That was 10 years ago."

> ⭐ HAPPY TRAILS
>
> Virginia contains 560 miles of the AT, more than any other state. Of the 2,500 hikers who attempt the hike each year, only about 250 finish. The Virginia Creeper Trail is more of a draw for Damascus, bringing in as many as 600 bikers and hikers in a single weekend.

Around Town

It would be a full year before we set foot in town ourselves. We, too, came off a mountain slope – Iron Mountain in nearby Mount Rogers National Recreation Area – and quickly realized how that artist, an ex-

Southwest Virginia

patriate of Washington DC, found hospitality. Many homes double as part- or full-time bed & breakfasts that service AT thru-hikers, as well as the many day-trippers who come to enjoy the extensive recreation facilities around Damascus. And yes, nearly every home has a front porch, painted white, with a cat napping on a wicker chair or rocker.

Damascus, with slightly fewer than 1,000 people, embraces its nickname of "Friendliest Town on the AT." The postmaster holds mail for thru-hikers and public computer terminals permit out-of-towners to receive news from home. Sixty percent of the town's population are senior citizens. Many take in thru-hikers, offer them food, rides or a place to bed down.

Main Street doubles as the Appalachian Trail; where hikers leave trees and wildflowers behind, they'll find a "Friendship Path" instead. A fund-raising project allows folks to commission bricks for the path from a local artist. Hand-fired and each with a unique design, they become a permanent record of special events and people with a connection to Damascus. Bricks memorialize beloved residents, celebrate anniversaries, and bear trail names of thru-hikers.

Each May Damascus plays host to anyone who ever hiked the AT, or even thought about it. Trail Days swells the town with 22,000 visitors and coincides with a time when the greatest number of northbound AT hikers reach Damascus on their 2,167-mile trek from Georgia to Maine. (Such is the draw, however, that thru-hikers who've already passed Damascus often backtrack.) A hiker talent show illustrates the life-altering rite-of-passage that completing the trail has become. Poems, skits and songs are comedic or highly personal, but always heartfelt. Festivities end with a Main Street parade for hikers who gamely dodge water balloons lobbed at them by crowds on the sidewalk.

★ READING LIST

Bill Bryson's **A Walk in the Woods**, which highlights the author's travels along the Appalachian Trail, became a national bestseller in 1999. For another good read from someone who actually thru-hiked the entire trail, raising money for charity, see Jeff Alt's **A Walk for Sunshine** (www.awalkforsunshine.com).

"Friendliest Town on the Appalachian Trail"

This anonymous letter sent to the Trail Days Web site sums up the character of this small town.

Who We Are

(Used with permission from the author)

We are local business owners, doctors, lawyers, police officers, volunteer fire fighters, factory workers, senior citizens, and college students. We invite you over to dinner during the week and go to church with you on the weekend. We are there when you have a question. The person you call at midnight to help you with a problem. We help you plant your crops in the spring and harvest them in the fall. We let you borrow the car when yours is broken and drive you to the store when you can no longer see. We say hello when we meet on the street and call when we haven't seen you for a while. We were there when your baby was born. We watched it grow and enter school. When they got their license we heard about how cool they were and how much they loved life. We were there when they lost that life and you cried all night on the phone with us. We grew up with you and you watched us grow up before your eyes. We watched you grow old during our lives, but listened with joy to stories from you that make you young again. We sat in the backyard and on the front porch swing with you on warm summer days. We shared plates of food and cold lemonade while we visited, didn't matter whether it was homemade or store bought, it was the best food in the world. We loved you with all our hearts and cried when it was time to say good-bye and let you go home to God.

We spend time in the woods enjoying nature and God's wonders. Some people call us hikers.

Most of you call us your friends and neighbors.

Southwest Virginia

Recreation

Did we mention that Damascus' other nickname is "where trails cross"? Besides the AT, the Transcontinental Bicycle Route passes through en route from Yorktown, Virginia, to Oregon, as do the Virginia Creeper, Historical Daniel Boone, and Iron Mountain trails. The **Virginia Creeper Trail** runs 34 miles from Abingdon to the North Carolina line.

The Virginia Creeper Trail

Originally an Indian footpath, the railroad claimed the route at the beginning of the 20th century for logging timber-rich forests. It was so steep in places the engines slowed to a crawl, hence the name creeper. Reclaimed as a recreation trail in 1977, it's a favorite with bikers who pedal to the top of Whitetop, then glide 17 miles downhill to Damascus.

There are a number of businesses that outfit and guide visitors. Several specialize in taking hikers to trailheads or driving bikers up Whitetop Mountain, from which they descend 1,700 feet through national forest along the Virginia Creeper Trail. Each business also rents equipment. See **Adventure Damascus** (128 W. Laurel Avenue, ☎ 888-595-BIKE, www.adventuredamascus.com); **Blue Blaze Shuttle Service** (226 W. Laurel Avenue, ☎ 800-475-5095, http://blueblaze.naxs.com); **Mount Rogers Outfitters** (110 Laurel Ave., ☎ 276-475-5416, www.mtrogersoutfitters.com).

For **fishing**, three trout streams flow off the mountains and through town. Fifty miles of streams and two lakes in the area have both stocked and natural trout. For current conditions and regulations, call **Virginia Creeper Fly Shop** in Abingdon (16501 Jeb Stuart Highway, ☎ 276-628-3826, http://vcflyshop.naxs.com).

The **Virginia Highlands Horse Trail** (☎ 276-783-5196) runs through the Mt. Rogers Recreation Area, and **Grayson Highlands State Park** has horse camping facilities (☎ 276-579-7092, reservations: 800-933-7275, www.dcr.state.va.us).

If you'd rather experience nature from the car, take the 34-mile **Mount Rogers Scenic Byway** (US 58) from Damascus to Volney, climbing Whitetop along the way. It's the highest road in Virginia.

Dining

Eating in Damascus is casual. At **Side Track Cyber Café** you can check your e-mail while having a sandwich (103 S. Shady Avenue, ☎ 276-475-6106). **Dot's Inn** is a bar that can get smoky and loud, but the food is great, made to order and quick (338 Douglas Drive, ☎ 276-475-3817).

Cowboys is in a gas station/convenience store at the corner of Douglas Drive and Laurel Avenue that serves three meals a day. Their southern country breakfast of biscuits, gravy, pancakes, sausage, bacon – you name it – is wholly satisfying (☎ 276-475-5444). There's also the **Country Kettle** at 21894 Jeb Stuart Highway (☎ 276-475-3380) and **Sicily's Pizza**, 132 W. Laurel Avenue (☎ 276-475-5753).

Lodging

For its size, Damascus has a surprising number of inns and private homes offering rooms to the thousands of visiting recreationists. Here are a few:

The Apple Tree Bed & Breakfast is a restored 1904 home with beautiful tiger oak floors, a two-suite cottage on a hill and an Apple Blossom Wedding Chapel. The hosts will arrange for a wedding in the chapel, on top of Whitetop or on the AT (115 E. Laurel Avenue, ☎ 877-36APPLE, www.appletreebnb.com, $).

The Maples Bed & Breakfast is a 1904 guesthouse with wicker chairs on the front porch to watch the world go by (203 Laurel Avenue, ☎ 276-475-3943, themaplesbedandbreakfast.com, $).

Mountain Laurel Inn is a 1903 Queen Anne Victorian with three guest rooms and a suite (22750 Jeb Stuart Highway, ☎ 276-475-5956, www.mountainlaurelinn.com, $$).

The River House is a fully furnished three-bedroom house on the south fork of the Holston River (21636 Delmar Road, ☎ 276-475-5257, www.riverhouse.homestead.com, $$).

Buchanan Inn at The Green Cove Station is next to an old train station (41261 Green Cove Road, ☎ 877-300-9328, $$). **Green Cove Inn** is a renovated schoolhouse at the foot of Whitetop Mountain (41070 Chestnut Mountain Road, ☎ 276-388-3479, $$$).

Southwest Virginia

You can stay at 4,000 feet at **Greer's Whitetop Mountain Cabin** on Whitetop Mountain (☎ 276-388-3477, www.wtmcabin.home-stead.com, $$).

Visitors who require only the bare necessities can inquire at **Mount Rogers Outfitters** about space in their hostel across the street: $10 for a two-bunk room (☎ 276-475-5416, $).

Information

Call the **Town of Damascus** at 866-DAMASCUS, or check their Web site, www.damascus.org.

Festivals

In addition to **Trail Days** the third week in May (☎ 866-DAMASCUS, www.traildays.com), the nearby community of Whitetop hosts several festivals celebrating the area's abundance. The **Maple Festival** is the last full weekend in March; the **Ramp Festival** is held the third Sunday in May and features an eating contest for the pungent wild on-ion; and the **Molasses Festival** is the second Sunday in October. For more information about these three events, contact Grayson County Tourism, ☎ 276-773-3711.

Big Stone Gap

Authors have built careers telling tales about this small Southwest Virginia town. Whether it's the historical, coal-mining romances of John Fox Jr., or Adriana Trigiani's bestsellers, the real Big Stone Gap keeps popping up in books. And who wouldn't be inspired to write af-ter witnessing that panorama of Appalachian Mountains that encircle this town?

Residents take pride in this literary history. They count Trigiani (author of a trilogy of *Big Stone Gap* novels) as a native daughter (look for a pamphlet on store counters that points out places in her books) and John Fox Jr. as an adopted son. Fox, a native Kentuckian, featured many locals as characters in his many novels and short stories.

Around Town

Generations of locals have acted in Virginia's official outdoor drama based on Fox's *Trail of the Lonesome Pine*. The **John Fox Jr. Museum** (☎ 540-523-2747) on Shawnee Avenue memorializes his former home. Furnishings and memorabilia of the family give it an authentic touch. He's most famous for *The Trail of the Lonesome Pine*, published in 1908, thrice a movie and now the longest running outdoor drama in America. Set during the rise of the local coal industry, it follows a mountain girl, June Tolliver, from her hill country home to Big Stone Gap. She was a real person, and her home is the **June Tolliver House** at Jerome and Clinton Streets (☎ 540-523-4707). It has a great gift and book shop, and makes a convenient stop right before a showing of the **Trail of the Lonesome Pine Outdoor Drama** (☎ 800-362-0149), performed next door on an outdoor stage from late June to early September. It's been running since 1963, with most townspeople having some connection to it, some even growing up in it, playing different roles over the past 40 years.

The Trail production is Big Stone Gap's chief draw, a far cry from iron and timber that lent the town the nickname "Pittsburgh of the South." Discovery of coal and iron ore deposits in the 1870s seemed to offer northern coal and timber barons all the ingredients for wealth. Hotels were built, streets were laid out methodically on a grid, and the railroad came, bringing with it the outside world.

But the thirst for wealth depleted much of the valuable timber by 1915. The iron ore reserves turned out to be much less than estimated. Coal proved more profitable. Neighboring Wise County still produces 40% of all coal mined in the state. **The Harry W. Meador Jr. Coal Museum** (☎ 540-523-4950) at E. Third Street and Shawnee Avenue displays artifacts from the industry that shaped this town and remains a major employer. The museum's namesake was a union laborer in the mines who rose to vice president of the coal company. The museum has displays of photographs, equipment and tools that go back to the pick-and-shovel days.

The **Southwest Virginia Museum** (☎ 276-523-1322) at W. First Street and Wood Avenue is located in a gem of a mansion built of locally quarried limestone. The house, built in the 1880s by Rufus Ayers, a Virginia attorney general, has been a museum since 1948. Three floors of exhibits vividly describe the boom and bust years of the town, describe Native American life as well as that of the pioneers who passed through on their way west through the Cumberland Gap. The grounds of the museum are nearly as fascinating as the interior. There's

Southwest Virginia

a separate brochure describing both the manmade and natural, from cultivated plants to a gigantic iron kettle brought over from France before 1776 to boil seawater for salt. Open Memorial Day to Labor Day, Monday-Thursday, 10am-4pm; Friday, 9am-4pm; Saturday, 10am-5pm; and Sunday, 1-5pm. Closed Mondays the rest of the year. Admission is charged.

Last is a stop that really should be your first, the **101 Car** on US 23 at the edge of town. The restored 1870 train car houses the **Lonesome Pine Tourist & Information Center** (☎ 276-523-2060), offering brochures, friendly advice, as well as a 50¢ tour of the plush conveyance, once the private car of the president of the Interstate Railroad.

⭐ **FILM CLIPS**

The 1937 film *Trail of the Lonesome Pine*, starring Henry Fonda, wasn't filmed here, and some residents still resent it. Parts of *Coal Miner's Daughter* were shot here, and a movie of Adriana Trigiani's 2000 best-selling novel *Big Stone Gap* is scheduled to be filmed in the area.

Dining

Stringer's on Fifth Street (☎ 276-523-5388) has long been the most popular place to eat on a Friday night (fried food, buffet-style). There's also **Red Flower Chinese Restaurant** on Wood Avenue (☎ 276-523-2498), **Little Mexico** in Powell Valley Square (☎ 276-523-3992), and **Huddle House**, next to the Comfort Inn, specializing in 24-hour breakfast (☎ 276-523-6530). **Mutual Drug** on Wood Avenue has cafeteria-style dining (☎ 276-523-1123). The nicest place to eat in terms of atmosphere is **Ms. Fritzi's Tea Room** in the 1908 Victorian House on Wood Avenue, serving lunch and dinner Tuesday-Saturday (☎ 276-523-6245).

Lodging

The **Country Inn Motel & RV Park** is really the only place to stay in town and, luckily, it takes pets for a $2 charge. It's a modest, old-fashioned motel, but the view of the mountains is first rate, and the 101 Car and Lonesome Pine Tourist Information Center are right next door (the motel is on US 23, ☎ 276-523-0374).

There's a **Comfort Inn** two miles from town (☎ 276-523-5911), and more lodging in nearby Norton.

Information

Heart of Appalachia Tourism, ☎ 888-798-2386, www.heartof-appalachia.com.

Lonesome Pine Tourist & Information Center, ☎ 276-523-200, www.BigStoneGap.org.

Q&A with Author Adriana Trigiani

How to write a book about your hometown
(and still be welcomed back)

Trigiani's main character, Ave Maria, is a 30-something life-long resident of Big Stone Gap. While Adriana moved away after college to write for television in New York City, her books are the imagined life she might have lived had she stayed there. Her parents still live in Big Stone Gap and, when she returns for book signings, she's embraced by the community.

Q: *How did you write a book about a town where you haven't lived in nearly 20 years, from a New York City apartment?*

A: That's the best way. I deliberately didn't go and spend long stretches there; I wanted to have the feelings I had back then. Art helped me – I had a giant painting of a house in a clearing in the Blue Ridge Mountains and I would stare at it. It looks a lot like the cover of the first book.

Q: *Did you think about what it might mean for this little town to have a novel set there?*

A: I didn't think about that at all. I thought it was like naming it "Philadelphia." When I went home I realized how important it was to them. If it helps them, that's great.

Southwest Virginia

69

Q: *There are some names in the book similar to real people's; are the characters based on those people?*

A: No, they're all fictitious characters, though I did steal some nicknames and parts of real names. Iva Lou is the name of a friend, but she's so far from that character. I used surnames that were authentic to the area. I saved a lot of obituaries.

Q: *Are you Ave Maria?*

A: No, but the first book catches the sense of living in a place and time that, while it's enchanted, you're dreaming of what's to be. She's not me, but she became a real person to me and really dictated how things would go and took over the twists and turns of the plot. I did get books from the Wise County Bookmobile, like she did, about three a week.

Q: *Would you ever consider moving back to your home-town?*

A: I think it's just the most beautiful place; I think it's America. But when I've had the experience of something, I don't have to repeat it.

Trigiani's first book in the trilogy, *Big Stone Gap* (Random House, 2000), is set to become a movie and will be filmed in town. The second, *Big Cherry Holler*, was published in 2001, and the third, *Milk Glass Moon*, in 2002.

★ TIP

If you meet anyone in town with a name similar to characters in Adriana Trigiani's *Big Stone Gap* books, *don't* assume it's really them in the book. "Adri," as she's affectionately known here, borrowed parts of some real names, but maintains all her characters and their shenanigans are fictitious. Local landscaper Jack McClanahan was astonished when he read the book and found his nickname – Jack Mac – was the same as the main character's love interest. The similarity ends there. McClanahan says he's 17 years older than Trigiani, and vaguely remembers her as a kid who watched him perform in the outdoor drama *Trail of the Lonesome Pine*.

Central Virginia

Central Virginia is the land of farms and wineries, railroad towns and historic plantation homes. Its now tranquil landscape witnessed both the opening and closing salvos of the Civil War. Throughout the **Piedmont**, as the region is often called, undulating roads roll away to the horizon, connecting once busy, dusty depots, built originally to handle the great harvest of the land. Today, they rely on the visitor in search of a quiet weekend get-away or a historical pilgrimage to Civil War sites.

THE TOWNS
▓ Little Washington
▓ Culpeper
▓ Fredericksburg
▓ Charlottesville
▓ Ashland
▓ Appomattox
▓ Bedford

Getting Here

The East Coast's main north/south thoroughfare, **I-95**, runs through Central Virginia, with **I-64** running across it. Additionally, **US 360** and **US 460** both cross the length of the southern Piedmont.

Central Virginia is serviced by **Richmond International Airport**, ☎ 804-226-3000, www.flyrichmond.com.

Regional Information

Virginia Tourism Corporation has Virginia Highway Welcome Centers on I-85 and I-95 at the Virginia/North Carolina state line, and at the Bell Tower on Capitol Square in Richmond (☎ 800-VISIT-VA, www.virginia.org).

Little Washington

What's there to do in Washington, Virginia? If you ask a local, as I did one hot afternoon, he might tell you to sit on the corner and see if anyone famous gets out of the limos. If you've got the money, the

Central Virginia

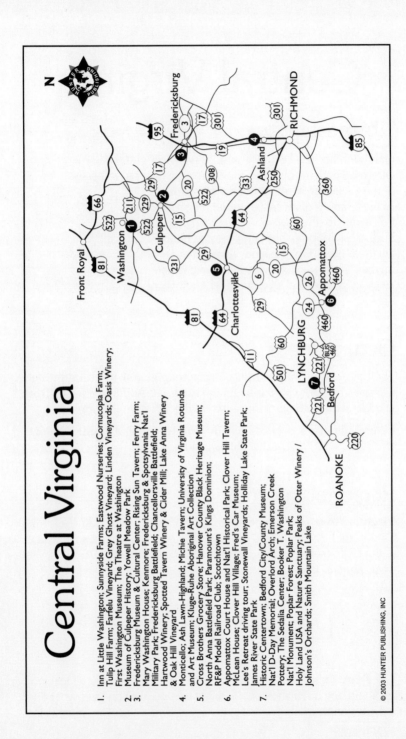

1. Inn at Little Washington; Sunnyside Farms; Eastwood Nurseries; Cornucopia Farm;
   Tulip Hill Farm; Farfelu Vineyard; Grey Ghost Vineyard; Linden Vineyards; Oasis Winery;
   First Washington Museum; The Theatre at Washington
2. Museum of Culpeper History; Yowell Meadow Park
3. Fredericksburg Museum & Cultural Center; Rising Sun Tavern; Ferry Farm;
   Mary Washington House; Kenmore; Fredericksburg & Spotsylvania Nat'l
   Military Park; Fredericksburg Battlefield; Chancellorsville Battlefield;
   Hartwood Winery; Spotted Tavern Winery & Cider Mill; Lake Anna Winery
   & Oak Hill Vineyard
4. Monticello; Ash Lawn–Highland; Michie Tavern; University of Virginia Rotunda
   and Art Museum; Kluge-Ruhe Aboriginal Art Collection
5. Cross Brothers Grocery Store; Hanover County Black Heritage Museum;
   North Anna Battlefield Park; Paramount's Kings Dominion;
   RF&P Model Railroad Club; Scotchtown
6. Appomattox Court House and Nat'l Historical Park; Clover Hill Tavern;
   McLean House; Clover Hill Village; Fred's Car Museum;
   Lee's Retreat driving tour; Stonewall Vineyards; Holliday Lake State Park;
   James River State Park
7. Historic Centertown; Bedford City/County Museum;
   Nat'l D-Day Memorial; Overlord Arch; Emerson Creek
   Pottery; The Sedalia Center; Booker T. Washington
   Nat'l Monument; Poplar Forest; Poplar Park;
   Holy Land USA and Nature Sanctuary; Peaks of Otter Winery /
   Johnson's Orchards; Smith Mountain Lake

Inn at Little Washington (see more information on pages 76-77) is the real reason to come to this tiny village of just under 200 people, at the edge of the Blue Ridge Mountains.

Around Town

Just an hour and a half from DC, the inn has attracted all the high-falutin' folks from Hollywood and government. Movie stars Paul Newman and Barbra Streisand have lent their names and accolades to the inn's brochure. Locals have spotted the likes of Alan Greenspan, Andrea Mitchell and Linda Carter stepping out of the limos. Their drivers park in front of the tiny post office waiting for their passengers, and sometimes grab a sandwich from the **Country Café** next door.

That said, there are plenty of *other* things to do – in town and around it. Many outlying farms are open for tours. There are several wineries nearby, and, of course, the Blue Ridge Mountains.

For such a small town there's an unusually eclectic and sophisticated array of art galleries, gold and silversmiths, boutiques and antiques stores housed in quaint old homes. There are not one, but two community theaters.

It's safe to say all other business in town relies in some way on the Inn and its clientele. After all, no matter how luxurious the accommodations or pampering the service at the inn, guests have to get out and take the air at some point. What they find is basically a country village, still two-by-five blocks just as George Washington laid them out, where upscale boutiques and artisans have set up shop. Watch them at work in their studios painting, making furniture and pottery. In others, pre-Columbian art, antiques and Tibetan rugs are displayed. There are a couple of bed & breakfast inns and an organic farm market that also sells gourmet cheese and fine wine.

From the outside, the Inn at Little Washington is a modest country inn, but the interior has been transformed into a lavishly decorated European-style hotel and restaurant. You can easily drop a cool grand on one night's lodging and dinner, and it might take months to get a Saturday night reservation.

It's a place where you may be greeted by a Dalmatian wearing a pearl necklace; a place Barbra Streisand called "extraordinary," and *Travel + Leisure* rated the "Top Hotel in the World for Food."

Reinhardt Lynch and chef Patrick O'Connell opened the Inn in 1977, decorating it with their art and antiques collections, and with the help

Central Virginia

73

of a London stage designer. They themselves call it "utterly decadent in detail." It's five-star all the way, for both food and accommodations.

While there's bound to be some local jealousy towards out-of-towners who've "bought half the town," cooperation and good will between the Inn and the town is apparent. The proprietors installed a fountain and bench across the street for public use, have held tours of the Inn that benefit the neighborhood church, and they help support local farms by using their fresh herbs and produce on the menu.

The Inn has managed to blend in nicely with the character of the town and its country surroundings, where most locals refer to the neighboring valley as a "holler," and drive a pickup instead of a Mercedes. Just a few miles down the road, Ben Jones, who played Cooter in the *Dukes of Hazzard* television show, sells Moon Pies and RC Cola from **Cooter's Store** (there's even a replica of the "General Lee" on the front lawn). As a side note, Jones writes a weekly newspaper column and ran for the 7th congressional seat in the Virginia House of Representatives in 2002, challenging the incumbent to debate him in country stores, barbershops, beauty parlors, and corner drugstores.

The bulletin board in front of the post office serves as the visitor information center, with brochures on lodging and shops. It also serves as a reminder that this still is a trusting, small town community. A note from the town's administrative assistant is posted, giving her home phone number, as well as the mayor's, if they're needed after business hours.

Why "*Little* Washington?"

The town's nickname distinguishes it from its big sister, the District of Columbia. But Virginia's Washington actually came first. The town was surveyed in 1749 by then 17-year-old George Washington, who laid out the streets and gave it his name. However, even before Washington came, the crossroads was a thriving frontier trading post where whites set up trade with Indians. Several homes in town have clapboards over the log cabin structures, and are still occupied by descendants of the original owners.

Attractions

Sunnyside Farms, which supplies the Sunnyside Farm Market in town as well as many fine restaurants in the mid-Atlantic region, is one of Virginia's oldest working farms, dating to 1720. Tours of the farm, an experiment in sustainable agriculture using natural compost and heirloom plants, are given Saturdays, May-November, by appointment (☎ 540-675-2627, www.sunnysidefarms.com).

Eastwood Nurseries grows all kinds of Japanese Maples and gives tours by appointment (634 Long Mountain Road, Washington, ☎ 540-675-1234, www.japanesemaples.com).

Cornucopia Farm raises white doves for release at special events. Don't worry – they're homing doves and have no trouble returning to the farm. If you're considering a white dove release, they'll give you a tour and a free demonstration (394 Hunter Road, Washington, ☎ 540-675-2336, www.virginiadoves.com). At **Tulip Hill Farm** you can see miniature donkeys being raised (6 Midnight Lane, Castleton, ☎ 540-987-8566, www.tuliphillfarm.com).

Nearby **wineries** include: **Farfelu Vineyard** in Flint Hill open year-round, Thursday through Monday, 11am-5pm (☎ 540-364-2930, www.farfelu.com). In Amissville, **Gray Ghost Vineyard** is open Friday through Sunday and federal holidays, 11am-5pm; and weekends only in January and February (☎ 540-937-4869). **Linden Vineyards** in Linden is open Wednesday through Sunday, 11am-5pm; weekends only December-March. Weekends feature educational tours at 11:30am (☎ 540-364-1997, http://lindenvineyards.com). **Oasis Winery** in Hume offers tastings daily from 10am to 5pm, year-round ($5 charge), with tours at 1 and 3pm. You can have a gourmet lunch or purchase a Davidoff cigar and sit on the cigar patio (☎ 540-635-7627, www.oasiswine.com).

The First Washington Museum has an 18th-century kitchen, a one-room school, and an historic room detailing the history of Rappahannock County and the town of Washington. Open April 15 to October 15 (198 Main Street, ☎ 540-675-3352).

The Theatre at Washington stages professional dramatic and musical performances, including the Smithsonian at Little Washington chamber music series. Feature films are shown two Friday nights a month at 8pm (corner of Gay and Jett streets, ☎ 540-675-1253, www.theatre-washington-va.com).

Ki Community Arts presents programs, festivals and educational events in the Old Town Hall. Also housed here is **Ki Theatre,** a professional company that tours worldwide (310 Gay Street, ☎ 540-675-1615, www.kitheatre.com).

Central Virginia

Dining

In the dining room at **The Inn at Little Washington** (see below), fresh flower arrangements adorn every table. Luxurious fabrics hang from the ceilings, fringed silk-shaded lamps over each table. The wine cellar boasts 14,000 bottles. You'll need to make a reservation at least two weeks in advance, and plan on spending at least $100 per person for dinner (Middle and Main streets, ☎ 540-675-3800).

The Country Café serves breakfast, lunch and dinner daily in a casual setting. Chicken, seafood, pork, fresh salads, homemade soup, desserts and ice cream. Located in the same building as the post office, across from the fountain (389-A Main Street, ☎ 540-675-1066).

Sunnyside Farm Market, located in one of the oldest mercantiles in the country (circa 1835), sells organic beef, pork, lamb and produce from nearby Sunnyside Farms as well as gourmet condiments, imported cheeses, and wines. Nearly everything in the store is original, down to the wooden counters that were tracked down after they'd been sold. We tried something we'd never had before: Torta, a sheep's milk cheese layered with roasted red peppers and basil pesto. Scrumptious! You can pick out a gourmet sandwich or salad from the cooler and eat outside on the backyard patio under an umbrella table. Open daily, 10:30am-6pm (337 Gay Street, ☎ 540-675-1074, www.sunnysidefarms.com).

That's it for dining right in Little Washington. Nearby Sperryville has several restaurants – the **Blue Moon** (☎ 540-987-3162) is fun – and in Flint Hill, **The Flint Hill Public House** (☎ 540-675-1700) and **Four & Twenty Blackbirds** are real treats (☎ 540-675-1111).

Lodging

The Inn at Little Washington has 14 bedrooms and suites, each decorated in a unique way with European fabrics and antiques. Breakfast is served in the glassed-in porch looking out onto a courtyard; just ask and you can have a picnic lunch packed for a drive in the country. Rooms start at $350 per night during the week and go up to nearly

$900 on peak weekends. There are no televisions, but ask for anything else and your wish will be granted (Middle and Main streets, ☎ 540-675-3800, $$$$).

If you can't afford to stay at the inn, but want to soak up some of what draws celebrities to Little Washington, there are several great bed & breakfasts in town:

Fairlea Farm Bed & Breakfast is a five-minute walk from town to a fieldstone manor house overlooking a sheep farm, gardens and mountain views. Three guest rooms and one suite with fireplace, all with private baths. The hosts will set up a horseback trail ride for you (636 Mt. Salem Avenue, ☎ 540-675-3679, http://bnb-n-va.com/fairlea.htm, $$).

Arrivals at the **Foster Harris House** are greeted with either fresh iced lemonade or hot apple cider, depending on the season. The 1900 country Victorian B&B has mountain views, fireplaces, whirlpool, and five guest rooms with private baths (189 Main Street, ☎ 800-666-0153, www.fosterharris.com, $$).

The Heritage House B&B is an 1837 manor house where the rooms are decorated with heirlooms and afternoon tea is served in the parlor. All private baths; full gourmet breakfast (291 Main Street, ☎ 540-675-3207, www.heritagehousebb.com, $$).

Middleton Inn is an 1850 home on five acres with mountain views, eight fireplaces, four bedrooms with private baths, and full breakfast served. There's also a guest cottage with fireplace and Jacuzzi (☎ 540-675-2020, www.middleton-inn.com, $$$$).

 The **Gay Street Inn B&B** welcomes dogs with advance notice and no extra fee, but they must be on a flea protection program. The restored 1860s stucco farmhouse has four guest rooms with views of the Blue Ridge. It's furnished with some pieces made by the innkeeper, Robin Kevis, who's also a carpenter. Donna Kevis, a graduate of Johnson & Wales College of Culinary Arts, prepares the breakfasts. They have a cat of their own and a chocolate Lab named Kaulua. Children are welcome (160 Gay Street, ☎ 540-675-3288, www.gaystreetinn.com, $$).

Information

Town of Washington, ☎ 540-675-3128, www.town.washington.va.us.

Rappahannock County, www.rappguide.com, for information about lodging, dining, things to do, weather reports and the like.

Event

Trinity Episcopal Church's **annual house tour** the third weekend in October is a great time for leaf peeping as well as peeking into some fabulous private homes. The ladies of First Baptist Church serve boxed chicken lunches, and high tea is served at the last house on the tour. Contact the Rappahannock Association for Arts & the Community, ☎ 540-675-3193. For other events, visit www.raac.org.

Culpeper

Around Town

It took a little time, but after walking up and down Davis Street, popping into shops and talking to local business owners, we finally met a person born and raised in Culpeper – 73-year-old Dorothy Inskeep James, an employee in Clarke's Hardware. She wanted to make sure I included her maiden name – Inskeep is a very old name in these parts, but just how old, she couldn't quite say. She also wanted me to know that the vitality of Culpeper's downtown, Davis and Main streets, isn't just a recent phenomenon. When she was a girl, Davis Street was just as busy with shoppers as it is now. There were three hardware stores (she worked at one for 21 years, and when it closed, she came to Clarke's), and everyone knew everyone.

Today, eclectic shops, art galleries and cafés blend fairly well with older businesses that have become local institutions: the 100-year-old **Clarke's Hardware**, **Gayheart's Drug Store**, where patrons have been meeting at the soda fountain for half a century, and **Knakal's Bakery**, where creamy confections have been satisfying generations of sweet tooths.

Some might call the recent gentrification of Culpepper a bit "artsy-fartsy," but downtown is still a place where folks can get a haircut, get their shoes repaired, or buy the right size wrench for a plumbing job. And no one can complain about what Culpeper Renaissance, Inc., through Virginia's Main Street program, has done for the heart of the city that had suffered a period of long decline and neglect that began in the 1970s. Where drug dealers and prostitutes loitered on street corners only a half-dozen years ago, now tourists and local shoppers patronize businesses and eat in sidewalk cafés. The renovated historic train station houses the visitor center, and is still the stop for two daily Amtrak trains – it's just 2½ hours to Washington DC's Union Station.

Culpeper's location has a lot to do with its recent resurgence. At the junction of Routes 29 and 3, it's on the way for folks traveling between DC and Charlottesville. Artists Rich and Kris Schluter of Fredericksburg found Davis Street a successful location for their **Thistletree Forge** gallery. They even expanded the gallery in 2002, taking advantage of the large, open spaces of a former hardware store to display their metal work along with pottery, candles, and pieces by other local artists. The gallery is open Thursday-Saturday (☎ 540-829-8440).

★ DON'T MISS

Ace Books & Antiques, with more than 250,000 used books, is believed to be the largest used bookseller on the east coast (120 W. Culpeper Street, ☎ 540-825-8973).

Across the street, another former hardware store houses the **Wine & Cheese Shop** and the acclaimed **Hazel River Inn**, where an Austrian chef does his magic in the oldest commercial building downtown, which was once used as a Civil War jail. The original rear of the building is circa 1790, while the 1835 painted brick front still proclaims "Yowell Hardware Co. – Stoves & Ranges – Electrical and Plumbing Supplies." It's definitely part of Culpeper's charm that such vestiges of its past remain. Lerner's Department Store is no longer, but the large sign remains atop the building that now houses a portrait and photography studio, hair salon, driving school and other businesses.

A barrel full of rakes and shovels, a line of tomato and herb plants, bright red Radio Flyer tricycles and wagons, and shiny metal trash cans crowd the sidewalk outside the Corinthian-columned Masonic Building. The Masons still meet upstairs, but **Clarke's Hardware** has been the downstairs tenant since 1970. When Claude Minnich bought the hardware store from Mrs. Clarke 22 years ago, he vowed not to change a thing, not the sign, the name, or the commitment to personal service the store had been known for since the turn of the century (☎ 540-825-9178).

"I give good service, so people have kept coming all along, even when this end of the street was basically a slum. The Wal-Mart opening didn't bother me at all," says Minnich. He adds that business has picked up in the last five or six years as other shops have opened and tourists have

Central Virginia

come. While they might not be in the market for a mop or a blender while visiting town, tourists love "old-time" hardware stores like Clarke's, where a bushel of locally grown garlic cloves sits on the counter.

The **Cameleer** was one of the first of the new, boutique-type shops to open 10 years ago, at the beginning of the revitalization. After spending three years in Australia, Sue Bernhardt returned home to Virginia to open up shop selling Aboriginal art and handcrafts (☎ 540-825-8073). The store has expanded to represent items from 50 countries and occupy three buildings on the corner of Main and Davis (for a good idea of what the corner looked nearly 100 years ago, see the cover of the booklet *In & Around Culpeper*, available in the visitor center). "Culpeper is a great place to live and do business. The merchants really work together," Bernhardt says. A strong sign of the confidence entrepreneurs hold for Culpeper is the 2002 opening of a four-screen theater right in the heart of downtown. A bold statement, when most other small-town theaters in the country have closed due to the opening of mall cinema complexes outside of town.

Another historic landmark was saved when Libba and Bo Chase purchased the old **Lord Culpeper Hotel** on South Main Street several years ago. After they moved in, the Chases first reopened the restaurant, and then the 20 guest rooms as each was renovated. In the bargain they believe they also got a couple of spirits – that of Jack Eggborn, former mayor and proprietor of the hotel, and his dog, Happy. In addition to being a great host known for lavish parties, Eggborn was also a prankster, and apparently continues to be. The current proprietors say they've seen dishes fall for no reason, lights and water coming on in empty rooms, and the sound of golf balls bouncing under tables (Jack was also a golfer, apparently).

To explore more of Culpeper's past, visit the **Museum of Culpeper History**, a state-of-the-art museum that traces local history back to the dinosaurs, through Native Americans, Colonial settlers, the Revolution and the Civil War. Open Monday-Saturday, 10am-5pm. Also open on Sundays, 12:30-4pm, May through October. Admission is a $3 donation for those 18 and older (803 S. Main Street, ☎ 540-829-1749, www.culpepermuseum.com).

On the first and third Saturdays of each month from June through October, Virginia Morton gives a Civil War Walking Tour of Culpeper. She's even written a book on the subject, called *Walking through Culpeper,* available at the Museum of Culpeper History. Tours start at 10:30am at the Visitors Center. $8 adults; children free. Call for the schedule (☎ 888-285-7373), or to arrange a special group tour (☎ 540-825-9147).

Recreation

For a break from shopping, keep heading west on Davis Street, take a wooden staircase down, and cross the road to **Yowell Meadow Park**. There's a beautiful pond with a fountain and ducks, walking trails, playing fields, and picnic tables.

Dining

For a quick bite downtown, there's **Baby Jim's Snack Bar**, an old-fashioned outdoor burger and milkshake joint (701 N. Main Street, ☎ 540-825-9212), the 1950s luncheonette and soda fountain at **Gayheart's Drugstore** (101 E. Davis Street, ☎ 540-825-3600), and a couple of coffee houses.

For sit-down dining, **It's About Thyme Café** has sidewalk tables in addition to indoor dining of "European Country Cuisine." Open for lunch Monday-Saturday, dinner Tuesday-Saturday (128 East Davis Street, ☎ 540-825-4264).

The gourmet dinner selections at **Hazel River Inn** include quail, veal, lamb, duck, Virginia bison and seafood. Open for lunch and dinner, closed Tuesdays (195 E. Davis Street, ☎ 540-825-7148, www.hazelriverinn.com).

Café Fairfax is a coffee bar with a full menu for breakfast, lunch, dinner and cocktails. There's weekend entertainment and outdoor seating (219 E. Davis Street, ☎ 540-829-8400).

Rex's Sports Bar and Grill serves up ribs, hot wings, nachos and live music. Open daily for lunch, dinner and late night (110 E. Davis, ☎ 540-825-3955).

Central Virginia

The Lord Culpeper Restaurant and B&B serves lunch and dinner daily, American fare with a Caribbean flair. There's also the **401 South Night Club** for late night entertainment (401 S. Main Street, ☎ 540-829-6445, lordculpeper.8m.com).

Lodging

There are several motels out on Route 29, as well as several bed & breakfast inns and an historic hotel downtown.

Fountain Hall Bed & Breakfast is in a Colonial Revival home renovated in 1985 as Culpeper's first bed & breakfast. The land was originally owned by Virginia's Royal Governor, Sir Alexander Spotswood. The inn has a sweeping walnut staircase and six guest rooms, some with private porches and whirlpool tubs. The first floor is handicapped-accessible (609 S. East Street, ☎ 540-825-8200 or 800-298-4748, www.fountainhall.com, $$).

Peter and Karen Stogbuchner, who own **The Hazel River Inn** restaurant in town, also operate an inn by the same name out on Eggbornsville Road. The century-old home has three bedrooms with private baths. There's a heated pool/spa (open May-October), a stream and great views. The hostess is a horticulturist, so the five acres of gardens are superb, as are the gourmet dinners prepared by the host/chef using herbs and produce grown on the grounds (☎ 540-937-5854, www.hazelriverinn.com, $$).

The moderately priced **Lord Culpeper Restaurant and B&B** is located in a 1933 hotel that was known for lavish parties and quality food. They recently renovated 20 rooms, including two suites. The current owners believe the spirit of the original proprietor is still in residence, along with his dog, Happy. Not surprisingly, they will accept small pets with a $5 charge. There's a nightclub in the hotel, but they say the sound doesn't carry up to the rooms (401 S. Main Street, ☎ 540-829-6445, www.lordculpeper.8m.com, $).

It's nine miles outside Culpeper, but worth the drive for a unique lodging experience at **The Funny Farm Inn**. Guests can bring their horses and well-behaved house pets (with prior notice) to the 85-acre horse farm. Three fully furnished homes with kitchens are available for lodging; two are 1800 log homes, renovated with all the modern amenities (2437 Funny Farm Road, Reva, ☎ 540-547-3481, www.bbonline.com/va/funnyfarm, $$).

Information

Culpeper Visitors Center and Chamber of Commerce, 109 S. Commerce Street, in the train depot, ☎ 888-285-7373, www.visitculpeperva.com.

Culpeper Renaissance, Inc., ☎ 540-825-4416, www.culpeper-downtown.org.

Event

Culpeper's annual **Fourth of July** celebration brings 10,000 people to downtown. Davis Street is closed for an antique car show and parade (☎ 888-285-7373).

Fredericksburg

Around Town

Old Town Fredericksburg on an unseasonably warm February Saturday is alive with activity. Shoppers going in and out of antiques galleries and boutiques; college students with backpacks; artists at work in their studios. It's even warm enough for lunch-goers to sit out at sidewalk café tables, soaking up the late winter sun hitting Caroline Street at just the right angle.

In one block of this street we noted a fascinating diversity of businesses: a tarot card reader, a train, coin and stamp shop, a tobacco shop and an all-natural café. Around the corner on Hanover Street we found a silver and goldsmith shop, **Art First Gallery & Studios** (☎ 540-371-7107, www.artfirstgallery.com), a cooperative outlet for local artisans, and **Dan Finnegan's** pottery studio, where you can watch him work on his salt-glazed stoneware, a skill he learned in England (☎ 540-371-7255). Across the street, Dan is helping to create new artists through **The Back Door Pottery**, which offers classes and workshops to aspiring potters (same phone number). For even more opportunities to see artists at work, purchase their art, or try your hand at your own, there's **Liberty Town Arts Workshop** in the former Fredericksburg Plumbing Supply on Liberty Street. Its 12,000 square

Central Virginia

83

feet provides work and exhibit space for 40 artists and dozens of students (☎ 540-371-7255).

The moniker "Liberty" isn't merely window-dressing. These are the very streets Thomas Jefferson and George Mason walked down on their way to **The Rising Sun Tavern**, where they hammered out a draft of Virginia's Statute of Religious Freedom.

Rare is the Virginia town or city without some claim to Revolutionary or Civil War fame, but few capture that spirit as well as Fredericksburg. George Washington's mother lived on Charles Street. His sister, Betty, lived a few blocks away in the **Kenmore Plantation** on Washington Avenue. And George grew up on nearby **Ferry Farm** in Stafford County on the north bank of the Rappahannock River. Tours of his home reveal the origin of two enduring myths: his chopping down a cherry tree and tossing a silver dollar across the river.

On river bluffs west of downtown, Confederate artillery defended the city from Union attack in 1863. Farther west on Route 3, battlefields at **Chancellorsville** and **The Wilderness** preserve acres of contested field and woodland.

Like Alexandria and Richmond, natural attributes helped build Fredericksburg's early fortunes. The falls of the Rappahannock made an ideal trading point for inland farmers and seafaring merchants. Today, modern businesses and manufacturers cluster west of the city, along Route 17. There, too, a visitor will find large outlets and shopping malls.

Merchants of a different stripe occupy storefronts in downtown's national historic district. Like Gettysburg, a town equally rich in Civil War history, Fredericksburg's galleries and bookstores stock all kinds of military-themed prints and books. Antique and artifact shops sell swords, maps and relics.

Given the ravages war inflicted, whatever survived – especially the great old river plantations – has become special. General Ambrose Burnside, Union commander, chose the plantation at **Chatham Manor**, in Stafford County, as his headquarters. From heights that afforded commanding views of the city on the opposite shore, Burnside ordered ill-fated attacks on Confederate defenses on Mayre's (pronounced Marie's) Heights. Sunken Road in the historic district marks where rebel soldiers, lined up behind a stone wall, allowed Union soldiers within 100 yards before commencing fire.

Guided tours at battlefield visitors centers, on Lafayette Boulevard in Fredericksburg or at Chatham Manor, recount these battles. If summer weekend plans call for staying overnight in one of Fredericksburg's historic inns, a free concert at Chatham's re-created plantation-era garden is a pleasant way to wile away an evening.

Attractions

Fredericksburg Area Museum & Cultural Center in the Old Town Hall tells the story of the area's history, from prehistoric times through to the 20th century, in six galleries. Admission is $5 adults, $1 children ages six-18. Open Monday-Saturday, 10am-5pm; Sunday, 1-5pm; closes at 4pm from December through February (907 Princess Anne Street, ☎ 540-371-3037, www.famcc.org).

At the **Rising Sun Tavern,** serving "wenches" entertain visitors with an interpretation of 18th-century tavern life. Built in 1760 as a residence, the building was later the only "proper" tavern in the city. Admission is $4 adults; $1.50 children ages six-18. Open Monday-Saturday, 9am-5pm; Sunday, 11am-5pm; closes at 4pm from December through February (1304 Caroline Street, ☎ 540-371-1494).

George Washington grew up at **Ferry Farm,** now an active archeological dig site. Admission is $2 adult, $1 children ages six-18. Open Monday-Saturday, 10am-5pm. Open weekends only in January and February. Located across the Rappahannock River from Fredericksburg on Route 3 (☎ 540-373-3381, ext. 28, www.kenmore.org).

The **Mary Washington House** (1200 Charles Street, ☎ 540-373-1569) is the home George purchased for his mother in 1772 so she could live near her daughter, Betty, for the last 17 years of her life. Betty lived at **Kenmore**, which is also open to the public (1201 Washington Avenue, ☎ 540-373-3381, www.kenmore.org).

The four battlefields just outside Fredericksburg make up the world's largest military monument, the 9,000-acre **Fredericksburg and Spotsylvania National Military Park**. Two visitor centers, a self-guided driving tour, wayside exhibits and interpretive trails help tell the story. It was here, at Guinea Station, where Stonewall Jackson died from battle wounds. A seven-day pass for all sites costs $3 adults, children 16 and under free. Open daily, 9am-5pm, with extended summer hours. **Fredericksburg Battlefield Visitor Center** (1013 Lafayette Blvd., ☎ 540-373-6122); **Chancellorsville Battlefield Visitor Center** (Route 3 West, ☎ 540-786-2880).

Wineries near Fredericksburg include **Hartwood Winery,** offering free tours and tastings Wednesday-Sunday (345 Hartwood Road, ☎ 540-752-4893); **Spotted Tavern Winery & Cider Mill,** open for free tours and tastings weekends, April-December (Route 612, Hart-

Central Virginia

wood, ☎ 540-752-4453); and **Lake Anna Winery and Oak Hill Vineyard,** open for tours and tastings Wednesday-Sunday (5621 Courthouse Road-Route 208, Spotsylvania, ☎ 540-895-5085, www. lawinery.com).

Dining

For a comprehensive listing, pick up the *Fredericksburg Dining Guide* in the Caroline Street Visitor Center, which has a menu carousel. Here are a few samplings:

Apparently, there are only a handful of places that serve breakfast in Old Town. Two are **Beans in the Burg** coffee shop, which opens at 8am weekdays and 9am weekends (813 Caroline Street, ☎ 540-654-5555), and **Old Town Grill & Café,** which opens at 7am and starts serving lunch at 11am (722 Caroline Street, ☎ 540-899-9199).

Dining in historic settings abounds, with **The Smythe's Cottage's** Colonial fare (303 Fauquier Street, ☎ 540-373-1645), **Sammy T's,** serving light, fresh and vegetarian/vegan fare in an 1805 building (801 Caroline Street, ☎ 540-371-2008, www.sammyts.com), and **Bistro 309**, located in an 1833 storefront with a bar made of 300-year-old heartpine and revolving exhibits by local artists (309 William Street, ☎ 540-371-9999).

623, American Bistro and Tapas Bar serves Spanish appetizers and contemporary American fare in a National Historic Landmark (623 Caroline Street, ☎ 540-361-2640).

Ethnic fare is well represented in Fredericksburg. There's **Bangkok Café's** Thai cuisine (825 Caroline Street, ☎ 540-373-0745), **Andrew's Mediterranean Bounty** (600 William Street, ☎ 540-370-0909), **Aztlan's** authentic Mexican cantina (3105 Spotsylvania Mall Drive, ☎ 540-548-4860), **Renato's** Italian food (422 William Street, ☎ 540-371-8228), **La Petite Auberge's** French cuisine (311 William Street, ☎ 540-371-2727), and several Japanese restaurants serving sushi.

Two places you can get homemade ice cream are: **Lee's Homemade Ice Cream** (821 Caroline Street, ☎ 540-370-4390), and **Cards and Cones** (201 William Street, ☎ 540-373-2422).

Lodging

To get the historical experience of staying right in Old Town in an historic lodging, there's **The Richard Johnston Inn,** constructed in the 1700s by one of the original signers of the Declaration of Independence (711 Caroline Street, ☎ 877-557-0770, www.bbonline.com/va/richardjohnston, $$); **The Fredericksburg Colonial Inn's** 30 antique-filled rooms (1707 Princess Anne Street, ☎ 540-371-5666, www.fci1.com, $); the 1745 **Charles Dick House B&B** (1107 Princess Anne Street, ☎ 540-372-6625, www.charlesdickhousebnb.com, $$$); and **The Kenmore Inn's** bed & breakfast, fine dining and pub (1200 Princess Anne Street, ☎ 540-371-7622, www.kenmoreinn.com, $$$).

Outside Old Town, the full gamut of chain hotels and motels are available, several of which take pets.

Information

Fredericksburg Visitor Center, 706 Caroline Street, ☎ 540-373-1776, 800-678-4748, www.fredericksburgvirginia.net.

Events

The mid-March **Fredericksburg Fine Arts Exhibit** draws artists from throughout the state for a weeklong exhibit and sale. The show has been running for more than 50 years.

The Annual **Fredericksburg Area Wine Festival** is held in early October (☎ 540-371-6522, www.bgcc.com/fbrgwinefest).

 TIP

Pick up a free copy of *The Virginia Heritage Times* magazine in the visitor center. The monthly glossy is packed with articles on Virginia history.

Central Virginia

Charlottesville

Around Town

By returning time and again to a favorite place, one risks losing touch with the very reason you love it. This is the traveler's oxymoron: Familiarity breeds unfamiliarity. The cure to this dilemma is, I believe, to tarry a while. Tarrying — the art of staying in one place longer than you should just for the guilty pleasure of it — is a traveler's luxury.

We tried this in one of our favorite small towns. Technically a city with a population of 45,000 that is swelled by the University of Virginia, Charlottesville nonetheless has small town charm. We strolled down the pedestrian mall one warm winter Sunday, absorbing all the many sights, sounds and smells. T-shirt and jewelry vendors dropped the hard sell for a friendly smile. Bells ring-a-tinged whenever a shopper entered or exited a shop. It was lunchtime and a delicious smell drew us into **The Immigrant Soul**, a vegetarian lunch-and-dinner spot.

The **Downtown Mall** is a seven-block pedestrian open-air mall in the historic district, packed with chic boutiques, artsy galleries, antiques shops, coffeehouses, trendy restaurants to down-home cooking. **The Blue Ridge Country Store**, set up like an old fashioned general store, has its own line of dressings and preserves, fresh baked goods, produce and a great salad bar. Mixed in with shops selling French linens and homemade gourmet ice cream are the more mundane, but necessary vendors: CVS, A&N and Foot Locker. There are several theaters – the Jefferson, Regal and the Paramount. **Read & Co.,** billed as "Purveyors since 1750," is a wonderland of exotic imported objects: handmade terra cotta pots from Crete, hand-carved antique pillars and furniture inlaid with camel bone, both from India. For the kids, **the Virginia Discovery Museum** is at one end of the mall; at the other is the **Charlottesville Ice Park**, offering daily public skating indoors.

Just off the mall is **Galerie LaParliere** where the magical hand-painted furniture, murals and art of French-born Maryvonne LaParliere can be seen. Her client list reads like a Hollywood movie bill, and include Steven Seagal, Priscilla Presley and the Prince of Indonesia, to name a few. We couldn't afford her beautiful works, but we enjoyed browsing and meeting the effervescent and friendly owner (414 E. Jefferson Street, ☎ 434-245-1365).

Our afternoon of tarrying was a success, in part because it broke the mold of past trips to Charlottesville, which had become somewhat routine – dinner at the Buddhist Biker Bar and Grill, music at a club, late-night breakfast at The White Spot.

The beauty of Charlottesville is that it can accommodate tastes far more simple, or sophisticated, than our own. Don't care a hoot for pricey wine lists, but can't resist an expensive piece of art? Skip the Old Mill Room and browse any number of art galleries on the Downtown Mall. Can't bear to look at art you can't afford? Museums, including the startling **Kluge-Ruhe Aboriginal Art Collection**, are free and open to the public. Bothered by crowds? Slip off the mall and onto 2nd Street or Water Street, where older buildings with fresh façades have been retrofitted to house thoroughly modern pursuits of consulting, investing, analyzing, publishing and healing. I find deciphering names of some of these businesses a pursuit all its own.

This is a city defined by history, and by the **University of Virginia**, with its 22,000-plus undergraduates. It also supports a viable and serious arts community. Live theater, readings, films and holistic pursuits fill the monthly calendar of events.

Historically, the name given to a short row of shops and restaurants directly across West Main Street from the University of Virginia is **The Corner**. Although it stretches barely two-tenths of a mile, it offers foreign cuisine from Mexican to Irish to famous late-night munchies at **The White Spot** (home of the Gus Burger), which is also a breakfast hangout. There's a **Roots, Rock, Reggae** shop, a **Starbucks**, **Bodo's Bagels**, and, of course, the Student Bookstore, where you can get all things UVa, from teddy bears to miniature Monticellos. **Plan 9** is a music shop where Dave Matthews worked. The club scene offers everything from **Rapture**, with expensive martinis, to various watering holes around **The Corner**, just outside University gates.

Today, the exotic – be it art or ideas – is part of Charlottesville's fabric. The town enjoys a cachet inherent in a place chosen by the rich and famous as their home (or second home). Yet what endears it to travelers is how within-reach it all is. The stuff of fine living is to be had in Charlottesville, whether it's wine, books or art. Far from intimidating, it is what draws us time and again.

Attractions

Two miles southeast of Charlottesville, Jefferson's home, **Monticello**, sits lovingly restored, atop a hill. Amid stately tulip poplars, the surpris-

Central Virginia

ingly small home, built in Greek Revival style, is a statement of the architect, owner and resident's embrace of foreign influences and styles. Jefferson's political ideals were influenced by French philosophers. So, too, was his cooking and decorating. Do take the guided tour of the gardens as well as the house, and don't miss the restored slave quarters. Open every day of the year, except Christmas; 8am-5pm from March through October, 9am-4:30pm the rest of the year. Admission is $11 for adults, $6 for children ages six-11. Located on Route 53, Exit 121 from I-64 (☎ 434-984-9800, www.monticello.org).

★ TIP

The **Presidents' Pass** is a combination discount ticket for touring Monticello, Ash Lawn-Highland, and Michie Tavern ca. 1784 Museum; it's $22, a $5 savings if you visit all three sites. Residents of Albermarle County receive a discount. The Pass is available at Charlottesville visitors centers; ☎ 877-386-1102.

The **Monticello Visitor Center** is before the turn onto the mountainside road leading to Monticello. Here you can see exhibits of memorabilia and artifacts, as well as an orientation film. Open daily, 9am-5:30pm, March-October, closing at 5pm the rest of the year; closed Christmas Day (600 College Drive, ☎ 434-984-9822, www.monticello.org).

Just a few miles past Monticello is the home of the nation's fifth president and close friend of Jefferson, James Monroe. His 550-acre estate, **Ash Lawn-Highland,** re-creates a working farm where peacocks strut, and interpreters demonstrate weaving, cooking and give tours of the house and gardens. Open daily, 9am-6pm, April-October, 10am-5pm the rest of the year. Admission is $8 for adults and $5 for children ages six-11 (1000 James Monroe Parkway, ☎ 434-293-9539, http://monticello.avenue.org/ashlawn).

Also near Monticello, **Michie Tavern ca. 1784** is one of the oldest homesteads in Virginia. Have a tour of the tavern and perhaps lunch served daily by staff in period costume. Tours are given daily 9am-5pm (683 Thomas Jefferson Parkway, ☎ 434-977-1234, www.michietavern.com).

No trip to Charlottesville would be complete without at least a stroll on the grounds of the university Jefferson founded. **The University of**

Virginia Rotunda and the lawn were designed by Jefferson as an "Academical Village." The Rotunda building is well worth a peek inside, if there isn't a lecture or event taking place (☎ 434-924-3239, www.virginia.edu/academicalvillage/).

The **University of Virginia Art Museum** features changing exhibits of fine art from around the globe (Rugby Road, ☎ 434-924-3592, www.virginia.edu/artmuseum/).

The **Kluge-Ruhe Aboriginal Art Collection of UVa** is one of the newest additions to the university, founded in 1997 through a gift of one of the foremost private Australian aboriginal art collections in the world. Open 9am-3pm Tuesday-Saturday; free admission (400 Peter Jefferson Place, ☎ 434-244-0234, www.virginia.edu/kluge-ruhe/).

Dining

Like most college towns, Charlottesville dining is eclectic and diverse. Here's a sampling from different areas of the city, including some of our favorites. For a full listing, see www.soveryvirginia.com.

The C & O Restaurant offers fine dining in an unexpected venue, a century-old diner across from the Chesapeake and Ohio Railroad station, saved from ruin in 1976. The three floors offer different atmospheres, the formal upstairs, the cozy and quiet Mezzanine, and the lively Bistro. The food is French Provincial, but with southwest and Pacific influences (515 E. Water Street, ☎ 434-971-7044, www.cando-restaurant.com).

Rococo's is a hip, upscale Italian restaurant serving homemade pasta and fabulous desserts (2001 Commonwealth Drive, ☎ 434-971-7371).

On the Downtown Mall, **Immigrant Soul** serves healthy food from all over the world (310 East Main Street, ☎ 434-977-8200). **Michael's Bistro & Taphouse** is a fun and lively place for microbrews and good food on the Corner (1427 University Avenue, ☎ 434-977-3697).

Out on Barracks Road is **Wild Greens,** an American grill where all entrées include their signature wild green salad (2162 Barracks Road, ☎ 434-296-9453).

For the finest of dining, nothing around beats **The Old Mill Room** at the Boar's Head Inn. It may be a restored gristmill, but the dress is semi-formal. The fare uses local ingredients with Southern and continental themes (200 Ednam Drive, Route 250 West, ☎ 434-972-2230).

Central Virginia

Lodging

Guesthouses Bed & Breakfast, Inc. is a reservation service for 60 private homes and estate cottages offering accommodations to guests (☎ 434-979-7264, www.va-guesthouses.com).

To stay right where the action is, **200 South Street Inn** is actually two restored houses right in the heart of downtown (200 South Street, ☎ 800-964-7008, www.southstreetinn.com, $$$) **The Inn at Court Square** in the historic area has five guestrooms with working fireplaces and private baths (410 E. Jefferson Street, ☎ 434-295-2800, www.bbonline.com/va/courtsquare, $$$).

Farther out in the country are several manor homes offering lodging. **Sunset Mountain Bed & Breakfast** is on top of a mountain (3722 Fosters Branch Road, ☎ 434-973-7974, www.sunsetmt.com, $$$).

Clifton – The Country Inn and Estate is an 18th-century manor house with 40 acres of gardens and a wine cellar (1296 Clifton Inn Drive, ☎ 888-971-1800, www.cliftoninn.com, $$$$).

Foxfield Inn is an elegant 50-year-old country home with five guest rooms (2280 Garth Road, ☎ 434-923-8892, www.foxfield-inn.com, $$$).

The **Inn at Monticello,** just a mile from Jefferson's home, is an 1850s manor home with five guestrooms (1188 Scottsville Road, ☎ 434-979-3593, www.innatmonticello.com, $$$).

 Keswick Hall at Monticello is a magnificent 600-acre estate of Italianate architecture, rolling lawns and elegance. There are 48 guest suites, several restaurants and bars, indoor/outdoor pools, a spa, and golfing at the adjacent Arnold Palmer-designed course. Pets are allowed with a $50 non-refundable cleaning fee (701 Club Drive, ☎ 800-274-5391, www.keswick.com, $$$$).

 For more modest accommodations, the closest to Monticello, **Holiday Inn Monticello** is just off I-64 and accepts pets (1200 5th Street, SW, ☎ 800-977-9991, $$), and, near UVa, **Quality Inn University Area** takes pets with a $10 charge (1600 Emmet Street, ☎ 434-971-3746, $$).

Information

Charlottesville/Albemarle Convention & Visitors Bureau, Main Visitors Center, Route 20 South, ☎ 877-386-1102, www.SoVeryVirginia.com.

Charlottesville/Albemarle Downtown Visitors Center, located near the Historic Downtown Mall, 108 Second Street, ☎ 434-977-6100.

Charlottesville Downtown Foundation, ☎ 434-296-8548, www.cvilledowntown.org.

University of Virginia Information Center, Route 250 Business, ☎ 434-924-7166, www.virginia.edu.

> TIP
>
> For the latest in fashion, rumors, art and music offerings, pick up a free copy of **C-VILLE Weekly**. Published every Tuesday, it's available on nearly every street corner.

Events

Covering books, wine, film, horses and nature, Charlottesville's festivals offer many opportunities to discover what makes this city exciting and lively.

There's **Virginia Festival of the Book** in March (☎ 434-296-4714 or www.vabook.org), and the 10-day **Dogwood Festival** in April (☎ 434-961-9824).

The **Foxfields** steeplechase events are in April (☎ 434-293-9501), and the **Monticello Wine and Jazz Fest** in early October offers samplings of a dozen Charlottesville-area wineries (☎ 434-296-4188).

The **Fridays After 5** free outdoor concert series runs late April to early October at Charlottesville's Downtown Amphitheater (www.FridaysAfter5.com). The **Virginia Film Festival** is held the last week in October (☎ 434-982-5277).

Central Virginia

Ashland

Around Town

A two-year-old boy repeats the word "train" in an excited voice, pointing out to his mom an Amtrak rumbling through town. His sister looks more interested in her double-scoop ice cream cone from the **Whistle-Stop Ice Cream Parlor**. A block away, a sidewalk café is filled with lunch-goers. A bicyclist, laden down with saddlebags, pedals slowly by on his cross-country route.

Forty trains a day pass through Ashland, a small town a dozen miles north of Virginia's capital city of Richmond. And we do mean *through* town. The east coast's main train route from Maine to Florida splits the main street – appropriately called Railroad Avenue – down the middle. Only eight stop daily, mostly Amtrak passenger service. But passengers still embark from the 1923 train station, which also houses the **Ashland Visitor Center**. Remarkably preserved, considering the continuous use it has had, the station has two original benches (a third is on display at the Smithsonian). The separate waiting rooms and window tickets are a somber reminder of the days of segregation.

The town exists here because of the railroad. In 1836 the Richmond, Fredericksburg and Potomac Railroad (RF&P) laid tracks north from Richmond, and began to develop the land along the right-of-way. In the 1850s, mineral springs were discovered where Randolph-Macon College now sits, and a resort retreat sprang up called Slash Cottage. The railroad encouraged people to buy building lots and relocate to the new town, named Ashland in 1855 after the Kentucky estate of Henry Clay, who was born in Hanover County.

Most of the finest houses in town face the tracks, and business names spin off easily from the railroad theme: Whistle-stop Ice Cream, the Caboose Wine Shop, the Ironhorse restaurant. All the buildings on the block burned to the ground in 1893, although the fire was fought valiantly by a bucket brigade of residents and a fire engine sent on a flatbed railroad car. The buildings standing today were built of fire-resistant brick between 1894 and 1913. A century after the fire, in 1993, another brigade of residents helped move the library's collection of 30,000 books across the tracks to the new library.

Many of the train passengers are students at **Randolph-Macon College**, which is across the street from the station. The co-ed liberal arts college moved here from Boydton, Virginia in 1868. Founded in 1830, it's the oldest Methodist college in the country.

Others passing through town are on bicycles. The **Transcontinental Bicycle Route** goes right down Railroad Avenue on its way from Yorktown, Virginia, to Oregon. While we were there, a biker stopped for directions. A little saddle-weary, he'd already been to the see the Yorktown Battlefield, and was now heading back west across the country.

★ FILM CLIPS

Christmas Every Day was a television movie filmed in Ashland in the fall of 1995. They picked the colorful leaves off the trees and sprayed the streets with a soapy fake snow. Scenes from the 1995 movie *Major Payne,* starring Damon Wayans, were filmed just outside the train station.

Attractions

Downtown on Railroad Avenue, **Cross Brothers Grocery Store** has been open since 1912. They still provide home delivery and charge accounts. In the back of the store are old photographs and store memorabilia. It's open Monday-Saturday, 8am-6pm; till 7pm on Friday (☎ 804-798-8311).

Hanover County Black Heritage Museum houses the history of local African-Americans. Open Monday, Wednesday and Friday by appointment. Free (204 Virginia Street, ☎ 804-798-5774).

North Anna Battlefield Park has interpretive walking trails and preserves Confederate earthworks which Grant attacked in May, 1864. Located three miles west of Route 1 on Route 684 (☎ 804-730-6165).

Six miles north of Ashland, **Paramount's Kings Dominion** is 400 acres of fun, fun, fun. Eight themed areas with a dozen roller coasters, live shows and a water park. Open late-March through October. Take Exit 98 off I-95 in Doswell (☎ 804-876-5000, www.kingsdominion.com).

Railroad buffs should check out the elaborate layouts of the **RF&P Model Railroad Club** in Hanover Springs Shopping Center, at routes 54 and 1. An open house is held each second Saturday, 10am-5pm (☎ 804-798-0250).

Central Virginia

Patrick Henry, Virginia's first elected governor, rode from **Scotchtown**, his home nine miles west of Ashland, to Richmond to deliver the famous words that helped spark the Revolution: "Give me liberty or give me death." Scotchtown is open Tuesday-Sunday, 10am-4:30pm, April-October (off SR 54, ☎ 804-227-3500).

Dining

Ashland Coffee & Tea serves quesadillas and grilled specialties. Live music Thursday through Saturday night attracts nationally known blues, jazz, bluegrass and folk artists. Wednesday is comedy night. Grab a coffee, sink into a deep cushioned chair or sit out on the deck (100 N. Railroad Avenue, ☎ 804-798-1702).

Brunch on the porch of the **Henry Clay Inn** is a real treat, served weekends only, along with the popular nouvelle cuisine dinner buffet. This Georgian Revival-style building is actually a 1992 replica of the 1906 original that burned in 1946. Photographs inside the lobby tell the story (114 N. Railroad Avenue, ☎ 804-798-3100).

The deli counter at **Homemades by Suzanne** makes dozens of different salads, fresh sandwiches and quiches daily to take-out or eat in at the café tables. Open for continental breakfast and lunch (102 N. Railroad Avenue, ☎ 804-798-8331).

The Ironhorse Restaurant is located in the old Cox Department Store, built in 1900. Descendants of the Cox family, and many who remember their parents shopping here, are lunchtime regulars. The restaurant's name is from the 1960s Dale Robertson movie, *The Iron Horse*. The menu features tapas, bison steaks, seafood, lamb, salads of field greens, and an extensive wine list. Open for lunch and dinner (100 S. Railroad Avenue, ☎ 804-752-6410).

Lodging

The Henry Clay Inn may have been built to replicate a 1906 inn, but the amenities are modern all the way. Twelve guest rooms, including two suites, all have telephones, cable TV, computer modem hook-ups, and private baths. There's a handicapped-accessible room, corporate and honeymoon suites, Jacuzzi tubs in some rooms, balconies and canopy beds in others. The front porch is a great place for train-spotting. Continental buffet breakfast included (114 N. Railroad Avenue, ☎ 800-343-4565, www.henryclayinn.com, $$).

There are nearly 20 chain hotels, motels and motor lodges in the Ashland area. The closest ones to downtown are a **Hampton Inn** at 705 England Street and Route 54 (☎ 804-752-8444, $$), a **Quality Inn** at 810 England Street (☎ 804-798-4231, $), and a **Comfort Inn** at 101 N. Cottage Greene Drive (☎ 804-752-7777, $$). For a complete list, contact the visitor center for the visitor guide to Ashland & Hanover County (☎ 800-897-1479).

It's surprising that there aren't any B&Bs in town, what with the abundance of fine old homes and the college, which draws visiting parents and alumni. Perhaps by the time you read this, someone may have decided to open one.

Information

The **Ashland Visitor Center** is open daily, 9am-5pm; ☎ 800-897-1479, www.ashlandhanoverva.com.

Events

The **Fourth of July** parade sometimes has more participants than onlookers, as anyone who shows up 15 minutes before the start can march. It's non-motorized, so townsfolk use their imaginations to come up with clever and humorous themes. There's been the croquet brigade, the folding chair brigade, and every year the Bassett Brigade brings hounds from throughout central Virginia. No one seems to mind that they slow the parade down a bit. "They have to sniff and lick all the children along the way," said Barbara Franklin, manager of the visitor center.

The **Strawberry Faire** in May is a celebration of spring under the big oak trees of Randolph-Macon College.

Central Virginia

⭐ DID YOU KNOW?

Ashland received national attention in 2001 as the community that dared to fight a Wal-Mart Supercenter. Many feared it would draw business away from downtown and change the small-town atmosphere. The battle was the subject of a PBS documentary called *Store Wars* that aired in June, 2001, and a *New York Times* article entitled *Incursion of a Superstore Galvanizes a Quiet Town* (June 4, 2001). Despite the protests, the Wal-Mart was eventually built in 2002.

Appomattox

Around Town

Appomattox Court House exists largely intact from its heyday of 1865 thanks to a railroad, a fire, and benign neglect. Unlike every other battlefield in the south, this place where Robert E. Lee surrendered Confederate troops to the Union received no memorial or acclaim in the aftermath of the conflict. No monuments were built by either side. When the railroad came to Appomattox Station, a few miles to the south, commerce moved there as well. No longer was the Richmond-Lynchburg Turnpike, which ran through town, a main thoroughfare for commerce. Serving travelers on the road had been the reason for the town's existence, which grew up around a tavern. The final straw came in 1892 when the courthouse burned. Rather than rebuild what had become a ghost town, town fathers moved the county seat to the now bustling railroad town.

But misfortunes had a silver lining for this historic spot. No fast food restaurants or gas stations ever paved over what, to many, remains hallowed ground. In the 1930s, the National Park Service began acquiring land and restoring buildings. In 1954 the **Appomattox Court House National Historical Park** opened as a re-creation of a town looking much as it did in 1865.

Today costumed interpreters and park rangers bring to life the events that took place on the quiet gravel roads and rolling fields surrounding the tiny town of a half-dozen buildings. Here, on April 12, 1865, Confederate soldiers lined the roads with their forfeited weapons. In exchange, a truly remarkable war-time agreement: The near-starving soldiers received food, paroles to go home and permission to take whatever they had brought to the war, even their own horses and rifles. Anything the Confederate Army had given them had to be surrendered, including their flags.

The **Clover Hill Tavern** is the oldest building in the park, built in 1819 to serve travelers on the turnpike. The visitor center is located in the reconstructed courthouse. There's a law office, a jail and a store. The largest house in town, the **McLean House**, has been reconstructed to the way it looked when Lee and Grant worked out the surrender terms in the parlor of the local merchant.

The McLean House has an interesting chronology. The original brick building was dismantled in 1893 and packed up. The plan was to take it to Washington DC for a war museum. But the recession of 1893 came along and funding disappeared. The building materials were left there, and for decades passersby took souvenir bricks. Of 80,000 original bricks, only about 5,000 were used in the reconstruction.

To this day, the national park receives at least one or two bricks a year in the mail with a note, usually to the effect that a grandfather or great-grandfather had it for years and the current owner feels the park should have it back. Since the house has been rebuilt, the bricks are stacked in the basement of the visitor center. The park is open daily, 8:30am-5pm, year-round. Admission in the summer is $4 per person, with a $10 maximum per vehicle. The rest of the year, it's $3 and $5, respectively. Pets are allowed on a leash throughout the park, but not in any of the buildings (☎ 434-352-8987, www.nps.gov).

A few miles south of the battlefield stands modern **Appomattox**. The railroad station on Main Street has seen its last train passengers. Freight trains still pass close by the 1930 station, but they don't stop there anymore. Inside is the **Appomattox Visitor Center** (☎ 434-352-2621), with historic displays, including the original scales used to weigh everything from passenger baggage to cattle, and an Arts & Crafts Center. Just a block long, Appomattox's Main Street could be the shortest Main Street in Virginia. Here visitors find a handful of quaint shops and eateries, and the beginning of a 44-stop self-guided tour of historic homes (exterior only), all within a half-mile. On some weekends, a horse-and-carriage tour is available. Ask inside the visitor center.

Central Virginia

Attractions

A half-mile past Appomattox Court House National Park, **Clover Hill Village** re-creates Appomattox history before and after Lee's surrender. The six-acre village has a general store, blacksmith shop, one-room schoolhouse, chapel and log cabin, many donated and moved here by the Appomattox County Historical Society. Open daily, during daylight hours, no admission charge.

Fred's Car Museum houses more than 65 automobiles, from a 1906 "horseless carriage" to cars of the 1980s. Located on Route 24 between Appomattox and the national park. Admission is $5. Open Monday-Saturday, 10am-5pm; Sunday, 1-5pm (☎ 434-352-0606).

Lee's Retreat is a 20-stop driving tour tracing the 100-mile retreat of Lee's Army from Petersburg to Appomattox. Brochure, map and historic markers detail the events.

Stonewall Vineyards on US 460 west of town, offers tours, tastings and a wine shop. Open Monday-Saturday, 11am-4pm (☎ 434-993-2185, www.stonewallwine.com).

Recreation

Holliday Lake State Park off Route 24 has camping, swimming, boating, fishing and hiking around the man-made lake (☎ 434-248-6308). **James River State Park** encompasses 1,400 acres on the James River, which runs along the northern border of Appomattox County. Canoeing and fishing are popular, with this section of the James claiming to have the best smallmouth bass fishing east of the Mississippi (☎ 434-933-4355).

Dining

The **Babcock House** is a bed & breakfast (see below), but it's also one of the best places for fine dining in the area. Lunch is served during the week, dinner by reservation. The candlelit tables are set with white linens, fine china and fresh flowers (106 Oakleigh Avenue, ☎ 804-352-7532, www.babcockhouse.com).

Otherwise, dining in Appomattox is quite casual. **Granny Bee's** on Main Street can fill you up with home-style cooking for $4 or less (breakfast or lunch). Dinner is served Wednesday-Sunday, breakfast daily, and lunch Monday-Friday (☎ 434-352-2259). There's also the

Caboose Sub Shop (☎ 434-352-2638), **Rayford's Café** (☎ 434-352-3196), and **Golden China** (☎ 434-352-8596).

Lodging

The **Babcock House Bed & Breakfast Inn** is a restored century-old inn with five guest rooms and one suite (106 Oakleigh Avenue, ☎ 800-689-6208, www.babcockhouse.com, $$).

Longacre Bed & Breakfast is a 1933 English Tudor House on two acres of gardens. There are three guest rooms, all with air conditioning and cable TV (107 S. Church Street, ☎ 434-352-9251, www.long-acrebb.com, $).

Spring Grove Farm Bed & Breakfast is a restored 1842 house on a 200-acre plantation with 16 fireplaces and 11 guest rooms and suites, all with private baths. There is one handicapped room and bath. Slip into a terry robe after a whirlpool bath, then curl up in front of the fire or on your private porch. There's a kennel for pets nearby (Route 613, ☎ 434-993-3891, www.springgrovefarm.com, $$).

 The **Super 8 Motel** just off US 460 at Route 24 takes pets for an additional charge of $10 (☎ 434-352-2339, $).

Information

The **Appomattox Visitor Information Center**, located in the restored railroad depot on Main Street, is open daily, 9am-5pm (☎ 434-352-2621, www.appomattox.com).

Events

In early May the community pays tribute to the inventor of the five-string banjo, born in the county in 1810. The **Joel Sweeney Banjo & Old-Time Music Festival** takes place at Paradise Lake Campground in Appomattox with a highly competitive banjo contest. Sweeney became a national celebrity with his banjo minstrel act, and even performed in England for Queen Victoria. Period costume is encouraged. Banjo players get in free (☎ 434-352-2621).

In June the **James River Batteau Festival** at James River Park celebrates the boats that once transported cargo on the river. Costumed pilots pole their batteaux down the river from Lynchburg to Richmond, camping along the way (☎ 434-352-2621).

The town's premiere event is the **Historic Appomattox Railroad Festival** taking place for two days in October. Parades, live bands, train exhibits, fireworks and hundreds of vendors have made this commemoration of the Norfolk & Southern Railroads' donation of the train depot to the town one of the largest festivals in the state (☎ 434-352-2621).

Bedford

Around Town

The hand-drawn sign and map of Bedford in the window of Arthur's Jewelry marks its spot with an arrow and declares: "You are here – Best Little Town in the World."

Plenty of small towns in the world would take exception to this motto, which locally is traced back to the mid-20th century, when a similar sign hung in the window of Wildman's Barbershop. But there's a lot to be said for the effect of such strident community pride. The streets of Bedford's **Historic Centertown** are clean, nicely landscaped, pedestrian-friendly and lined with more than 200 historic buildings. Even the local radio station takes its call letters from the acronym of Best Little Town – WBLT. Simply put, everyone here believes it to be true.

Bridge Street has half a dozen antiques shops, furniture and jewelry stores, and unique local shops selling used books and stained glass artwork. The **J.J. Newberry Co. 5-10 & 25 Cent Store** (the glass sign is still over the door) now houses two curious enterprises: the **Global Gallery** – "Whole Life for the Whole World" – and **Northbridge Gifts**. Next door is **House of Gargoyles**, a gift shop carrying the theme of the ghoulish little critters.

Main Street is all about business, with an impressive complex of courthouse buildings, monuments to both the Confederate and World War II dead, and the **Bedford City/County Museum** (open Monday-Saturday, 10am-5pm, ☎ 540-586-4520), located in the Masonic Building, an imposing brick structure called "the handsomest building in town" when built in 1895. A walking tour brochure, available at the museum or the Bedford Visitors Center, describes the highlights of Centertown.

But the main source of pride lately is Bedford's status as home to the **National D-Day Memorial,** opened in 2000 to honor those who served in the invasion of France on June 6, 1944. Set atop a hill overlooking the city is the 44-foot-tall granite **Overlord Arch**. In case you're wondering about the name, Overlord was the Allies' code name for the Normandy landing. It's more than simply a stone monument, however. A realistic experience awaits those who pass through the arch. In an attempt to make visitors feel just a sliver of what it was actually like in the battle, a boat with an open ramp onto a beach has figures of soldiers struggling and helping each other. There's the sound of gunfire and splashing water as if bullets were hitting around them.

Why build the D-Day Memorial here, in central Virginia, when most other national war memorials are in Washington DC? In the battle, Bedford lost the highest number of men per capita of any community in the nation. Of the 35 Bedford men who landed, 21 were lost. The small, rural town is emblematic, organizers say, of the sacrifices made by hundreds of communities across the nation. A total of 150,000 servicemen participated in history's largest air, land and sea operation that signaled the demise of Nazi domination of Europe. Two eight-foot walls bear the 4,000 names of those who never returned.

Since the memorial's opening, scores of World War II veterans have made the moving pilgrimage to Bedford; for some, now in their 80s and 90s, the trip is a feat in itself. Open 10am-5pm daily; admission is $10 per vehicle (Route 122 and US 60 Bypass).

Attractions

Watch pottery being made and painted at the **Emerson Creek Pottery** factory outlet, located in an 1825 log blacksmith's cabin (☎ 540-297-7884, www.emersoncreek-pottery.com).

The Sedalia Center promotes the arts, from pottery-making to bluegrass music, through festivals, exhibits and programs (☎ 434-299-5080, www.sedaliacenter.org).

Call ahead for an appointment to see handmade furniture being made at **The New Henderson's Country Furniture** (☎ 800-755-8546, www.hendersonsfurniture.com), or **Maxwell Furniture Co (☎** 800-686-1844, www.maxwellfurniture.com).

Central Virginia

Booker T. Washington National Monument is a tobacco farm and the birthplace of the African-American leader who overcame slavery to become an educator, writer, founder of Tuskegee Institute in Alabama, and advisor to three presidents. Located on Route 122 in Hardy, near Smith Mountain Lake. Open daily 9am-5pm (☎ 540-721-2094, www.nps.gov/bowa).

Thomas Jefferson built the octagonal brick house at **Poplar Forest** in Bedford County in 1806 as a summer retreat. The restored home is open for tours April through November, 10am-4pm daily; admission is $7 for adults and $1 for children ages six-16. Located east of Bedford on Route 221 (☎ 434-525-1806, www.poplarforest.org).

Poplar Park on Smith Street is home to the world's largest yellow poplar tree and is the largest tree of any kind in the state (☎ 540-587-6061).

Holy Land USA and Nature Sanctuary depicts Bible scenes of Israel on 250 acres. Open year-round; admission is free, though there is a nominal fee for primitive lodging, wagon tours and hiking tours (1060 Jericho Road, ☎ 540-586-2823, www.holyland.pleasevisit.com).

Peaks of Otter Winery is open for tours and tastings at **Johnson's Orchards**, where you can pick your own fruit, purchase bushels, or products like apple wine, cider and butter. Open daily August through mid-fall. Call ahead the rest of the year. Six miles northwest of Bedford on Route 680 (☎ 800-742-6877, www.peaksofotterwinery.com).

Outdoors

Ten miles to the north of Bedford, the famed Peaks of Otter – **Flat Top** and **Sharp Top** – are clearly visible. From the Blue Ridge Parkway Visitor Center it's a short (1.6 miles) but strenuous and steep climb to the Sharp Top summit's 360° view. Flat Top is a longer hike (4.4 miles), rewarded by scattered rock outcrops at 4,000 feet. **Peaks of Otter Lodge** has lakeside dining and accommodations with terrific views of both peaks (☎ 800-542-5927, www.peaksofotter.com).

Twelve miles south of Bedford is **Smith Mountain Lake**, an engineering marvel created in the 1960s. Recreation abounds at the state park, with boating, camping, fishing, hiking and swimming (☎ 540-297-6066, www.dcr.state.va.us/parks/smithmtn.htm).

Dining

The **Duchess of Bedford Bakery and Olde Shoppe** is a take-off on the fact that Anna, the 7th Duchess of Bedford, is credited with starting the tradition of afternoon tea in England. The duchess apparently couldn't wait until dinner and started having a small meal of dainty sandwiches, tiny pastries and tea with her friends in the afternoon. The shop doesn't actually serve afternoon tea, but sells the items to have your own (1842 Forest Road, ☎ 540-587-8777).

Forks Country Restaurant serves home-style cooking and breakfast all day (1619 Forest Road, ☎ 540-586-9041).

For exceptional food and wine in an unusual setting, there's the **Millstone Tea Room**, 10 miles north of Bedford on Route 122. The renovated general store serves specialties like roasted quail and rack of lamb. The wine list carries more than 50 vintages from Virginia, California and France, and more than 20 beers. Sorry, they don't serve afternoon tea here either – the name comes from the restaurant, grocery and gas station opened here in 1939. There's a heated patio for outdoor dining. Open for dinner Wednesday-Saturday and Sunday Brunch (9058 Big Island Highway, Sedalia, ☎ 540-587-7100).

Olde Liberty Station takes its name from Bedford's original name of Liberty and is located in an historic 1905 train depot. The menu is cleverly titled with railroad themes: desserts are "Cabooses" and side dishes are "Side Cars." Serving beef, pork, chicken, salads, seafood and pasta for lunch and dinner (515 Bedford Avenue, ☎ 540-587-9377).

R-U-Up is a cheerful double storefront on Main Street serving breakfast and lunch Monday-Saturday and Sunday brunch. Gourmet coffees, ice cream, sandwiches, salads, vegetarian selections and delicious pastries (140 West Main Street, ☎ 540-587-0145).

Other Centertown restaurants include **Hunan Chinese** (207 N. Bridge Street, ☎ 540-586-3591); **Abby's Place** for breakfast and lunch (302 Court Street, ☎ 540-586-4281); and the 1950s-style **Snack Shop** (104 N. Bridge Street, ☎ 540-587-8780).

Lodging

There are three bed & breakfasts within walking distance of Centertown, and chain motels on US 460 just outside the city limits. Cozy

Central Virginia

mountain cottages, inns and cabins await at Peaks of Otter and Smith Mountain Lake.

The Bedford House is in the historic district, furnished with antiques and reproductions (422 Avenel Avenue, ☎ 540-586-5050, $$).

The Inn on Avenel is a 1915 Greek Revival home with rockers on the porch where refreshments are served every afternoon. Four guest rooms and full breakfast served (416 Avenel Avenue, ☎ 540-586-5978, www.innonavenel.com, $$).

Liberty House Inn is like going back 50 years, with World War II memorabilia, a 48-star flag and 1940s décor (602 Mountain Avenue, ☎ 540-587-0966, www.wp21.com/liberty, $$).

 The **Days Inn** at US 221 and 460 accepts small pets with a $5 charge (☎ 540-586-8286, $).

Information

The **Bedford Visitors Center** is open daily, 9am-5pm. It's located on Burks Hill Road at the foot of the hill leading up to the D-Day Memorial. Inside are all the brochures and information visitors need. On the porch are rocking chairs to rest on, donated by a local woodworker, and inside free apples donated by a local orchard (☎ 877-HI-PEAKS, www.visitbedford.com).

Bedford Main Street, Inc (☎ 540-586-2148, www.bedfordmainstreet.org).

Events

The **Farmer's Market** on Washington Street is open Monday-Saturday, 7am-noon, year-round, with arts, crafts, food and local produce. Contact Bedford Main Street, Inc (above).

Centerfest draws more than 10,000 visitors to downtown for street dancing and craft vendors the last Saturday in September. For information, contact Bedford Main Street, Inc.

Northern Virginia

More than just a bedroom community to the nation's capital, Northern Virginia still has plenty of villages with small-town charm. West and north of the Capital Beltway stand genteel estates of Virginia's horse country. Hidden from view of I-95 are small towns packed with antiques shops. Farther afield still, in the foothills of the Blue Ridge Mountains, small towns host artist communities, fine inns and wineries.

THE TOWNS
▓ Leesburg
▓ Waterford
▓ Old Town Manassas
▓ Middleburg
▓ Occoquan
▓ Warrenton
▓ The Plains

Getting Here

Ronald Reagan Washington National Airport (☎ 703-419-8000, www.metwashairports.com/National) and **Washington Dulles International Airport** (☎ 703-419-8000, www.metwashairports.com/Dulles).

Regional Information

The **Virginia Tourism Corporation** operates Highway Welcome Centers in this area; these are found along I-95 between US 17 and SR 3; on I-66 between US 29 and SR 234; and at 1629 K Street NW in Washington DC (☎ 800-VISIT-VA, 800-934-9184, www.virginia.org).

Leesburg

Leesburg is the county seat of the third-fastest-growing county in the nation, which means if you want to see it while it's a small town, hurry. Every year, it swells with more new families and couples attracted by the small town charm unimaginable a mere 35 miles from Washington DC. This town is the frontier of DC's urban range, and the countryside between the capital and this one-time farm community is now referred to as the **Dulles Corridor** (after the airport, Dulles Inter-

Northern Virginia

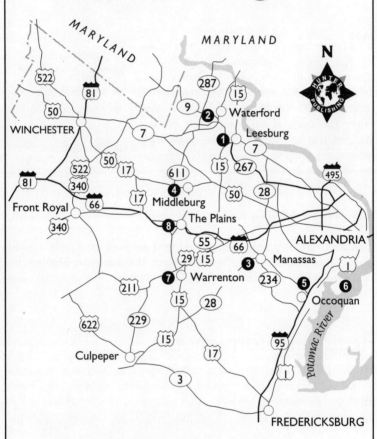

1. Market Station; Washington & Old Dominion Trail; Loudoun Museum & Shop
2. Waterford Foundation; Waterford Market; Waterford Mill
3. Walking & Driving Tours; Manassas Museum; Manassas Industrial School; Manassas Volunteer Fire Company Museum; Manassas Battlefield Park
4. Red Fox Inn; Middleburg National Sporting Library; Piedmont Vineyards & Winery; Swendenburg Estate Vineyard; Wankopit Community Trail
5. Riverwalk; Mill House Museum; Harbor River Cruises; Prince William National Forest Park
6. Gunston Hall
7. Old Jail Museum; Jimmie's Market
8. RR Arts Depot; Afro-American Historical Association of Fauquier County; Great Meadow

national). Instead of farms, there are spacious campuses and glass-enclosed offices of high technology companies.

Amid growth and busyness, Leesburg's historic core brings things down to a human scale. Local customers in a coffee bar chat about fine art and the owners' newest puppy. Storefronts are pressed right up against the street, separated only by a bumpy, brick-paved sidewalk. Clustered along King, Loudoun and Market streets are hip shops and restaurants, vintage and antiques stores, art galleries and cafés.

Throughout its history, first as a farming community and later as the commercial center of Loudoun County, Leesburg seems a place to which people escaped. That was literally true during the War of 1812, when the British advanced on Washington and burned the White House. For a brief period, Leesburg became America's capital city and repository for the Constitution and Declaration of Independence. South of Leesburg stands Oak Hill, the home of President James Monroe. He would retreat here for respite and, it's said, wrote the Monroe Doctrine here, a document that embodied the principles of America's "manifest destiny" and justified westward exploration and expansion. From 1941 to 1959, General George Marshall, a soldier and statesman known for his far-reaching ideas and policies, resided in town. His Marshall Plan helped reconstruct Europe after World War II and earned him a Nobel Peace Prize.

Northern Virginia

★ DID YOU KNOW?

Leesburg was originally called "George Town" to honor the king of England.

Around Town

The town's character isn't just about famous people, though. Leesburg's charm is as much about its old buildings and the smaller towns on its periphery that were the farm communities of German and Scotch-Irish settlers. A few stone homes and mills date from the pre-Revolutionary period, but most are turn-of-the century – which is still old in as dynamic a region as Northern Virginia. That old-time feeling is certainly what developers of **Market Station** on Harrison Street, Leesburg, had in mind. The re-created mill complex has historic buildings relocated from other states, and it's a unique setting for restaurants, shops and a courtyard with outdoor tables. A log house built in 1840 in Rectortown MD, made entirely of American chestnut, is now home to a teddy bear gift shop. The centerpiece is the Osterburg Mill, moved here from southwest Pennsylvania in 1984.

As you mill about Market Station, you might see people in bike shorts and helmets carrying water bottles. Leesburg is a pit-stop on the **Washington & Old Dominion (W&OD) Trail**, and is popular with bikers who love the paved, 100-foot-wide rail-to-trail that runs 45 miles from the suburbs of Arlington, just outside Washington DC, to Purcellville at the edge of the Blue Ridge Mountains. The railroad opened in 1860, and was an attempt by merchants of port cities like Alexandria to get western goods across the Blue Ridge and onto their tidewater docks. But commercial success was not in the cards for this railroad. The most prosperous years came after the Great Depression and through World War II, when it transported tourists and vacationers out to the countryside; the trip included a stop at Leesburg. For more information on the W&OD Trail, contact the Northern Virginia Regional Park Authority at ☎ 703-352-5900 (or the W&OD park at ☎ 703-729-0596), or visit their Web site, www.nvrpa.org (click on "Trails" under "Park Facilities"). Another organization, the non-profit Friends of the Washington and Old Dominion Trail (FOWOD), provides information on its site as well, www.wodfriends.org.

If you're looking for a good introduction to town, visit for a **First Friday Gallery Walk**. The evening might feature a wine tasting at one gallery and music at another. Downtown shops are open until 9pm the first Friday of every month (except January), and many serve wine and cheese and other refreshments. Check online at www.leesburgfirst-friday.com for more information.

Leesburg is probably as well known for the shopping outlet mall just outside town, with some 110 brand name retailers. But if it's a one-of-a-kind art object, an antique treasure or unique home decorative piece you're looking for, explore downtown. There's a restaurant at every turn, some with Colonial fare that will keep you refueled. And if you want to keep the old-fashioned theme going, you can stay at a historic bed & breakfast within walking distance of the shops.

The **Loudoun Museum & Shop** chronicles town and county history through exhibits, videos and a walking tour. Trace its beginnings in 1758, through the revolution when the county was known as "the bread basket of the revolution," through the Civil War, to the present. There are 5,000 objects in the collection, from Native American to locally crafted silver. Of particular note is a collection of seven letters sent by the Lucas family to their former masters, the Heatons of Loudoun County. The emancipated slaves returned to Africa in 1830, but kept in close contact with the Heatons. The museum is open

Monday-Saturday, 10am to 5pm, and Sunday from 1 to 5pm. Admission is $2 for adults, $1 for students, teachers and seniors, and free to children under 10 and members (14-16 Loudoun Street, SW, ☎ 703-777-7427, www.loudounmuseum.org).

Dining

Eating in historic Leesburg can mean a century-old diner, a candlelit Colonial-style dinner, or fish and chips and a game of darts in a British pub. **Georgetown Café and Bakery** has an elevated dining deck in the back with a pergola for shade (19 S. King Street, ☎ 703-777-5000, www.leesburgcolonialinn.com).

The **Green Tree Restaurant** serves "early Colonial cuisine" using 1700s recipes. They light candles on the tables – even for lunch (15 S. King Street, ☎ 703-777-7246, www.leesburgcolonialinn.com).

King's Court Tavern is an English Pub serving fish and chips from an authentic British menu (2C W. Loudoun St SW, ☎ 703-777-7747, www.leesburgcolonialinn.com).

Leesburg Restaurant is reminiscent of an old-style small town diner. It first opened for business in 1865 as Beuchler's Bakery and Ice Cream Shop. Consistency is its middle name – the place opens every day at 7am, serving breakfast, lunch and dinner seven days a week (9 S. King Street, ☎ 703-777-3292).

Lightfoot Restaurant is in a restored 1900 bank building and serves American cuisine (11 N. King Street, ☎ 703-777-2233, www.lightfoot-restaurant.com).

At Market Station, **Tuscarora Mill Restaurant** serves American cuisine in either a formal dining room, the more casual café, or outdoors on the terrace. They have 21 beers on tap (☎ 703-771-9300, www.tuskies.com).

Nido Italiano Ristorante is open for lunch and dinner (☎ 703-777-7786).

See also the Laurel Brigade and Leesburg inns under *Lodging*, below.

Lodging

There are several bed & breakfast inns in the historic district. The **Laurel Brigade Inn** has five Colonial guest rooms with private bath and air conditioning. Their restaurant overlooks the garden, and they

they serve afternoon tea and Sunday brunch; call for details and reservations (20 W. Market Street, ☎ 703-777-1010, $$).

Leesburg Colonial Inn & Bella Luna Restaurant has 10 guest rooms with four-poster beds and Oriental rugs, but with all the modern amenities. The restaurant serves Northern Italian cuisine in an elegant atmosphere (19 S. King Street, ☎ 703-777-5000, www.leesburgcolonialinn.com, $$).

The **Norris House Inn & Stone House Tea Room** is a stately 1760 inn at 108 Loudoun Street SW. Three of the bedrooms have fireplaces; there's a parlor, library, sunroom and veranda. On weekend afternoons tea is served in the stone house or in the gardens. (☎ 800-644-1806, www.norrishouse.com, $$$).

It's outside town a few miles, but wouldn't it be neat to stay on a working vineyard? **Tarara Vineyard, Winery and Bed & Breakfast** is on a 475-acre farm on the Potomac River. All rooms include a bottle of wine, two souvenir glasses and a light breakfast (13648 Tarara Lane, ☎ 703-771-7100, www.tarara.com, $$$).

Amazing – on two counts! A Holiday Inn in an 18th-century mansion 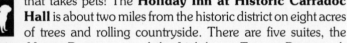 that takes pets! The **Holiday Inn at Historic Carradoc Hall** is about two miles from the historic district on eight acres of trees and rolling countryside. There are five suites, the Mansion House Restaurant and the Lighthorse Tavern. Pets are allowed (no extra fee), but they request that you not leave them unattended in the rooms (1500 E. Market Street, ☎ 703-771-9200, www.leesburgvaholidayinn.com, $$$).

Information

Loudoun County Visitor Center at Market Station, Harrison Street is open 9am to 5pm, daily (☎ 800-752-6118, www.visitloudoun.org).

Waterford

Five miles northwest of Leesburg is a village time has forgotten, or so it seems, thanks to benign neglect in the first half of the 20th century, and national recognition of its historic value in the second.

Driving through the tiny, storybook town of Waterford, just 40 miles from Washington DC, you might feel a bit like an intruder. While the 1970 designation of the entire village as a National Historic Landmark preserves this gem for everyone, these are private homes, so tread lightly. Park the car, get out and walk the narrow, winding streets, paved with brick and lined with old, mossy stone walls. Tone it down a notch, and get in step with the country pace. There are no restaurants or hotels, no trendy boutiques, and not a whole lot to do, so take your time.

If you'd like to know the stories behind the buildings, pick up the "Walk With Us Through Waterford" publication at the **Waterford Foundation** office located in the Corner Store at Main and Second. It details the history of practically every structure in town – 120 of them. The office is open weekdays only, 9am-5pm, so if you're there on a weekend, look for a brochure rack outside, or ask at the **Peaceable Kingdom** art gallery.

Stop in at the **Waterford Market** on Second Street, a general store since 1883. Play a game of checkers, or sit by the pot-bellied stove on a cold day.

Time your visit with the bi-monthly Sunday **Waterford Concert Series** at the Old School, which is preceded by a guided walking tour (☎ 540-882-3018, www.waterfordva.org).

The **Waterford Mill** has peaceful, park-like grounds with picnic tables and benches along a tinkling stream. The rushing waters of Catoctin Creek persuaded Pennsylvania Quaker Amos Janney this was a good place to settle in 1733. The brick mill was built in the 1820s, the third one at this location. The Waterford Foundation had the foresight to buy and preserve it way back in 1944. The mill isn't open regular hours, but there are interpretive signs outside. It operated until 1939, and now serves as the headquarters for the **Waterford**

Homes Tour & Crafts Exhibit. Held the first weekend in October, this is one of the few times when Waterford sees a crowd – up to 40,000 people come to get a peek inside the historic buildings. The three-day festival features traditional crafts for sale and demonstration, military re-enactments, art exhibits and tours of homes. Several homes and the Old School may also open to the public during Historic Garden Week in April.

Private tours for groups can be arranged through the **Waterford Foundation** (☎ 540-882-3018, www.waterfordva.org). Contact the foundation for more information about Waterford.

Old Town Manassas

Our entry into this small town was delayed by, of all things, a 30-car eastbound container train that crosses the main road into Manassas. The Norfolk Southern train was no doubt headed to Norfolk International Terminal where cargo would be loaded onto huge barges.

As inconvenient as it might be to 21st-century drivers, the railroad is the reason this town sprang up. The Orange & Alexandria and the Manassas Gap railroads joined here in the 1850s, and this tiny hamlet known as Tudor Hall was renamed Manassas Junction. The railroads formed a long-awaited transportation link between the Shenandoah Valley and port cities below the Great Falls of the Potomac, serving as a means of shipping farm goods to larger East Coast towns and cities. Overnight the small village became a bustling railroad depot. It was such an important location that in 1861 the Confederates built a ring of earthen forts around the entire town. The same year they built the world's first military railroad, which supplied the Confederate Army at Centreville during the winter of 1861-1862. Union and Confederate troops twice fought battles over this town, with the northern army burning many of the buildings around the railroad in March 1862. The rebuilt 1914 **train station** houses the visitor center and a small railroad exhibit.

Around Town

Manassas is still an important link for Virginia produce, evidenced by the Farmer's Market held every Thursday and Saturday morning on

Church Street. Vendors come from as far away as the Shenandoah Valley. Whether you're talking pork products or scones, it's all hand-grown, raised or baked. It was the smell of baked good that drew us to two stalls adjacent to one another. In one, a local family, immigrants from West Africa, sold a variety of breads. In the other, an older couple from West Virginia sold their own assortment of baked goods.

John and Brenda "Mama" Bowling have been bringing their goodies to the Manassas market for 16 years. "Mama makes 10 flavors of scones," says John of his wife, whose name and likeness grace their company's labels: "Mama's Goodies."

"And they're not dry like some scones; they're extra sweet. Cross between a biscuit and a cookie. That's how my mama and hers made them back in West Virginia for us kids to eat during the day."

"Back home" is Coalwood, West Virginia, the setting for the film *October Sky*. John went to school with "those boys," and played in the same fields. Their fathers were all coal miners. John and Brenda married there, then moved to Manassas about 20 years ago.

In the next booth over, the two young West African boys press the hard sell for goods their family of eight bakes at home in Sterling, Virginia. Originally hailing from Togo in West Africa, the family named their baking enterprise "Becky's Pastries," after their littlest daughter.

"Our sweet Portuguese bread is like no other – you won't find it in any store," says Komlan Sessou, an enthusiastic teenage businessman. Jalapeño cheese bread is another specialty the family makes.

You'll likely find these vendors, and a dozen others – many Hispanic farmers with vegetables and plants – at the Farmer's Market April through October. It's open Thursdays from 7am to 1pm and Saturdays from 7am to 2:30, although we noted that several were packing up by 1pm, so get there early!

Such ethnic diversity and the entrepreneurial spirit exemplify Northern Virginia. Old Town Manassas is a remnant of a small town surrounded by urban sprawl. There are even traffic jams in Old Town on any given summer Saturday. Just across the tracks, "real" Manassas, a modern city of more than 35,000 people, is a bedroom community for Washington DC, just 30 miles away. That makes the gem of Old Town all that more special.

Northern Virginia

Attractions

At the visitor center in the railroad depot, pick up the **Walking Tour** and **Driving Tour** brochures of Old Town Manassas. Old Town is best experienced walking – it's only about six blocks long and three wide. The walking tour includes the 1914 Old Town Hall, a 1908 candy factory, the 1875 red sandstone Old Presbyterian Church, the community's first bank, built in 1896, and the Connor Opera House, where the last reunions of Mosby's Rangers were held. **The Manassas Museum** is the last stop on the walking tour, but you could spend a couple of hours here alone, exploring the history of the railroad junction and of the Virginia Piedmont. Open Tuesday-Sunday, 10am to 5pm. $3 adults, $2 seniors and children age 6-17 (9101 Prince William Street, ☎ 703-368-1873, www.ManassasMuseum.org).

Located about a mile southwest of Old Town on Wellington Road is the **Manassas Industrial School/Jennie Dean Memorial**, an intriguing re-creation of the Manassas Industrial School for Colored Youth that opened in 1894. Its founder, Jennie Dean, was born a slave in 1852 in Prince William County. Her dream was to create a school where young black men and women could learn marketable trades. It remained a segregated school until 1966. The original buildings are gone, but a bronze model of the campus, outlines of the foundations and historical markers tell the story. It's an outdoor memorial park, so it's free and open during daylight hours every day (☎ 703-368-1873).

The **Manassas Volunteer Fire Company Museum** at 9322 Centreville Road (☎ 703-368-6211) displays hundreds of antique fire equipment and memorabilia in a working, modern fire station where visitors can talk with firefighters. Open Sundays noon-4pm. Free (☎ 703-368-6211).

Manassas Battlefield Park, five miles north of Old Town Manassas, tells the story of the two great Civil War battles of 1861 and 1862, also known as the Battles of Bull Run. The national park encompasses more than 5,000 acres – a one-mile walking tour of the first battle, a 12-mile driving tour of the second battle, as well as 30 miles of hiking trails, 20 miles of bridle paths and a visitor center. Open 8:30am to 5pm daily, until 6pm in summer; closed Thanksgiving and Christmas days. Admission is $3 for adults, under age 17 free (12521 Lee Highway, ☎ 703-361-1339, www.nps.gov/mana).

Shopping

More than two dozen specialty shops in Old Town line **Center Street** – the main drag – and its side streets. You'll find antiques, country crafts, artists' studios and art galleries.

Dining

For such a small area, Old Town has a great diversity of restaurants. You can eat Cajun at **Okra's Louisiana Bistro** (9110 Center Street, ☎ 703-330-2729), Thai at the **Thai Secret** (9114 Center Street, ☎ 703-361-2500), Italian and Portuguese at **Carmello's & Little Portugal**, located in the old Cocke Pharmacy (9108 Center Street, ☎ 703-368-5522), or Philly specialties at the **Philadelphia Tavern** (9413 Main Street, ☎ 703-393-1776). Have English tea at **The Victorian Tea Room** (9413 Battle Street, ☎ 703-393-TEAS), a cool treat at **The Old Town Scoop** (9360 Main Street, ☎ 703-396-7151), or hot coffee at **Java Jacks** (9112 Center Street, ☎ 703-330-5124).

Lodging

Bennett House Bed & Breakfast is a Victorian inn that serves a full country breakfast, a great start for a day of walking in Old Town. Your return or arrival in the afternoon is greeted with a cup of tea or wine and cheese. Then take some time to relax on the porch or in the hot tub (9252 Bennett Drive, ☎ 800-354-7060, www.virginia-bennetthouse.com, $$).

Olde Towne Inn is a modest motor lodge right in the heart of Old Town (9403 Main Street, ☎ 703-368-9191, $).

Best Western Manassas is located just outside the Old Town area at 8640 Mathis Avenue (☎ 703-368-7070, $$).

 Nearly all the major chain motels are represented close to the battlefield area at Route 234 and I-66. The **Red Roof Inn** at Route 234 and I-66 takes pets at no extra charge (☎ 703-335-9333, $).

Information

The **Historic Manassas Visitor Center** in the historic railroad depot is open 9am to 5pm daily (☎ 703-361-6599, www.visitmanassas.org).

> ★ TIP
>
> Parking is free on Old Town's streets and in public lots, but it is timed. If you don't want to worry about getting a ticket, pick up a free all-day parking permit at the visitor center.

Events

The **Loy E. Harris Pavilion**, next to the train station, is the center of activity in Old Town Manassas, with a full schedule of concerts, festivals, art shows and holiday celebrations June through October (☎ 703-361-6599, www.harrispavilion.com). A highlight is the annual **Manassas Heritage Railway Festival** the first Saturday in June (☎ 703-361-6599).

> ★ LOCAL HISTORY
>
> The First Battle of Manassas (Bull Run) on July 21, 1861, was the first major battle of the Civil War. It was during this battle that Confederate General Thomas J. Jackson earned the name "Stonewall." The Confederates defeated federal troops in their first encounter, although an argument could be made that both sides were staggered by the vicious fighting and heavy casualties. "The Confederate army was more disorganized by victory than that of the United States by defeat," wrote Confederate General Joseph E. Johnston.

Middleburg

The Piedmont countryside is dissected by stone walls and split rail fence. Past gated entrances, long driveways lead to estates such as Westview, where the Piedmont Foxhounds, the nation's first hunt club, hold their traditional first meeting of the year. This Federal-style home boasts a provenance of ownership that fought for the "right" side in both the Revolutionary War (American) and Civil War (Confederate).

As the epicenter for Virginia's hunt country, Middleburg holds a rather exclusive status. It serves the scions of industry and sport – particularly horse racing – who reside in neo-plantation estates out in the surrounding countryside. In this world of polo matches and wine tastings, Middleburg is where they dine and shop. As such, amenities are of high quality and priced accordingly. Mercedes and Jaguars line the streets in front of art galleries and equestrian-themed boutiques.

Around Town

Middleburg is a lovely village of just 600 people, with more than 160 buildings listed on the National Register of Historic Places. Washington Street and a surrounding six-block area make for great window shopping. Irish crystal, cigars, designer clothing at the Finicky Filly, or gourmet kitchen supplies, antiques, guns, sporting art and clothing are just a sample of what can be bought. At Christmas, stores are decorated to the nines for a holiday season that begins with a parade of hounds and equestrians in full attire.

Middleburg is also home to the second-oldest tavern in America (although the sign out front says *the* "oldest original Inn"). Originally called Mr. Chinn's Ordinary, **The Red Fox Inn** has been hosting travelers since 1728, including a young George Washington on a surveying trip, and John F. Kennedy who occasionally held press conferences here. (Jackie attended hunt breakfasts at Westview.) During the Civil War, John Mosby ran his raids from Middleburg and held meetings at the same yellow fieldstone tavern. Thus Middleburg earned its other reputation, as the center of the area that became known as "Mosby's Confederacy."

One of the newest buildings in town is the **Middleburg National Sporting Library,** housed in a whitewashed brick building built to resemble a 19th-century carriage house. A life-sized bronze statue of a

Northern Virginia

horse sits in the center of a circular driveway, commissioned as a memorial to the 1.5 million horses and mules killed or wounded in the Civil War. Inside, there's 15,000 square feet of space housing some of the world's most prized volumes on turf and field sports, from 16th-century books on horse care to a handwritten manuscript of Theodore Roosevelt's "Riding to the Hounds on Long Island." Visitors can sit and peruse books from the 15,000-item collection in one of two alcoves furnished with comfy chairs and sofas. Open Monday, 1-4pm; Tuesday-Friday, 10am-4pm; Saturday by appointment (102 The Plains Road, ☎ 540-687-6542, www.nsl.org).

Loudoun County has several vineyards; two just outside Middleburg. **Piedmont Vineyards and Winery,** established in 1973, is Virginia's oldest Chardonnay producer, also acclaimed for its Semillon and Cabernet Sauvignon (2546D Halfway Road, off Route 626 south of Middleburg, ☎ 540-687-5528, www.piedmontwines.com). **Swedenburg Estate Vineyard** is one mile east of Middleburg off US Route 50 on a circa-1762 farm. Open daily, 10am-4pm (☎ 540-687-5219).

Outdoors

The **Wankopin Community Trail** winds for three miles through a 500-acre plat in the upper Wankopin Creek Watershed. The trailhead is at Hill School, 180 S. Madison Street, Middleburg (☎ 540-687-5897).

Dining

The Red Fox Inn offers fine dining in seven Colonial dining rooms – Windsor chairs, low ceilings of exposed wood beams, plenty of fireplaces. Proper attire is required. The extensive wine cellar was added in 1812 (2 East Washington Street, ☎ 800-223-1728, www.redfox.com).

For a completely different experience, pop in to **Scruffy's Ice Cream Parlor and Thrift Store**, a few doors down from the Red Fox. Proceeds from sales go to the Middleburg Humane Foundation. The sign on the door reads: "Fur coats not welcome, unless you have four feet." One has to wonder what they think of fox hunting (☎ 540-364-3272).

Back Street Café serves fresh food with an Italian flair, and hosts live jazz on the weekends (☎ 540-687-3122). The **Hidden Horse Tavern** is indeed hidden down a lane on the side of Middleburg Plaza. Live jazz during Sunday brunch (7 W. Washington Street, ☎ 540-687-3828).

Magpie's Café is more of a tavern with outdoor dining for people-watching and live music on Thursday and Sunday (118 West Washington Street, ☎ 540-687-6443). **Mosby's Tavern** is a fun eating and drinking establishment at 2 West Marshall Street, near the Pink Box visitor's center (☎ 540-687-5282).

Lodging

The Longbarn is a renovated 100-year-old barn in the woods. That might sound rustic, but it has air conditioning, fireplaces, and a library; it is furnished elegantly in Italian country style (37129 Adams Green Lane, ☎ 540-687-4137, http://members.aol.com/thlongbarn, $$).

The Middleburg Country Inn, circa 1820, has eight period guest rooms, serves a full breakfast daily, dinner on weekends, and afternoon tea in the parlor or out on the terrace. Canopy beds, fireplaces, and an outdoor hot tub make for romantic weekends combining the best in historic elegance and modern comfort (209 E. Washington Street, ☎ 800-262-6082, www.midcountryinn.com, $$$).

Accommodations at **The Red Fox Inn** are in 30 guest rooms and suites located in four adjacent historic buildings. Rooms start at $150 and go up to $325 for the Belmont Suite (2 East Washington Street, 800-223-1728, www.redfox.com, $$$).

Welbourne is a 1775 home with six guest rooms and two cottages on Route 1 (☎ 540-687-3201, $$).

The **Goodstone Inn** is a manor house and carriage house on 265 acres in the midst of hunt country (36205 Snake Hill Road, ☎ 540-687-4645, www.goodstone.com, $$$$).

Information

The **Pink Box** at 12 North Madison Street (turn off Washington Street at the Red Fox Inn) serves as the visitor's center. The little whitewashed brick house does look kind of pink (☎ 540-687-8888, www.middleburgonline.com).

Loudoun County Tourism Council, ☎ 800-752-6118, www.visitloudoun.org.

Northern Virginia

Events

Glenwood Park hosts the **Middleburg Spring Races** in April and the **Virginia Fall Races** the first weekend in October (☎ 540-687-5662, www.vafallraces.com).

The **Farmers' Market** is held every Saturday, 9am-1pm, May-October, behind the community center. The market features produce such as fruits, vegetables, flowers, herbs, honey and eggs, as well as canned and baked goods and even wine (☎ 703-777-0426).

In September, the **Middleburg Classic Horse Show** comes to Great Meadow in the Plains (☎ 757-357-1775, www.middleburgclassic.com).

Virginia's annual **Historic Garden Week** in April offers outsiders rare glimpses of private gardens and homes in the area (☎ 804-644-7778).

★ DID YOU KNOW?

Established in 1787, the name of Middleburg comes from its location midway on the commercial route between Winchester and Alexandria.

Occoquan

In the language of the Dogue Indians, "at the end of water" translates as "Occoquan," a term English settlers adopted when they built a small industrial and commercial center near the falls of this Potomac tributary. Once a thriving 19th-century mill town, Historic Occoquan is a small village with barely 800 residents. It's also a charming oasis of shops, restaurants and inns. The Occoquan River was the conduit of commerce of the community's early industrial days. That job is now handled by nearby Interstate 95. Yet it remains a striking feature of this town how closely it exists to the East Coast's major interstate, yet in such undisturbed and relative quietude.

It helps that the village sits in a bowl – well, not exactly a bowl, but at the base of a hill along the Occoquan River. It is bounded by water and by hills, and buffered by both from distraction. On a spring day, the sun will set a few minutes earlier downtown than it does on the hilltops south and east, which are fringed with town homes. The sun's last rays play on a front porch packed with wooden rocking chairs halfway up Union Street, while restaurants down at the water's edge have already struck evening lights to attract dinners.

Around Town

Occoquan merchants carry no illusions: Theirs is a weekend town for day-trippers who find it convenient to I-95 (Exit 160), people who are more interested in fine arts and crafts, jewelry or antiques than the mass-produced goods available, say, at nearby Potomac Mills. Occoquan's shops and galleries – nearly 100 at last count – occupy original 18th- and 19th-century buildings that have survived both fire (which destroyed much of the town in 1916) and a hurricane (Agnes, in 1972).

Riverwalk, with its Victorian stylings, is not one of those historic buildings. But it catches a visitor's eye first, and there is much to explore in the small shops. Eventually, the eye wanders up Mill Street to the crooked buildings and colorful signboards. Behind them, nearly obstructed, flows the Occoquan River. **Harbor River Cruises** (see below) conducts daily boat rides, while guests in the waterfront restaurants enjoy seafood, or the atmosphere of a haunted inn or Victorian tea room.

Outside its historic district, Occoquan is surrounded by condominiums, starter homes and townhouses. Where there is an empty field or a bit of woods, there's likely to be a sign declaring what new housing development is coming. Seeing this, as you leave Occoquan, makes you you appreciate the bit of the past that has been preserved.

Attractions

The town had the nation's first automated grist mill and one of the first cotton mills in Virginia. The only remaining building of the mill and foundry complex is operated as the **Mill House Museum,** open daily, 11am-4pm, with free admission (413 Mill Street, ☎ 703-491-7525).

Harbor River Cruises offers a 40-minute sightseeing trip. Catch the boat dockside at 201 Mill Street, behind Riverwalk; the cost is $11 for adults and $8 for children (☎ 703-385-9433).

Northern Virginia

Outdoors

You're as apt to see wildlife as you are another person in **Prince William National Forest Park**. Small waterfalls make for scenic viewing along South Branch and North Branch Quantico River. Between them lie a mix of open fields and eastern hardwood forests. There are 35 miles of trails spread over 17,000 acres, a scenic driving loop, and camping either in a tent, RV or cabin. Located on State Route 619 near Triangle (☎ 703-221-7181).

Shopping

Ye Olde Dominion Wine Shoppe carries Virginia wines exclusively and offers daily tastings year-round (408 Mill Street, ☎ 703-494-1622, www.ecounties.net/yeolde).

For 21st-century shopping, just south on I-95 is the **Potomac Mills Outlet Mall**, a mile-long array of designer outlet and off-price retail stores. It also has an indoor/outdoor in-line skating complex, a 20-screen cinema and food court (☎ 800-VA-MILLS).

Dining

The **Garden Kitchen** is a café and bakery serving specialty sandwiches and homemade desserts. Dine inside in one of the Colonial dining rooms or out in the terraced gardens (404 Mill Street, ☎ 703-494-2848, www.gardenkitchen.com).

The **Occoquan Inn and Virginia Grille** are fine dining and casual counterparts under the same roof. The central part of the building is the original 1810 residence. Legend has it that a Dogue Indian sometimes haunts the upstairs ladies "necessary." The story goes that the Indian, one of the last remaining in the town, was having a relationship with the innkeeper's wife. The jealous husband caught him coming down the stairs and shot him (301 Mill Street, ☎ 703-491-1888, www.occoquaninn.com).

Sea Sea & Company is a large seafood restaurant on the water next to Riverwalk, with deck dining and a nautical theme (201 Mill Street, ☎ 703-690-2004).

Toby's Café is worth searching out, set back in a courtyard with a couple of boutiques. Pasta, soup and sandwiches on fresh-baked French bread are the specialties. Dine inside or out on the patio courtyard where there is often live music on the weekends. Choose from more than two dozen flavors for your coffee or soda (201 Union Street, ☎ 703-494-1317).

Lodging

There's no place to stay in town, but several major chain hotels operate in nearby Woodbridge. The closest is a **Hampton Inn**, about a mile away (☎ 703-490-2300).

Information

The **Prince William County Tourist Information Center** is open daily, 9am-5pm, at 200 Mill Street; ☎ 703-491-4045, www.occo-quan.com.

Prince William County/Manassas Conference and Visitors Bureau, ☎ 800-432-1792, www.visitpwc.com.

Events

The **Historic Occoquan Spring Arts and Craft Festival** is in June, and a fall show takes place in late September (☎ 703-491-2168).

Christmas in Occoquan begins with Santa's arrival by boat in late November (☎ 703-491-1736).

> ★ TRAVEL TIP
>
> Be sure to pick up a *Shopping & Dining Guide* at the Visitors Center. Inside is a street map and self-guided haunted walking tour with great tidbits about the historic buildings.

Northern Virginia

Trip Journal

Gunston Hall

Dogwood may be the state tree (and flower), and azaleas may be the unofficial (and ubiquitous) flowering shrub, but to me, what really says "Virginia" is the scent of ancient boxwoods. There are plenty of these at Gunston Hall, where George Mason planted the long row of boxwoods that very likely predate the Revolution.

Kept trimmed to only a few feet tall while Mason was alive, the shrubs now tower overhead and have overgrown a pathway that was once 12 feet wide. Walking through the now-narrow tunnel of greenery, the pungent, slightly sweet smell overwhelms. Take a minute to peer through the branches at the thick, gnarled, ancient trunks.

Archeologists are using soil sampling to unearth what Mason's original Colonial gardens looked like and what else grew in them. According to journals kept by John Mason, his son, the elder Mason did his best thinking in these gardens. In good weather, he left his study several times a day to walk and meditate, and it was understood during these meditations no one should disturb him. It was likely here in these very gardens that founding father Mason mentally framed the *Virginia Declaration of Rights*, the first document in America that called for freedom of the press, religion, and the right to a trial by jury. Based on the writings of philosopher John Locke, it influenced the *Declaration of Independence* and the *Bill of Rights*.

Ironically, Mason's slave quarters were probably visible just outside the gardens, a painful reminder of the contradictions that people like Mason, Thomas Jefferson and George Washington lived with. Inalienable rights did not apply to all residents of the fledgling nation.

Even while he wrote of slavery as a "slow poison," an act of "Despotism & Cruelty," and fought for the abolition of the slave trade in the *Constitution*, Mason was the second largest slave holder in Fairfax County (Washington was first). Nor is there any record that Mason ever freed any of his slaves. His writings reveal him to be painfully conflicted on the matter. While he wrote that the practice of slavery made men "callous to the Dictates of Humanity… to regard part of our own Species in the most abject & contemptible Degree below us," he could devise no means of ending slavery that would preserve the prosperity of the plantations – and by association, his own large family of 12 children.

Roger Wilkins, author of *Jefferson's Pillow*, said "The founding fathers led lives cushioned by slavery." Yet it is refreshing to see lives of America's early African-Americans interpreted in more candid ways than before at places like Gunston Hall, where a new exhibit opened in 2002 with reconstructed slave quarters and outbuildings. Museum interpreters here, and at the museum homes of Monticello and Mount Vernon, are moving away from shameful avoidance of slavery, to acknowledgement that it was African-American labor that built the vast plantations and wealth, making it possible for the founding fathers to enjoy lives of thought, politics and travel that enabled them to form a new nation.

In 2002, the first memorial to a non-president was dedicated on the National Mall in Washington DC. The larger-than-life bronze statue of George Mason is surrounded by stone walls inscribed with his portentous words. Appropriately, the memorial has a re-created 18th-century historic garden, near the area known as the Pansy Garden.

Gunston Hall Plantation is open daily, 9:30am to 5pm (closed on Thanksgiving, Christmas and New Year's day), with tours on the half-hour. Admission charged (10709 Gunston Road, Mason Neck, ☎ 800-811-6966 or 703-550-9220, http://GunstonHall.org).

Northern Virginia

Warrenton

Around Town

A set of stocks greets visitors to Warrenton at the **Old Jail Museum** – or "Gaol" as the sign outside reads. The 1808 jail has been restored to more or less how it looked before the "new" and larger jail was built next door in 1823. In the Old Kitchen three layers of plaster were removed to expose a fabulous brick fireplace that was used to cook for the prisoners. Inside the hearth it was found that whoever walled it up had thrown in some treasures – iron lamps, utensils and even cast iron pots with blackened food still inside. The Old Jail is said to have a resident ghost, an elderly man who died there while a prisoner. Docent Leona Keen says she's never seen him, but she has heard strange noises.

The museum tells the history of The Warren Green Hotel, which now houses school board and county offices. Before closing in 1960, the guest list read like a Who's Who of American history, including General Lafayette in 1825, presidents James Monroe, Andrew Jackson and Theodore Roosevelt. Here, General McClellan said goodbye to his troops after President Lincoln relieved him of his command, and Henry Clay announced his candidacy for president.

Scandal sells, and it is an infamous guest who probably garnered the most attention. In order to get a quiet divorce in a small town, Wallis Warfield set up temporary residency in the hotel in 1927. Originally from Baltimore, she had friends in Fauquier County from her boarding school days. In the year she lived here, she carried on a relationship with her next husband, Earnest Simpson. By the mid-1930s she was seeing the Prince of Wales, and we all know where that led – to the King of England abdicating his throne to marry an American divorcee. She may have been fickle in love, but Simpson kept her ties to Warrenton. The couple returned for a visit in 1941 as the Duke and Duchess of Windsor.

We were told old-school Warrentonians don't really like to flaunt such notoriety. They like things relatively quiet and conservative. When an Irish pub opened in 2001 on Main Street, it caused quite a flutter because it was one of the first bars to open on Main Street since World War II, when many lined the street. The movie theater was closed down in 1971 when Marlon Brando's *Last Tango In Paris* shocked the community.

Several other pubs and bistros have opened as well, and the Old Town that once rolled up its sidewalks at 5pm with all shops closed on Sundays now brings in night and weekend crowds – people who want to have a drink and hear live music. Main Street is a happening and busy place during the week, with businesspeople going to lunch, and lawyers and police officers coming to and from the courthouse. On the weekends diners and shoppers patronize the more than 50 antiques shops, boutiques, restaurants, coffee shops, ice cream parlors and art galleries.

It seems to be everything that an American Main Street should be. Yet there's a nice dash – just enough – of the sophisticated and hip. The local newspaper has called it "Little Georgetown."

A walking tour of Warrenton's historic area starts at the Old Jail Museum. Inside the jail are exhibits on the county's history and visitor information. It is open Tuesday-Sunday, 10am-4pm. Admission is free, but donations are welcome (corner of Main & Ashby streets, ☎ 540-347-5525).

Jimmie's Market is a place that's been catering to the discriminating lunch crowd and shopper since the 1970s. A store since 1939, the small, narrow shop at 22 Main Street has original tin ceilings and is packed with all kinds of imported and gourmet groceries, 80 kinds of beer, local wines, deli items, even some antiques. At a counter you can sit and browse through the cookbooks for sale, or have a flavored coffee and a European pastry brought in from New York City. A small café in the back seats about eight. The deli sandwiches use the finest ingredients, and you can purchase locally produced Black Angus beef or organic meat from the freezer, including châteaubriand and veal scaloppine from Summerfield Farms in nearby Culpeper (☎ 540-347-1942).

Dining

There are several options for fine dining. The **Depot Restaurant** is located inside, you guessed it, an old train station, decorated with old railroad memorabilia and photographs. The fare is Mediterranean and American. Open for lunch and dinner Tuesday-Sunday (65 S. Third Street, ☎ 540-347-1212). **Fantastico-Ristorante Italiano & Inn** features authentic northern Italian cuisine. Open daily for lunch and dinner, plus brunch on Sunday, with live music Thursday-Saturday. Tuesday is open-mike night, if you'd like to bring your own entertainment (380 Broadview Avenue, ☎ 540-349-2575, www.fantastico-inn.com).

Napoleon's Restaurant is in a restored 1830s Greek Revival, serving continental fare. Open for lunch and dinner Monday-Saturday (67 Waterloo Street, ☎ 540-347-4300, www.napoleonsrestaurant.com).

Pubs, cafés and bistros include: The **Main Street Bistro**, one of the newer establishments, serving breakfast, lunch and dinner daily (32 Main Street, ☎ 540-428-1778); **Molly's Irish Pub**, open for dinner nightly and Sunday brunch, with live music on weekends (36 Main Street, ☎ 540-349-5300); and **Smokey Joe's Café**, serving American fare and live entertainment (11 Second Street, ☎ 540-341-2826).

The Earthly Paradise, a coffeehouse on Main Street, is open daily (☎ 540-341-7115). For ice cream, there's the **Creamery**, 61 S. Fourth

Northern Virginia

Street (closed in winter). **Old Town Café** is a renovated soda fountain serving daily specials and cocktails (79 Main St, Warrenton (☎ 540-347-4147).

Lodging

The **Black Horse Inn** is a 19th-century Colonial Estate with nine guest rooms, stables, a new reception facility and ballroom, and panoramic views of hunt country (8393 Meetze Road, ☎ 540-349-4020, www.blackhorseinn.com).

Fantastico Inn has 14 rooms with private baths, a restaurant and piano bar (380 Broadview Avenue, ☎ 540-349-2575, www.fantastico-inn.com, $$).

Stonehurst Farms is a secluded inn with great mountain views (6623 McRaes Road, ☎ 540-347-7710, www.stonehurstfarms.com, $$).

 Pet-owners, you're in luck, and you have choices! The **Hampton Inn** accepts pets without a charge (501 Blackwell Road, ☎ 540-349-4200, $). The **Comfort Inn** (7379 Comfort Inn Drive, ☎ 540-349-8900, $$) and **Howard Johnson** (6 Broadview Avenue, ☎ 540-347-4141, $) both accept pets for a $10 extra charge.

Information

Warrenton-Fauquier County Visitor Center, 183-A Keith Street, ☎ 540-347-4414 or 800-820-1021, www.fauquierchamber.org, is open daily. Pick up a walking tour brochure of the historic downtown.

Partnership for Warrenton Foundation, ☎ 540-349-8606, www.historicwarrenton.org, provides maps and information about events and historic attractions.

★ LOCAL HISTORY

Across the street from the visitor center is **The Warrenton Cemetery**, the resting place of Col. John Mosby and a memorial to 600 fallen Confederates.

The Plains

The Plains, a tiny village of 266 people, will forever be remembered as the place where we learned the difference between liver pâté and truffee. Truffee is creamier in texture, more like a mousse, and it spreads beautifully on a Carr's cracker. We enjoyed it with a nice, inexpensive (around $6) bottle of Spanish wine.

Hardly trivial, this distinction embodies The Plains, a crossroads community with one stoplight nestled between Warrenton and Middleburg. We picked up the truffee and wine in the rustic **Farm Store**, which is best described as a gourmet general store. Yes, this is the life and, judging by those who've bought second homes here, it's a good one. Robert Duvall has a farm here and he once owned the Rail Stop restaurant, but recently sold it. Willard Scott, who lives in nearby DelaPlain, comes into The Plains Pharmacy quite often, riling up the girls behind the counter, no doubt.

Getting to The Plains is a short, scenic drive on Route 626 from Middleburg. The road by itself is an attraction – rolling and winding through farmlands and past estates, with glimpses of the Blue Ridge to the west. Today a cutesy little hamlet with a handful of trendy artists' studios and shops, The Plains was once the outpost of civilization, hence the name. In 1726 the first settlers came through Thoroughfare Gap to the north and began farming the land.

Around Town

A post office came in 1831 to join the one store and one house in town. In 1862 Lee's entire army camped here, and it was considered part of Mosby's Confederacy. The Union Army twice sent search and destroy missions, burning many of the buildings. The Manassas Gap railroad had reached The Plains in 1852, and, after the freight depot was built in 1892 to pick up produce grown in nearby farms, the town started to thrive.

In the early 1990s, the train depot was narrowly saved from destruction by a citizens' group called "Save the RR Station." Enid Adams (☎ 540-253-5678), a fabric and garden designer, was the first artist to move her studio into the station's waiting room and encouraged other artists to join her. Large windows look into the various studios at **RR**

Northern Virginia

Arts Depot, where you might be able to catch artists at work during the week, or by appointment.

 TIP

Several shops and restaurants are closed on Mondays and Tuesdays, and artists are generally not in their studios on weekends, so the best days to visit The Plains are Wednesday through Friday.

Attraction

The **Afro-American Historical Association of Fauquier County** preserves and shares the history of the county's black population through photographs, genealogical records and educational programs (4249 Loudoun Avenue, ☎ 540-253-7488, www.afro-americanofva.org).

Great Meadow hosts a variety of equestrian events, from Friday night polo to the Middleburg Classic Horse Show (5089 Old Tavern Road, ☎ 540-253-5001, www.greatmeadow.org).

Dining

The **Rail Stop** on Main Street serves specials incorporating local Black Angus beef and smoked trout. Open for lunch and dinner, Tuesday-Sunday (☎ 540-253-5644, www.railstoprestaurant.com).

Just Breakfast & Lunch serves just that (4244 Loudoun Avenue, ☎ 540-253-5501).

Lodging

 The **Grey Horse Inn** is an 1880s mansion on four acres with six guest rooms, one of which is designated for guests with pets and has its own entrance. There's no extra charge for four-legged critters (4350 Fauquier Avenue, ☎ 540-253-7000, www.greyhorseinn.com, $$$).

Information

Information is available from the **Fauquier County Chamber of Commerce**, Warrenton, ☎ 800-820-1021, www.fauquierchamber.org.

Event

Each October is your chance to catch most of The Plains' artisans at work at one time during the **Open Studio and Walking Tour**. In addition to the artists in the RR Arts depot (☎ 540-253-5470 or 253-5678), there's also a potter, a sculptor and two harpsichord builders in town.

Northern Virginia

Coastal Virginia

From the Northern Neck down to Hampton Roads, the waters of the numerous rivers emptying into the Chesapeake Bay define life and recreation in Coastal Virginia. The great native tribes of Powhatan lived and fished along the banks of "river country." Our nation's Colonial history is acted out in daily ritual from its beginnings at Jamestown, to the middle period at Williamsburg, to the end of Colonial status – and the birth of a nation – at Yorktown. Old steamboat landings scattered up and down the shorelines of the many peninsulas serve tourists seeking peaceful waters, golfing vacations, antique hunting, and bountiful seafood restaurants.

THE TOWNS
※ Colonial Beach
※ Oak Grove
※ Reedville
※ Kilmarnock
※ Irvington
※ Urbanna
※ Gloucester
※ Yorktown
※ Williamsburg
※ Smithfield

Getting Here

Interstate 64 provides access to the towns of the Virginian Peninsula, including Williamsburg and Yorktown. **Route 17** runs north-south through Gloucester and the Middle Peninsula, and the Northern Neck is traversed by **routes 3, 202** and **360**.

Several airports serve this area: **Newport News/Williamsburg International Airport** (☎ 757-877-0221 or 757-877-0924); **Norfolk International Airport** (☎ 757-857-3200, www.norfolkairport. com); and **Richmond International Airport** (☎ 804-226-3000, www.flyrichmond.com).

Regional Information

Northern Neck Tourism Council, ☎ 800-393-6180, www.northernneck.org.

Williamsburg Area Convention and Visitors Bureau, 421 N. Boundary Street, Williamsburg, ☎ 800-368-6511, www.visitwilliamsburg.com.

Colonial Beach

With a deepwater port and long, sandy beach, Colonial Beach enjoys an enviable spot on the wide Potomac River. Never shy about exploiting these natural endowments, the town has endured boom and bust, fame and notoriety, and a cast of colorful characters, much of this originating from the town's proximity to the Maryland border.

The story of this town is tied equally to Maryland as to Virginia. In 1632, King Charles I granted to Catholic nobleman George Calvert land bounded on the north by the 40th parallel, and on the south by the Potomac. This gave his new colony, Maryland, ownership of the river proper, and placed Northern Neck towns literally "on the border" of Maryland. Inevitably, conflicts arose between the states over use of the river and, in an early stroke of diplomacy, George Washington helped formulate rules for use of the river by either state for commerce. Yet animosity persisted for two centuries, reaching a fever pitch during a period known as the Oyster Wars, from the late 19th century through 1960.

Colonial Beach kept to the sidelines in this drawn-out battle. It was focused on the good-time business of entertaining Washington DC tourists who came by the boatloads on summer weekends. An amusement park with a large ferris wheel operated until a hurricane in 1933 destroyed it and three popular "beer piers" built out into the Potomac. Because the piers crossed into Maryland, the owners operated under that state's laws, thus circumventing Virginia's strict alcohol regulations.

By the 1950s, business owners found a new way to exploit the border and draw crowds. Gambling was legal in Maryland, and a long pier and casino with slot machines extended from the Colonial Beach shoreline into the Potomac and across the border. Colonial Beach was instantly revitalized as a tourist destination, although the new enterprise brought a somewhat tawdry reputation as "the poor man's Las Vegas."

The end of World War II saw a violent resumption of the Oyster Wars, and this time, Colonial Beach was in the thick of it. A valuable oyster strike was found nearby and Colonial Beach oyster packers hired watermen to poach the beds. Maryland's specially commissioned oyster police pursued them with high-powered motor boats outfitted with machine guns. When, in 1959, Virginia waterman Berkeley Muse was killed in a hail of gunfire from the Maryland authorities, the hue-and-

Above: *Ponies at Chincoteague, on Virginia's Eastern Shore.*

Below: *A patriotic floral display at the Gloucester Daffodil Festival.*
(Photos by Mary Burnham)

Above: *Contestants at Crisfield's annual crab-picking contest, on Maryland's Eastern Shore.* (Photo courtesy of Crisfield Area Chamber of Commerce)

Opposite: *Hughlett Point Nature Preserve in Kilmarnock, on Coastal Virginia's Northern Neck.* (Photo by Mary Burnham)

Below: *The Watermen's Museum in Yorktown, Virginia.* (Photo by Mary Burnham)

The Laurel Brigade Inn, Leesburg, Virginia.
(Photo by Mary Burnham)

Damascus offers a warm welcome to hikers on the Appalachian Trail.
(Photo by John Reese)

Above: *The 101 Car in Big Stone Gap.* (Photo by Mary Burnham)
Opposite: *Colorful produce at a market in Mannassas, Virginia.* (Photo by Mary Burnham)
Below: *Ash Lawn-Highland in Charlottesville, Virginia, is now a working farm.*

Peppers
2 for 1.00

Furnace Town, north of Snow Hill, along Maryland's Eastern Shore.
(Photo by Mary Burnham)

A broom maker demonstrates his craft at Furnace Town.
(Photo by Mary Burnham)

Above: *Hungry Mother State Park, in Southwestern Virginia.* (Photo by Mary Burnham)
Opposite: *State House and garden, Historic St. Mary's City, Maryland.* (Photo courtesy of HSM
Below: *Carrying water from the creek at Historic St. Mary's City.* (Photo courtesy of HSMC

Street scene in Onancock, on Virginia's Eastern Shore.
(Photo by Mary Burnham)

cry led to formation of a bi-state commission that to this day governs use of the Potomac.

Outlaw days behind it, Colonial Beach is reborn as a popular boating destination and the last deepwater port for pleasure boaters heading north on the Potomac to Washington DC. The town's 2½ miles of beach, one of the longest stretches in the state, draws sun-bathers, fishing tournaments, Jet-ski competitions, music and seafood festivals. Boaters can pull up for free at the town pier and browse the many antique and specialty shops with land-lubbers, then choose from several waterside restaurants. There's still gambling – the off-track kind – at the Riverboat restaurant and bar. Thankfully, you don't have to have walk the pier into Maryland to reach this. Virginia legalized pari-mutuel betting in the early 1990s.

Calamity struck the town again in April 2002, when a fire devastated the town's largest marina. More than 50 boats and most of the docks were lost in a chain reaction explosion. But Colonial Beach Yacht Center, in business for half a century, quickly set about rebuilding "bigger and better" than ever.

Around Town

The Museum at Colonial Beach preserves all the town's rich history, going back to the first visit of Captain John Smith in 1608. There's a Victorian parlor, several vintage slot machines, a Watermen's Room, and lots of memorabilia from the old Colonial Beach Hotel. The museum is located at the corner of Hawthorne Street and Washington Avenue in a building with its own colorful past. Built in 1892 by Mayor William Billingsley, it served as the town's first private school in 1898 and has at different times housed the town's first newspaper, a clothing store, drug store, doctor's office, the town's telephone switchboard system, a barber shop, grocery store, bakery, a gas company and an antiques shop. In 1993 it was saved from destruction by a group of citizens, and in 1999 the museum opened. It's open Memorial Day through Labor Day on weekends and holidays, noon to 3pm. Open Saturdays only the rest of the year. Admission is free (☎ 804-224-5800 or 224-8020).

Outside Colonial Beach are the birthplaces of George Washington and Robert E. Lee. **George Washington Birthplace National Monument** is eight miles west of Montross on Pope's Creek Road. Costumed interpreters help portray the 18th-century plantation life George Washington experienced and that helped shape his character. There's a visitor center, the brick foundation of the house where he was

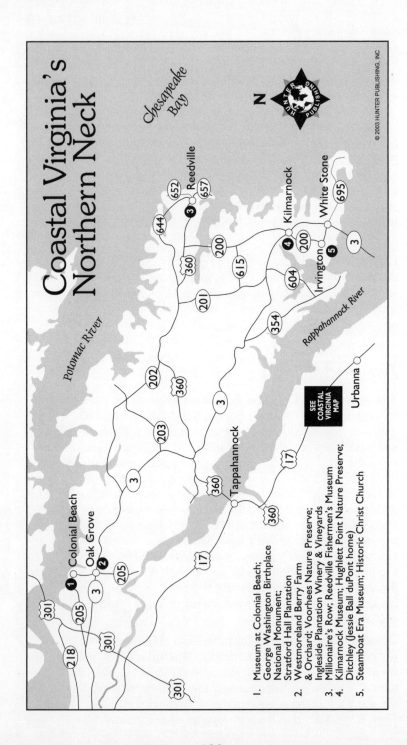

Coastal Virginia's Northern Neck

Chesapeake Bay

N

© 2003 HUNTER PUBLISHING, INC

Potomac River

Rappahannock River

Reedville

Kilmarnock

White Stone

Irvington

Colonial Beach

Oak Grove

Tappahannock

Urbanna

SEE COASTAL VIRGINIA MAP

1. Museum at Colonial Beach;
   George Washington Birthplace
   National Monument;
   Stratford Hall Plantation
2. Westmoreland Berry Farm
   & Orchard; Voorhees Nature Preserve;
   Ingleside Plantation Winery & Vineyards
3. Millionaire's Row; Reedville Fishermen's Museum
4. Kilmarnock Museum; Hughlett Point Nature Preserve;
   Ditchley (Jessie Ball duPont home)
5. Steamboat Era Museum; Historic Christ Church

born, and family burial grounds – although George and Martha are buried at Mount Vernon, further up the Potomac. There are nature trails, a picnic area and a Potomac River beach. Open daily, 9am-5pm, except Christmas and New Year's Day; admission is $3 for adults and free for those under age 16 (☎ 804-224-1732, http://www.nps.gov/gewa).

A visit to **Stratford Hall Plantation**, built in 1738 by Thomas Lee, lays bare the conflicted legacy of the Lee family, whose descendants, Richard Henry Lee and Francis "Lightfoot" Lee, signed the Declaration of Independence. Robert E. Lee was born here in 1807, and he went on to lead the Confederate army against the Union. Seemingly opposing forces – one generation for union, the other in conflict with union – find unity on the principal of self-determination. The 1,670-acre plantation is a working farm to this day and is open for tours. Have lunch in the plantation restaurant (11:30am-3pm). The visitor center and grounds are open daily, 9:30am-5pm, except on Thanksgiving, Christmas Eve and Day, and New Year's Day; house tours are given from 10am to 4pm. Admission is $8 for adults and $4 for ages six-17. Stratford Hall Road, near Montross (☎ 804-493-8038, 804-493-8371, www.stratfordhall.org).

Dining

The **Dockside Restaurant** at the Colonial Beach Yacht Center overlooks the Potomac and offers fresh seafood, a raw bar and steaks. The center also houses an authentic British Pub, the **Blue Heron**, operated by a Brit. Both restaurants close on Tuesdays (1787 Castlewood Drive, ☎ 804-224-8726, www.dockside-blueheron.com).

This could be the freshest seafood around. The proprietors of **The Happy Clam** often catch seafood for their guests right off the restaurant's dock. There are nightly dinner specials, a seafood buffet every Friday through Sunday, and the homemade pies are locally famous. Open daily for lunch and dinner, year-round (3700 McKinney Blvd., ☎ 804-224-0248, www.thehappyclam.biz).

Colonial Beach's gambling legacy on the Potomac is carried on at the **Riverboat on the Potomac**, where there's off-track betting, Keno, Virginia and Maryland lottery tickets, and an arcade. The food and water view are pretty good, too. **The Porch** is a fun place for a cocktail, with its whimsical island theme. Open daily, year-round, 8am to 1am (301 Beach Terrace, ☎ 804-224-7055, www.theriverboat.homestead.com).

Coastal Virginia

Lodging

The Bell House B&B is an 1882 Victorian on the Potomac River, once the summer home of Alexander Graham Bell. Guests can partake of a wine and cheese hour at 5pm or a Potomac River dinner cruise aboard the innkeeper's boat, *Apolonia*, on a Friday or Saturday evening (for an extra charge). The five-course meal with wine is offered May through November. The rest of the year, the dinner is served in the house (821 Irving Avenue, ☎ 804-224-7000, www.thebellhouse.com, $$).

The Plaza Bed & Breakfast is a 1903 Victorian with three guest rooms, a pool/spa, gardens and a wrap-around porch. A full breakfast and afternoon tea are served (21 Weems Street, ☎ 804-224-1101, www.colonialbeachplaza.com, $$).

Wakefield Motel – On the Point has rooms with kitchenettes. There's a fishing pier on the Potomac for guests to use, and a beach and public boat ramp nearby (1513 Irving Avenue, ☎ 804-224-7311, www.wakefieldmotel.com, $).

 The **Days Inn Colonial Beach** accepts pets for a daily charge of $10.75 (30 Colonial Avenue, ☎ 804-224-0404, $$).

Information

The **Colonial Beach Information Center**, ☎ 804-224-0732, is on the boardwalk, open in season only.

Colonial Beach Chamber of Commerce, ☎ 804-224-8145, www.cbvacc.org.

⭐ DID YOU KNOW?

Colonial Beach was originally called Monrovia, because it was first settled in 1647 by Andrew Monroe, a Scot and the great-great grandfather of President James Monroe.

Events

The **Potomac River Festival**, held annually for more than 50 years, is the first weekend in June, with parades, fireworks and music.

Side Trip

Oak Grove

Spend a perfect day enjoying the fruits of nature just south of Oak Grove. At the **Westmoreland Berry Farm and Orchard** you can pick your own in season, buy them by the pound, or purchase dessert for a picnic by the river. You can even feed the goats, who are sometimes 20 feet above your head! The "goat walk" is a series of platforms and ramps built to satisfy the goats' natural urge to climb. The farm has a harvest schedule online to help you plan a trip (☎ 800-997-BERRY [2377], www.westmorelandberryfarm.com).

Work off the calories on the six miles of trails at adjacent **Voorhees Nature Preserve**, with observation points along the Rappahannock River and marshes (☎ 804-224-9171).

End the day with a tour and tasting at **Ingleside Plantation Winery and Vineyards.** There's a museum on the 1834 plantation, which has been a winery since 1890. There are tours, tastings, and a gift and wine shop. Open Monday-Saturday, 10am-5pm; Sunday, noon-5pm (☎ 804-224-8687, www.ipwine.com).

Reedville

Around Town

This quiet fishing village on the Northern Neck may be the smallest town in Virginia serviced by a major four-lane highway. We're talking about Route 360, the high road from Richmond that dead-ends at an old wharf in Reedville, population uncertain. Our entrance, on a quiet Sunday afternoon during the off-season, proved a solitary event –

Coastal Virginia

there was nobody else on this wide, wide road. At a local restaurant we learned the answer to the mystery: Why would such a major highway service such a small town? Reedville is still a large commercial fishing center, as it has been since Elijah Reed built a fish processing operation here in 1867. Today's modern fish factories are the reason for the wide road, getting hundreds of commuters to work during the week.

Reedville is a Southern town built by a Yankee. It prospered, thanks to a one-inch, bony fish – or more accurately, millions of small, bony fish. Elijah Reed, originally of Maine, heard about the menhaden fish in the Chesapeake Bay. This fish is not for eating, but is prized for oil and fertilizer (they're also a mainstay in the diets of certain whales, like the humpback). So Elijah came down and built a menhaden-processing outfit in 1867. The town was established in his name in 1874, and became home to the Atlantic menhaden fleet.

Made wealthy by the harvest, the menhaden captains and plant owners built spectacular Victorian mansions along Main Street. Now known as **Millionaire's Row**, this Virginia Historic Landmark encompassing 70 buildings is a remnant of the days when Reedville had the highest per capita income of any US town.

> ★ THE "COME-HERES"
>
> Someone with a sense of humor came up with a bumper sticker seen around this town. It reads, "Elijah Reed was a come-here," poking fun at the practice of labeling people who settle in Virginia from other parts as "come-heres."

Conversely, the **Reedville Fishermen's Museum**, partly located in the Walker House, an 1857 waterman's home, preserves the lifestyle of that hardworking, hard-living set. The museum's Covington Building houses exhibits and collections on the Chesapeake Bay maritime history, basically the tools of the trade for crabbing, oystering and fishing. Docked outside are the *Claude W. Somers*, a 42-foot skipjack built in 1911, and the *Elva C.*, a 55-foot traditional workboat built in 1922, used for pound-net fishing and freight until 1989, when it was donated to the museum. Visitors can also enter a 1928 pilothouse on land and see a crabbing skiff, a menhaden striker boat and a Potomac River Nancy. Future plans include a boatbuilding facility, model workshop and boat livery. Open March-December, the hours are normally 10:30am-4:30pm daily, but check ahead for hours in March, April, November and December, when it may be open only on weekends. Admission is $3 for adults and free for those age 12 and under. (504 Main Street, ☎ 804-453-6529, www.rfmuseum.com)

Dining

The **Crazy Crab** at Reedville Marina has dockside and outdoor dining. They serve – what else – fresh seafood. There are daily specials and steaks, too. Located at the end of Main Street. Open Tuesday-Sunday in season; weekends only in the off-season (☎ 804-453-6789).

Another waterfront restaurant pays tribute to the town's founder. In the mid-1990s, Elijah Reed's great-great grandson, Taylor Slaughter, renovated the old mercantile and fish cannery into a quaint restaurant. The interior of **Elijah's Restaurant** has massive exposed beams and plank walls. Above the bar are the original ledger books of the mercantile, and some cans from the cannery. One of the owners of the cannery, Blundon & Hinton, Inc., was another of Slaughter's ancestors. Portraits of Reed and the first owners are prominently displayed. Diners get a view of Cockrell's Creek, and in warmer weather can eat on a glassed-in porch. As of spring 2002, Slaughter was leasing the restaurant to a couple doing business as **Tripp's at the New Elijah's**. But the sign out front still bears grandpa's name. Closed Monday and Tuesday. Open on weekends for breakfast, lunch and dinner; dinner only Wednesday-Friday (☎ 804-453-5359 or 453-3425).

Lodging

Coach House Inn at the Gables is a sea captain's brick mansion with an 1800s schooner mast built into it. Rooms have private baths and a water view of Cockrell's Creek; boat slips are available. Four guest rooms have cathedral ceilings. Located at the end of Main Street (☎ 804-453-5209, $$).

 Near Reedville, **Fleeton Fields** is a 1945 Colonial-style brick B&B on the Chesapeake Bay in the little village of Fleeton, a former steamboat wharf. The inn has three suites with antiques, fireplaces, sitting rooms and bay views. They accept pets at no extra charge (2783 Fleeton Road, ☎ 804-453-5014 or 800-497-8215, www.fleetonfields.com, $$$).

Coastal Virginia

The owners of **Grandview Bed & Breakfast**, on the Chesapeake Bay near the Tangier Island Cruises, have their own pets, so they prefer to take only friendly pets on the small side (no extra charge). Water views from every room, full breakfast, private pier (114 Riverside Lane, ☎ 804-453-3890, http://grandviewbb.freeyellow.com, $).

Information

Northumberland County Chamber of Commerce & Visitor Center, 410 Northumberland Highway, Callao, ☎ 804-529-5031, www.rivnet.net/chamber.

Events

The **Blessing of the Fleet** marks the opening of fishing season in early May.

A Small Boat Show and Model Boat Races are part of the **Fourth of July** festivities.

The **Oyster Roast** is the second Saturday in November, and in December Santa arrives by boat for **Christmas on Cockrell's Creek**. The contact for all these events is the Reedville Fishermen's Museum, ☎ 804-453-6529, www.rfmuseum.org.

★ TRAVEL TIP

Two ferries depart from the Reedville vicinity. Turn right down Route 702 for the ferry to Tangier Island (May-October, ☎ 804-453-2628). Make a left to Smith Point for the Smith Island Ferry (May-October, ☎ 804-453-3430).

Kilmarnock

Around Town

Signs for Kilmarnock's "Town Information Center" led us into a huge, but crammed-full, antique gallery. We were puzzled, but sure enough, the lady at the front desk pointed toward the customer lounge that doubles as a welcome center. Not only do they stock a good selection of brochures, but there are public restrooms and a soda machine. Now that's small town!

The antiques in the **Kilmarnock Antique Gallery** on School Street fill room after room – 22,000 square feet with more than 100 dealers. On the way out, the owner asked us to come by again and offered to work with us on prices. Later, we learned Stephen Spielberg's movie crew shopped there for props for *Minority Report*, starring Tom Cruise, portions of which were filmed in nearby Gloucester County.

> ⭐ HOW TO SAY IT
>
> Don't pronounce it "Kil-Mar-KNOCK." Say it fast, so the last syllable is like "nick" or "nuck," and the emphasis is on "MAR."

Kilmarnock grew out of Steptoe's Ordinary, a roadside inn established in 1719. Since then it's been the commercial hub of the lower Northern Neck. Before the automobile became popular, the town was extremely isolated. No railroad ever reached town, and ferries rather than bridges connected the tip of the peninsula to the outside world. For a time the steamboat era brought vacationers from Norfolk and Baltimore, but that died down when the storm of 1933 took out many of the steamboat wharfs. The millionaire Alfred duPont came on a steamboat – he liked to hunt on the Northern Neck. He met and married a local girl, Jessie Ball, of the Mary Ball Washington line (Mary Ball Washington was George Washington's mother).

The **Kilmarnock Museum** tells this and other great stories about the town. Like most local museums on the Northern Neck, Kilmarnock's exists thanks to volunteer effort, so the hours are a bit sketchy. If you're lucky, you might catch the museum's founder, Augusta Sellew, whose family has lived here for generations. On both sides of her family tree

Coastal Virginia

are important members of the Kilmarnock business community. Her grandfather Eubanks owned the general store and the hotel. Her grandmother ran the hotel and her mother was born and raised there. The brick building, which now houses offices, is the second reincarnation of the hotel. The first, a frame structure, burned in 1909. The brick store is now American Standard Insurance.

Selew is among those who remember the big fire of 1952, the third great conflagration in the town's history. The same section of north Main Street burned in 1909, 1915 and 1952 – the last one Sellew watched, horror-stricken as a teenager. Hopes of saving memories of the town prompted Sellew to pursue a museum. Word spread of a need for artifacts and photographs and all sorts of old things appeared on the building's door step – and still do. While we visited one afternoon, Sellew opened the sceen door to find an old aerial photograph someone had donated anonymously.

The museum also became the repository for a lot of things people might normally have thrown out. They call it "ephemera" on the PBS *Antiques Road Show* – items such as old theater programs and invitations from the town's Holly Ball, a debutante affair that's been held every year since 1895. There's a melted bottle salvaged from the dairy that burned in 1952, a spoon from the soda shop, and Coke bottles from the now-defunct Tidewater Bottling Co. Old crab traps, newspaper clippings and old photographs are carefully displayed. Separately, they might appear to be junk. Put together and shown in context with other items, they tell the story of a town that was once the center of commerce for the isolated Northern Neck. On sale is a book written by Sellew's aunt, Catherine Blake Hathaway, called *When Dabba was Young*, a story about growing up in Kilmarnock.

The collection has had to move a couple of times, but since 1999 the museum has been in a very appropriate home, a mid-1800s farmhouse on Main Street, one of the oldest homes in town. The Kilmarnock Museum is open March-December, 10am-4pm, Thursday-Saturday (76 Main Street, ☎ 804-436-9100).

Dining

There are a dozen or so restaurants in Kilmarnock. Here are a few:

Lee's is a popular, family-operated and affordable restaurant in the heart of downtown. Three home-style meals are served every day but Sunday (34 Main Street, ☎ 804-435-1255).

de'Medici Fine Italian Ristorante serves prime rib, veal, poultry, pasta and seafood in "casual elegance." (School Street, ☎ 804-435-4006).

Jimmie's Grille, which opened in 2001, provides an elegant atmosphere for wine and cocktails, lunch and dinner. Closed Sundays (North Main Street, ☎ 804-435-7799).

Lodging

The Holiday Inn Express is the first new hotel in town since Eubank's closed a generation ago. It has 68 rooms and an outdoor pool. They'll arrange golf and fishing packages for their guests (☎ 804-436-1500, www.holidayinnexpress/kilmarnock.com, $$).

The only B&B in town at this writing is the **Waverly House**, a chalet-style home built around 1930 on 3½ acres, just four blocks from Main Street. There's an indoor swimming pool, four guest rooms, and the innkeeper serves a big, hearty breakfast. Located at Waverly Avenue and Raleigh Drive (☎ 804-435-0458, $).

Information

Lancaster County Chamber of Commerce, ☎ 804-435-6092, www.lancasterva.com.

A satellite **Visitor Center** run by the Chamber of Commerce is located in Kilmarnock Antique Gallery, 144 School Street (see page145).

Trip Journal

Northern Neck

One of our favorite things to do is pack a lunch and head out by car or kayak for a day exploring the peninsulas, or "necks" of Chesapeake Bay's River Country. When you dispense with expectation and open yourself to wonder at simple things, serendipity strikes. We discover the best things – new to us, anyway – and meet the friendliest people.

Coastal Virginia

We have two rules: You can't be in a hurry to get somewhere, and you can't get upset if you take a wrong turn. Sometimes great finds are down the wrong road.

One unseasonably warm winter day we packed a lunch of egg salad sandwiches and headed north to explore the Northern Neck. After poking around **Kilmarnock**, we head out to the **Hughlett Point Nature Preserve** for a hike with the dog and a picnic. Good old Virginia had blessed us with a 75° first day of February, and we just couldn't stay inside and work any longer. We brought the camera and binoculars to check out this nature preserve on the Chesapeake Bay.

A mile's hike through woods with boardwalks and strategically placed observation decks looking out over the bay, and then we hit the beach. We munch our sandwiches while looking out onto the Chesapeake Bay, then walk along the narrow strip of sand to the point, the late afternoon sun filtering through fascinating cloud patterns. We stop to watch some little sandpipers dodge lapping waves, sticking their thin, pointy beaks into the sand for food. Suddenly the wind picks up. Cool, almost icy air from the southwest mingles with an unseasonably warm humid breeze behind us. It starts blowing so hard it whips a mix of sand and spray around us. It's a portent of the weather to come – the temperature is supposed to drop 40 degrees by tomorrow morning. We head back on the beach, as the sun comes out, warming us. I could live here, I think, it's so beautiful. Just make a camp right here on the beach.

I think that we haven't seen much wildlife, and then we hear geese honking. A *lot* of geese. In a semi-sheltered cove we watch from quite a distance hundreds of Canada geese and, interspersed among them, larger white swans with long graceful necks and black beaks – tundra swans (sometimes called whistling swans). Their more subtle voices were easy to distinguish from the honk of the geese. It's more of a plaintive cooing, like a mourning dove. (Don't confuse them with snow geese, which have shorter necks and pink bills.)

The Virginia Department of Fish and Game tracked a couple of tundra swans tagged in Essex County on the Middle Peninsula in spring 2001. They migrate an incredible 5,000 miles to Canada's Northwest Territories, diagonally across North America! (To see maps of the swans' routes, go to Tundra Trax at www.dgif.state.va.us/wildlife/swan.).

We get close enough to shoot a couple of pictures, then head back to the parking area, satiated by nature, but our stomachs hungry. The Jeep's thermometer said 76°. By morning, it will have dropped to 34°.

Leaving the preserve, we stop at an unassuming white building, set off in a field and looking a bit lonely. **Shiloh School** was the last one-room schoolhouse built in Virginia (the sign says it operated from 1909 to 1929). It might not even have had a sign, had it not been for a fairly famous teacher – Jessie Ball duPont. Famous by birth and by marriage, she was a member of George Washington's mother's lineage, and the third wife of Alfred duPont, the chemical king.

Back at Route 200, straight ahead is an irresistible little junk store. "New stuff and junk," the sign says. It's closed, but purchases can be made by the honor system. Buy anything on the porch and put the money in the door slot. Coffee mugs and glasses cost 25¢.

Bill decides to look for Jessie Ball duPont's ancestral home, **Ditchley**, which leads us down a winding road past modest homes. Ditchley is the exception. Large and brick, the 1752 house is used as a seasonal home. Bill chats up the caretaker and learns that the furnishings inside are as when Jessie lived there, until her death in 1970 (her slippers are still under the bed!). The caretaker gives tours by appointment to groups of five or more. (I'm *so starving* by now, I'm secretly relieved there are only two of us.)

I remembered a wine and cheese shop in Kilmarnock, but when we we got there, it was closed. Supremely disappointed, we head home through the tiny town of **White Stone**, where the White Stone Wine & Cheese shop is all lit up. A sign out front reads, "Wine Tasting Tonight, 4-7pm." I glance at my watch and see that it's just 6pm. Now *that's* serendipity. A perfect ending to a perfect day.

Coastal Virginia

Irvington

Around Town

An artful sense of humor has of late infected Irvington, population 673. Columns on the front porch of the town's dentist's office are 10-foot-tall toothbrushes. Lampshades at Hope and Glory Inn are made of silly hats and, in the garden, there's a bathtub for moonlight soaks. An outline of a giant bone graces the roof of Trick Dog Restaurant, where they hang a "sleeping dog" sign when closed.

These are all relatively new additions to this Northern Neck village. Once a thriving steamboat destination with an opera house, skating rink and markets, it succumbed to a fire in 1917 that destroyed buildings, but not spirit. The town is being re-created on a pedestrian-scale, rekindling that elusive vacation aura with the help of some moneyed and imaginative new residents. **The Tides,** Irvington's 50-year-old resort on Carter's Creek, underwent a multi-million-dollar renovation in early 2002 by its new owner, Sedona Resorts. The resort sits on a commanding spot on its own peninsula with a private beach, golf courses, marina and swimming pools.

In particular, one architect is responsible for much of Irvington's new look. Randall Kipp moved here in 1998 and has since helped with the Tides' update, designed the unusual dentist's office, the new Steamboat Era Museum, and a quaint-but-hip retail row that houses a restaurant and boutiques. That row of shops, while brand new and trendy, recall Irvington's small town roots. Each has a white picket fence, and the café's open courtyard and fountain creates a space where diners can interact with shoppers. There's a coffee shop, boutiques of designer clothing, and a kitchen shop that offers French linens, china, crystal and cooking classes. The owner of **Trick Dog Café**, Bob Westbrook, has scattered metal plaques bearing the paraphrased advice of Kurt Vonnegut, Jr. along the front walk to inspire passersby: "Do one thing every day that scares you." "You don't always need an umbrella." "Live in New York City once, but leave before it makes you hard." "Live in Northern California once, but leave before it makes you soft."

Irvington's **Village Improvement Association** has tried hard to revive small town charm with sidewalk benches, potted flowers, and new street lights. Summer nights are filled with the sounds of concerts at the gazebo, and the first Saturday morning of the month (April-December) the town is abuzz with a farmer's market once again.

A new museum interpreting the heyday of the Northern Neck of a century ago is in the planning stage. The **Steamboat Era Museum** should resemble the building travelers saw upon arriving at the wharf in Irvington a century ago: A cedar-sided dockside warehouse with a ticket and purser's office. Inside, exhibits will tell the story of the Chesapeake Bay steamboat era, 1826 to 1937, when big boats from Baltimore and Norfolk cruised the Bay, picking up local produce and fish at small town wharves, and dropping off manufactured goods. Vacationers soon began utilizing the steamboat routes to escape the heat of the cities, or even just to get ice cream in Baltimore, where the only ice cream plant existed, said Bruce King, the museum's director. To accommodate all this activity, ferry stops like Irvington grew larger with general stores, hotels and post offices. Call for updates about their opening schedule; ☎ 804-438-6888, www.steamboateramuseum.org.

Appreciatively, the recent gentrification in Irvington has not sacrificed too much its rural Virginia roots. Farming and fishing are still major industries. Watermen ply the waters beside mega-yachts, and a big red pick-up with crab traps in the back is just as likely to pull into "Mom & Pop's" gas station as is a retiree's silver Mercedes.

One thing that's virtually unchanged in nearly three centuries is **Historic Christ Church** (the "historic" is an important adjective, since Middlesex County also has a Christ Church). Unlike the newer buildings in Irvington, no one knows who was the architect of this church, which Frederick D. Nichols of the American Institute of Architects has called the finest Colonial church in America. Robert "King" Carter commissioned it in 1735 at his own expense, and it was built with a half-million bricks fired at a great kiln. The architecture is Georgian; the building is in the shape of a cross, with a three-tiered pulpit and three-foot thick walls. A quarter of the high-backed, enclosed pews were reserved for Carter's family – he had 15 children, plus servants who attended service in adherence to Church of England rules. One of colonial Virginia's most prominent citizens, Carter was a member of the House of Burgesses and, for a period, the acting Governor of Virginia. Unfortunately, he died three years before the church was completed. He's buried here, as are much of his family. His descendants include two presidents, three signers of the Declaration of Independence, eight Virginia governors and Gen. Robert E. Lee.

That the brick structure has remained intact for so long is due in part to serendipity, isolation and infrequent use for nearly a century. After the American Revolution, the new state confiscated all property belonging to the Church of England, but since Christ Church was privately owned, it was not subject to confiscation. In 1958 the Foundation for Historic Christ Church renovated the church. Today visitors can attend Episcopal services at 8am Sundays, Memorial Day weekend through Labor Day. In late April is the Kirkin o' the Tartan, a traditional Scottish celebration with bagpipes and kilts. The reception center/museum offers guided tours and is open April through November, 10am-4pm, Monday-Saturday, and 2-5pm on Sunday. The church is accessible year-round, during the office's hours, Monday-Friday, 8:30am-4:30pm. Group tours can be arranged ahead of time throughout the year. The church is off Route 200, on Route 646, about 2½ miles north of Irvington (☎ 804-438-6855, www.christchurch1735.com).

Dining

Trick Dog Café. The building may be new, but the name is from Irvington's past. The legend goes that after the 1917 fire someone found a statue of a dog in the basement of the opera house, sooty and black. He took it home, gave it to his son, saying it was a trick dog because it would always sit and stay. The menu uses plenty of seafood, local produce and has an eclectic flair. The bar serves chocolate martinis and 25 single malt scotches. Dinner is served Tuesday through Saturday, with brunch on Sunday (Tidewater Drive, ☎ 804-438-1055).

The Tides Inn (see below) serves award-winning, regionally inspired cuisine in five restaurants, all of which are open to the public as well as to inn guests. Jackets are required after 5:30pm in the formal dining room. The adjacent **Chesapeake Club** is more casual, and offers the same menu and panoramic view of Carters Creek, as well as live piano music. The service is five-star, and the dessert chef should be canonized (reservations are required for both dining rooms). **The Binnacle** is a casual, seasonal restaurant across the creek at The Tides Marina. For lunch, **Commodore's** serves light fare by the main pool, and **Cap'n B's** dishes up New Orleans-style atmosphere at the Golden Eagle Golf Club (480 King Carter Drive, ☎ 800-843-3746, www.tides-inn.com).

Lodging

The Tides Inn is one of the country's top resorts, tucked away on this scenic Virginia peninsula. The 2002 renovation resulted in larger rooms, redecorated with a British Colonial theme. The Inn has 106 rooms. There are two pools, one salt and one fresh water. After a game of tennis or croquet on the lawn, or a round of golf on one of the two courses, indulge in a treatment at the waterfront spa where all treatment rooms have water views. The 127-foot historic yacht *Miss Ann* departs from the marina for sunset cruises and trips on the bay. The yacht was christened in 1926 and used by the Navy in World War II. The original Tides owner acquired her in 1955, and named her after his wife (480 King Carter Drive, ☎ 800-843-3746, www.tidesinn.com, $$$$).

 The **Hope & Glory Inn** reopened in 1996 after an extensive renovation by Peggy Patteson and Bill Westbrook. It had been The King Carter Inn for years, but was originally built in 1890 as the Chesapeake Academy for boys and girls. The Victorian structure still has two front doors, one for boys and one for girls. The classrooms are now the lobby, with folk art and checkerboard floors. An outdoor "bathroom" has a claw-foot tub and sink in a privacy enclosure, and the unique moon garden is at peak fragrance and bloom in the evening. The innkeepers take guests on their two vintage yachts, lend out bikes, offer bocce ball or croquet, and can arrange a massage or a kayak trip. The town tennis courts are next door and there are three golf courses nearby. Children and pets are welcome in the four guest cottages (King Carter Drive, ☎ 800-497-8228 or 804-438-6053, www.hopeandglory.com, $$$).

Information

Village Improvement Association and **Irvington Chamber of Commerce**, ☎ 804-438-6287.

Town of Irvington, ☎ 804-438-6230.

Lancaster County Chamber of Commerce, ☎ 804-435-6092, www.lancasterva.com.

Events

Irvington's big events of the year are the **Fourth of July parade** and the **Christmas boat parade**. Contact the Irvington Chamber of Commerce, ☎ 804-438-6287.

Urbanna

Urbanna has ridden the boom-and-bust cycle that is a familiar story in many Virginia coastal towns. Founded as a Colonial tobacco port, it became a steamboat resort and, within the last century, an oyster-processing center. It was during one bust period that it lost the honor of being the seat of Middlesex County's, but despite that, it has held onto its biggest asset: water. Steadily, pleasure boats are replacing the workboats down on Urbanna Creek, a protected, deepwater harbor a short jaunt off the Rappahannock River with easy access to the Chesapeake Bay.

Even though the harvesting of Virginia's native oyster has fallen to a mere fraction of the days when millions of bushels were taken annually, enthusiasm here remains high for the "succulent bivalve." Urbanna's **Oyster Festival**, dubbed the state's official oyster fest by act of the state General Assembly, draws up to 80,000 people who crowd the streets of this small town. It's been held the first Friday and Saturday in November since 1958 (☎ 804-758-0368).

During the festival, vendors line Urbanna's Virginia Street selling oysters in every conceivable way – raw, roasted, steamed, stewed, fried or frittered. There are two parades and ceremonial crowning of the Oyster Festival Queen and Little Miss Spat (a spat is a baby oyster). The amateur shucking contest is quite entertaining, but it's all business during the official contest. Shuckers are judged primarily on speed, but also on more subjective qualities like the amount of shell fragments, clean separation from the shell and damage to the meat. Up for grabs is title as state champion and the right to represent Virginia at a national oyster-shucking contest. Urbanna residents Deborah Pratt and her sister, Clementine Macon, have each won the state contest more than a dozen times. Deborah has even gone on to the World Championships in Ireland.

Visiting peaceful Urbanna any other time really is "like traveling back 100 years," a claim many towns make, but few deliver as Urbanna can. Virginians have been coming here to buy and sell for more than three centuries. As one of 20 Colonial ports established by royal decree in 1680, all tobacco and imported goods had to pass through its customhouse. In colonial times, tobacco-laden carts trundled down Virginia Street to the creek to be loaded onto ships. Plantation representatives stopped at the Tobacco Warehouse to exchange their harvest for immediate cash and credit.

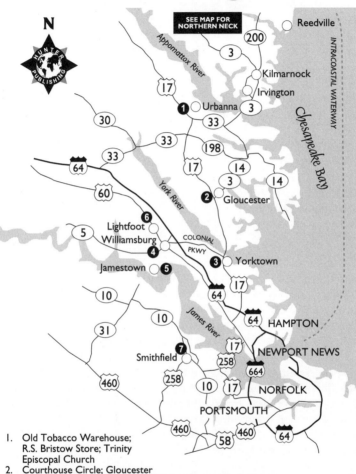

© 2003 HUNTER PUBLISHING, INC

Coastal Virginia

1. Old Tobacco Warehouse;
   R.S. Bristow Store; Trinity
   Episcopal Church
2. Courthouse Circle; Gloucester
   Museum of History; African-American Heritage Trails Tour;
   Abingdon Episcopal Church; Rosewell; Beaverdon Park;
   Gloucester Point Beach
3. Watermen's Museum; Victory Monument; Riverwalk; Yorktown
   Victory Center; Gallery at York Hall; Historical Museum
4. Colonial Williamsburg; Water Country; Busch Gardens; Williamsburg Winery;
   College of William & Mary; Muscarelle Museum of Art
5. Historic Jamestowne; Jamestown Settlement; James River Plantations
6. Williamsburg Pottery; Williamsburg Soap & Candle Company
7. Historic District Walking Tour; Old Courthouse of 1750;
   Isle of Wight Museum; Boykin's Tavern; Battery Park;
   Historic St. Luke's Shrine; Fort Boykin Historical Park

Around Town

Built in 1766, Urbanna's **Old Tobacco Warehouse** is the only surviving Scottish factor store in the country. Prior to its establishment, planters sent their tobacco and other crops directly to England and waited for months until supplies and goods came back on the ship's return voyage. Today's customers are tourists – the building has been converted into a visitor center. Pick up the self-guided walking tour brochure here. Continue on down the road to the historic waterfront where pleasure craft and fishing boats tie up at three marinas. If crabs are in season, pick up some live ones at **Payne's Crab House.**

Back up on Virginia Street, the **R.S. Bristow Store** is a must-see. In business since 1876, it had the county's first gas station and supplied generations of shoppers with live chickens, coal and groceries. When it was built, most goods came from Baltimore by steamboats that docked at Burton's Wharf at the foot of Watling Street. The store's main product today is women's designer clothing. Hats and gifts sit on the ceiling-high shelves that once held canned goods, but they're still reached by ladders that roll along on wood floors. The giant red mill used to grind coffee and pepper is still in the window. The post office in the back of the store now displays shoes in the mailboxes. This was once the largest retail store in the county and the owners were the first people to have electricity in Urbanna. Their house is two blocks down Cross Street. The block outbuilding behind the house contained batteries that provided the electricity.

Next door to Bristow's is **Marshall's Pharmacy**, where sodas are still served at the old-fashioned lunch counter. When was the last time you sat on a twirly stool and ordered an ice cream soda? If you're looking for some tips on fishing, eavesdrop on the watermen discussing that day's catch at the **Inn at Urbanna**. The town's 1748 Courthouse harkens to the days when Urbanna was a county seat. Today, it houses **Trinity Episcopal Church** and is the oldest building in town.

During the steamboat era of the 1870s, Urbanna was a popular resort and had several hotels. The Hotel Nelson on the waterfront had a dance pavilion, tennis courts, croquet and a screened bathing area to protect bathers from stinging nettles (or jellyfish). Only one of the hotels of that steamboat era remains, the Burton House at West Urbanna Wharf (Watling Street), which is now a private residence.

Dining

Virginia Street Café is located in an old five and dime store, across from the R.S. Bristow Store. Basic family fare, seafood, and breakfast served all day (☎ 804-758-3798). **River's Edge Ice Cream Parlor** is open year-round (217 Virginia Street, ☎ 804-758-1447), and **Colonial Pizza** serves Italian and Greek specialties (☎ 804-758-4079). Down on the pier, **The Boathouse Café** is a rustic former boathouse (☎ 804-758-4046).

Outdoors

Lazy Days Adventures is based in nearby Saluda, but most of their trips leave from Upton's Point Marina in Urbanna. They'll rent you a kayak, camping and fishing equipment if needed, and take you to great places for exploring. They lead guided camping trips on the river, and eco-tours of the Dragon Run Swamp (☎ 804-758-9302, ☎ 804-366-6915).

For boaters, there are several marinas serving the area: **Urbanna Yachting Center** (☎ 804-758-2342); **Dozier Port Urbanna** (☎ 804-758-0000); and the town-owned **Upton's Point Marina** (☎ 804-758-9773 or 758-2613).

Lodging

The old resort hotels may be gone, but there are several historic lodging options if you'd like to stay right in town. **Atherston Hall B&B** has four rooms, two with private bath, serving full breakfast and afternoon tea (250 Prince George Street, ☎ 804-758-2809, $$). **Hewick Plantation B&B** was built in 1678 by Christopher Robinson, member of the House of Burgesses and an original Trustee of the College of William & Mary. Robinson's 10th and 11th generation descendants still live here (Lord Mott Road off Route 227, ☎ 804-758-4214, www.hewick.com, $$).

Coastal Virginia

Out on Route 17, near Church View, the **Dragon Run Inn** is a 1913 farmhouse with a porch swing and rooms named for farm animals (☎ 804-758-5719, www.dragon-run-inn.com, $).

The **Bethpage Camp-Resort** is an RV resort on the Rappahannock River with a marina, sand beach, pool, charter boat fishing and sightseeing tours aboard a restored Chesapeake Bay workboat (☎ 804-758-4349, www.bethpagecamp.com, $).

Information

Town of Urbanna, ☎ 804-758-2613, www.urbanna.com.

Gloucester

Drive virtually any Gloucester County road between late February and May, and vestiges of a once-thriving industry are visible. County farmers were, in the early 20th century, among world leaders in cut daffodils, the "poor man's rose" whose popularity took off during our Great Depression. It's not the old farms you see, but rather the hardy multiplying bulbs that live on, reproducing year after year in the wild. It's called naturalizing, and come spring, enterprising local school children take to the woods and pick big bunches to hawk along the roadside.

Around Town

Gloucester capitalized on its flower fame with daffodil tours starting in 1938. After a long hiatus, civic leaders revived the **Daffodil Festival** in the late 1980s. Today, it draws some 15,000 visitors annually to tiny Gloucester Courthouse the first Saturday in April (☎ 804-693-2355, www.gloucesterva.info). The day starts with a 5K run, followed by a parade, and continues with more than 100 crafters and artisans in a juried show, live entertainment, and bus tours to a third-generation farm, **Brent & Becky's Bulbs** (www.brentandbeckysbulbs.com).

If you can't make the festival, a self-guided **Daffodil Driving Tour** highlights places in the county where they bloom in profusion. Featured sites are recent beautification efforts, like the 20,000 bulbs in front of Page Middle School where the annual Daffodil Show takes place. Farther out, the tour passes old daffodil farms and obscure spots where daffodils have naturalized around old homesteads. The latter make for striking – almost eerie – scenery off the shoulder of country roads. There you see an old, abandoned farmhouse, the roof caving in. And around it, in sharp contrast, are bright green stalks and cheerful faces of dozens of yellow daffodils, planted by the lady of the house so long ago. The house may be falling down, but her handiwork is still there, reproducing and spreading every year.

While Gloucester isn't well known as a weekend getaway (the county's first chain motel opened only a couple of years ago), it has plenty of history. The courthouse commons dates to the 1700s. Dr. Walter Reed, conqueror of Yellow Fever, was born here, and it was here that Pocahontas purportedly saved the life of Captain John Smith. Several restored plantation homes have been converted into elegant bed & breakfast inns. There are a handful of good restaurants, and a Main Street shopping district that so far has survived the Wal-Mart Super-center nearby.

Gloucester's **Courthouse Circle** survives as a classic early Virginia county seat, surprisingly intact, despite several fires through the centuries that destroyed county records. John Clayton, the world-renowned botanist, was Clerk of the Court in the 1700s. The Clayton House is being renovated into a visitor center. Strolling through the small circle is like stepping into a miniature version of Colonial Williamsburg – except the buildings, dating to the 1700s and 1800s, are all original. Whatever the season, a summer evening, or a crisp, winter morning, the circle is a delight, an oasis in the middle of a busy Main Street, which literally goes around it. Just outside the circle is **Lawyers Row**, a charming group of cottages built in the early 20th century as offices for the lawyers having business in the courthouse. Today, some still house law offices, while others are used as antiques shops and real estate offices.

> ★ DID YOU KNOW?
>
> In Colonial Virginia, the village hosting the county seat was known as "Courthouse." It's still that way in Gloucester County.

The Botetourt Hotel served as an ordinary or tavern for two centuries and now houses the **Gloucester Museum of History and Visitor Information**, where changing exhibits tell the county's history. Open Monday-Friday, 11am-3pm; Saturday, noon-4pm. ☎ 804-693-1234,

Coastal Virginia

www.gloucesterva.info/museum/historyhome.htm. At the top of Main Street is a statue of **Pocahontas**. Although her father, Chief Powhatan, moved his tribe around a lot, it's believed Pocahontas grew up in Gloucester County at a spot known as Werowocomoco, on the York River.

 TIP

Gloucester is pronounced GLAW-ster, with the first syllable rhyming with CLAW.

Attractions

Gloucester is a large, rural county, with lots of historic gems tucked down back roads. A good way to discover them is to pick up one of the driving tour brochures at the visitor center. The **African-American Heritage Trails Tour** details county sites important to local black history. Several of these sites are also included in *The Heritage and Culture of African Americans in Virginia: A Guide to the Sites* (available at www.virginia.org, click on "Publications"). The home of local black attorney **Thomas Calhoun (T.C.) Walker** is on lower Main Street, marked with a state historical sign. Walker founded the Agricultural and Industrial School for black students in 1888 and the Gloucester Training School in 1921, among the first secondary schools for blacks in the region. Orator Frederick Douglass, lyricist James Weldon Johnson, and singer Marian Anderson each visited the Agricultural and Industrial School for cultural enrichment programs.

Other stops on the tour are **Bethel Baptist Church**, a black church founded during the Reconstruction period; **The Servants' Plot,** where black indentured servants plotted a very early insurrection against their masters in 1663; and **Old Hayes Store**, where **Irene Morgan** boarded a Greyhound bus in 1944, then refused to give up her seat to a white passenger. She was arrested and the case was appealed to the Supreme Court, which ruled in her favor in 1946. It would be another 10 years before Rosa Parks did the same thing in Alabama, sparking the Civil Rights movement.

The award-winning brochure called **Driving Tours of Gloucester County's Country Stores & Rural Post Offices** has beautiful sketches by local artist Harriet Cowen. Before automobiles, the nearest four corners was your hub of activity, each with at least one store and a post office. They were scattered throughout the farming community, and many remain today, some still operating. The Bena store and post office are worth a trip down Guinea Road. The store is called **Mo' Stuff** now and sells country arts and crafts.

Abingdon Episcopal Church, on Route 17, dates to 1755, but the parish, one of the oldest in the nation, predates it by a century. Take a look at the ancient-looking graves of some of the county's earliest and most prominent residents.

In its day, **Rosewell** was purported to be the finest example of Georgian architecture in the English colonies. It takes some imagination to envision this today. Towering brick ruins are all that's left of the home. Preservation is fueled largely by private donations, and a new visitor center displays both history and restoration work. This is a great place for a picnic lunch, but don't stay past dark – many say the ruins are haunted. Open Monday-Saturday, 10am-4pm; Sunday, 1-4pm; admission is $2 for adults and $1 for students (☎ 804-693-2585, www.rosewell.org).

Dr. Walter Reed's Birthplace, a tiny slip of a one-room farmhouse, stands at the Belroi crossroads. The interior is open only during Historic Garden Week in April. Reed helped rid the world of yellow fever by proving mosquitoes caused the disease.

Outdoors

Rent a canoe at **Beaverdam Park**, hike the trails or fish in the lake. Take a dip at **Gloucester Point Beach** or fish off the long pier. Rent a kayak in nearby Mathews County from **Bay Trails Outfitters**. Explore on your own, or they'll guide you on some of the area's hundreds of miles of Chesapeake Bay coastline, rivers, and innumerable tidal creeks. You're on a peninsula, framed by the York and Rappahannock rivers, so water is everywhere.

Shopping

People come from all over Hampton Roads to visit the **Stagecoach Market & Antique Village** (☎ 804-693-3951), known locally as just "the flea market." More than 45 permanent shops sell antiques, jewelry and collectibles, with dozens more set up in the outdoor flea market on weekends, 7am-5pm. Gloucester County has half a dozen other antiques shops, including **Holly Hill** on Route 14, **Plantation Antique Mall** and **Marketplace Antiques** on Route 17, and **Lord Botetourt Antiques** in the Courthouse.

Coastal Virginia

Sarah Creek Potters is a cooperative on Tidemill Road where you might get to see local potters at work. Open Tuesday-Saturday, 10am-5pm. **Simple Gifts and Beehive Café** is a great place to shop for unique presents, then have lunch in the café, on Route 17 in Hayes.

Pick up some local produce at one of the **farm stands** along Route 17. **Ware Neck Produce** is on Main Street in the Courthouse.

Main Street is lined with quaint shops housed in historic buildings. The brochure *A Walk Through Historic Gloucester* gives a peek at the original uses. **Twice Told Tales**, the town's bookstore, was once a Colonial grocery store, and then a uniform factory. **Lord Botetourt Antiques** was built as a Ford Motor showroom in 1919, and the **Gift Garden** was originally a barbershop. The owner of the shop, Joanne Lawson-Whitten, is a relative of the barber, Phillip Lawson. Inside you can still see the wall mural of Courthouse Circle painted by Wilson Hibble in 1963. Lawson-Whitten sells prints of it to take home.

Other quality shops in town are **Heaven Sent Toys, Kelsick Gardens** wine shop, gourmet market, and dining room (once a Dollar General store!), **Feather Your Nest's** unique decorative items and art objects, **Emily's** boutique of unique clothing and accessories, and **Angelwing Stationers**.

Gloucester is the headquarters for **Peace Frogs**, the cute little frog that's become a national T-shirt and bumper sticker phenomenon. The design studio and outlet store (seconds and discontinued items, real cheap) is on Route 14 heading towards Mathews.

Dining

Our personal favorite place in Courthouse is **Stillwater's on Main,** not only because the food is a wonderful mix of regional seafood specialties with an eclectic flair but also, like Cheers, they know our names when we come in. It's our special place to go for a celebration or romantic dinner, or to bring out-of-town guests. The spacious dining room has tall ceilings, covered with punched tin, a long, old wooden bar, seating in wooden booths or around cozy tables in ladderback chairs. White linens add a touch of elegance, yet the dress is casual. It has a great wine list, and a regional beer, Mobjack Bay, on tap. The building was originally Gray's Pharmacy, run by Dr. Gray who lived next door (the house has been razed, unfortunately). Several different restaurant incarnations have occupied the building, but after three years in business the present owners recently replaced the stained-glass window over the door that said "Capers" (two owners ago), with

"Stillwater's" in elegant script. A good sign (pun intended) that they plan on sticking around (6553 Main Street, ☎ 804-694-5618).

The working lunch crowd on Main Street craves **Kelsick Gardens'** daily specials for take-out, dining in the café or outside under an umbrella table (6604 Main Street, ☎ 804-693-6500).

The **Old Courthouse Restaurant** is a local favorite for down-home cooking (6714 Main Street, ☎ 804-693-9905). For seafood there's **Cheryl's Shack and Raw Bar** (6597 Main Street, ☎ 804-694-0057) and **The Blue Fin** (6870 Main Street, ☎ 804-693-9390). For lighter fare, **Leigh and Nardozzi Caterers** serve daily soup, salad and sandwich specials, along with delicious baked goods (6672 Main Street, ☎ 804-693-3854), and **High's Ice Cream** is the place to get a sundae, cone or sandwich (6786 Main Street, ☎ 804-693-7857).

South of Courthouse on Route 17, **Seawell's Ordinary** is a "publick" house dating to 1757. The menu claims a tobacco burn on the floor came from a careless General Lafayette (☎ 804-642-3635).

Farther south, near Gloucester Point, **River's Inn** features elegant dining with views of the York River Yacht Haven, or casual feasting on the outdoor Crab Deck (☎ 804-642-9942, www.riversinnrestaurant.com).

Lodging

Airville Plantation has three guest rooms with period furnishings, fireplaces, and air conditioning. There's a pool, beach and fishing from a deepwater dock. Children over 11 welcome. Full breakfast served (6359 T.C. Walker Road, ☎ 804-694-0287, $$).

The **North River Inn** is a 17th-century estate on 100 acres surrounded by water on three sides. The eight guest rooms are in three historic structures, each at the end of private lanes on the water, and furnished with family antiques, private baths, air conditioning and telephones. Rent a single room or an entire house. Canoes are available for rent. Children over 12 welcome (8777 Toddsbury Lane, ☎ 877-248-3030, www.northriverinn.com, $$).

The fabulously renovated **Warner Hall** is a 1642 river plantation established by Augustus Warner, great-great grandfather of George Washington. There are gardens and horse pastures on the 38 acres remaining of the original plantation. Dining, for breakfast or dinner, is in the elegant dining room or the sun-filled enclosed porch with views of the Severn River. The inn has nine working fireplaces and a choice of places to curl up with a good book. The owners completed a fantastic

Coastal Virginia

restoration in 2001. Each of the seven guest rooms and two suites are fastidiously appointed down to every detail, with individual climate control, telephone, VCR, private bath, antiques, art and eclectic furnishings. Children ages eight and over welcome (4750 Warner Hall Road, ☎ 800-331-2720, www.warnerhall.com, $$$).

The **Willows Bed and Breakfast** has four guest rooms with private baths on a quiet country road. Full breakfast served. Children over 16 welcome (8335 Robins Neck Road, ☎ 804-693-7575, $$).

 The **Comfort Inn** on Route 17, near the Winn-Dixie shopping plaza, takes pets with a $10 charge. It's also child-friendly – kids stay free with an adult. It has 78 rooms, an outdoor pool and offers free continental breakfast (☎ 804-695-1900, $).

Information

Gloucester Parks, Recreation & Tourism, ☎ 886-VISITUS, 804-693-2355, www.gloucesterva.info.

> ★ DID YOU KNOW?
>
> Gloucester has dubbed itself "Land of the Life Worth Living." Its symbol is the beehive, for industriousness.

Yorktown

Around Town

A few days after September 11, 2001, a small crowd gathered at Yorktown's Victory Monument for a National Day of Prayer. The Fifes and Drums of Yorktown marched up Main Street dressed in their red uniforms and tri-cornered hats. As dusk fell, about 100 people passed around candles, held them in silence, then joined together in spontaneous song for "God Bless America."

It took a national calamity for us to revisit Yorktown, a small burg with a large presence in United States history as the site where the English surrendered to General George Washington. We live close by, but our visits tend to be once, maybe twice a year. Is it human nature for people to ignore treasures in their own backyard? Maybe it's the notion that because it's so close we can see it any time.

With renewed purpose, I strode forth on a spring morning to walk Yorktown's narrow streets and browse Colonial-themed shops and galleries. Inside the Watermen's Museum (see next page), volunteers were preparing for the spring Heritage Celebration. Over at the Yorktown Visitor Center, national park officials awaited arrival of a restored tent used by George Washington during the siege of Yorktown. Back in my car, I drove the **Colonial Parkway**, a national park draped in April's splendor – delicate blooming white dogwood and magenta redbud. This is truly one of America's most beautiful scenic drives.

Come winter, Yorktown hosts a different sort of holiday tradition on its riverfront. Cauldrons of cider steam over beach bonfires as folks draw nearer to the heat, bundled in their coats, scarves and mittens. Offshore, yachts, small sailboats, pleasure cruisers and even fishermen's workboats decked with holiday lights cruise proudly in single file. Held the first Saturday in December, the holiday boat parade is preceded by a candlelight procession down Main Street and ceremonial lighting of the community tree. The next day, private homeowners open their doors for a **Christmas Homes Tour**. Altogether, it captures nicely the community pride in a history of watermen and war.

A good place to start a walking tour of Yorktown is at the **Yorktown Visitor Center,** the entry to the battlefield, operated by the National Park Service. Inside, the story of the siege is told through exhibits and films. From the roof you get a panoramic view of the battlefield. The center is open 8:30am-5pm in spring, till 5:30 in summer, and 9am-5pm in winter; grounds are open till sunset. A seven-day pass is $5 for adults and free for children under age 16 (☎ 757-898-2410, www.nps.gov/coloYorktown/ythome.htm).

From here it's just a short walk (466 yards to be exact) on a shady pathway to the village of Yorktown, passing en route the massive **Victory Monument**. The Continental Congress authorized it in 1781, but construction didn't begin until 100 years later during the Centennial Celebrations of the Allied Victory over the English. The monument was completed in 1884.

If you're lucky, your visit may coincide with a performance of **The Fifes and Drums of York Town**. This local treasure provides a musical backdrop for historic events, festive Fourth of July celebrations and solemn Veterans' Day observances throughout York County. In summer they perform several times a week at the Yorktown Visitor Center and at the Victory Monument. Formed for the bicentennial celebration in 1976 of youth ages 10 to 18, the corps has performed at the Smithsonian Institute, before the Virginia General Assembly, and has opened for the Virginia Symphony (☎ 757-898-9418, www.fifes-and-drums.org).

Riverwalk along the York River beach has benches, hand-molded Virginia brick paving, granite seawalls, and wrought iron streetlights. Together, it gives the newly constructed walkway a historic appearance. About 20 cruise ships make brief stops at Yorktown's pier each year. Day visitors can take a sightseeing cruise May through October aboard the *Miss Yorktown* (☎ 757-879-8276) or the *Yorktown Lady* (☎ 757-229-6244). Riverwalk passes by the old **Freight Shed**, which was originally the steamboat landing and later housed the Yorktown Post Office. In spring 2002 the building was moved closer to the street to protect it from the beach erosion, and plans are to renovate it as an historic tourist attraction.

About a block farther along Riverwalk**, The Watermen's Museum** preserves and interprets the traditions of fishing, crabbing, oystering and clamming – trades by which a hardy few still make their living. During the Watermen's Heritage Celebration, third Sunday in May, they display the skills and boats that have evolved over two centuries. Exhibits tell of local aquaculture and African-American boat pilots who participated in the Battle of Yorktown. Schoolchildren love the nine-foot jawbone of a right whale that swam up the North River in Gloucester County in 1858. Their challenge is to locate the "tail of the whale" two rooms away, a graphic illustration of the length of a 43-foot-long whale.

The museum building itself is a conversation piece. Donated by a wealthy Gloucester couple in 1987, it needed to be floated across the York River to its present location. Local legend holds that en route, the barge carrying the building got caught up on a shoal. Veteran watermen who were called upon to aid advised simply waiting for high tide at the full moon, just a few days away. They did, and under power of gravitational pull between earth and moon, the house floated free. The museum is open April-November, Tuesday-Saturday, 10am-4pm and Sunday, 1-4pm. It's open only on weekends the rest of the year. Admission is $3 for adults and $1 for students (☎ 757-887-2641, www.watermens.org).

Future plans involve extending Riverwalk to the **Yorktown Victory Center**, making all of Yorktown's historic sites pedestrian-friendly. The Victory Center's re-created Continental Army Camp and a 1780s farm bring the Revolutionary period to life. Interpreters demonstrate 18th-century life, medical techniques, cooking and musket firing. You can even lend a hand tending the farm's garden. The center is open 9am-5pm daily, year-round; closed Christmas and New Year's days. Admission is $8.25 for adults and $4 for children ages six-12 (☎ 888-593-4682, www.historyisfun.org).

★ CORNWALLIS CAVE

Cornwallis Cave wasn't really the headquarters of the English general during the siege of Yorktown. Most likely it was used by other English officers and civilians to hide and store provisions. The cave can be seen along south Water Street.

Attractions

The **Gallery at York Hall** opened in 2002 in York Hall at Main and Ballard Streets (☎ 757-890-4490). Themed exhibits change every two months or so, and volunteers assist visitors with directions and information. Closed Mondays, but hours vary seasonally, so call first. Also in York Hall is the **Historical Museum** (☎ 757-890-4122), which displays many early Native American and Colonial artifacts that were discovered in 1992 at the Chischiak Watch archeological dig. Chischiaks were the local Indians who lived along the shores of the York River.

There are several antiques shops and art galleries scattered through the town. Keep in mind that several shops and galleries are closed on Mondays. The **Yorktown Shoppe** on Main Street is one example of several shops owned by the National Park Service that peddles all things Colonial: caps, shirts, flags, lanterns, hand-dipped candles, and – what every house needs – a deck prism, a reproduction of the colored triangular prisms of glass that were embedded in the decks of ships to give light to the quarters below (☎ 757-898-2984).

Across the street, **Period Designs** carries art objects based on 17th- and 18th-century originals: ceramics, prints, floor coverings, and more (401 Main Street, ☎ 757-886-9482, www.perioddesigns.com).

On the Hill Cultural Arts Center offers on commission the work of about 80 local artists and crafters – from watercolors and photographs to note cards and jewelry (Yorktown Arts Foundation, ☎ 757-898-3076).

Coastal Virginia

Dining

There are several restaurants on Water Street with some water-view tables and the opportunity to take a stroll along the beach after dinner.

Nick's Seafood Pavilion has been a landmark in Yorktown for half a century. The late owners, Nick and Mary Mathews, opened the Greek-themed seafood restaurant in 1944. Even though its seafood and Greek specialties are extremely popular in the summer, you'll rarely have trouble getting a table, as it seats 500. Choose a table under a crystal chandelier, or a booth lined in turquoise-colored vinyl. Statues and grapevines complete the Grecian atmosphere. In 2002 the county purchased the restaurant and land around it as part of ongoing Water Street revitalization. There is much speculation about what will happen to Nick's, but county officials vow they'll keep it open in some form (Water Street near the Coleman Bridge, ☎ 757-887-5269).

Water Street Landing could be called an upscale pizza shop, with a tantalizing list of gourmet toppings. But they also serve quiches, soups and sandwiches for lunch, and nightly dinner specials. Booths look out through large windows to the street and beach (114 Water Street, ☎ 757-886-5890).

The **Yorktown Pub** is very casual and, although basically a bar, it's also suitable for families. You might sit next to out-of-towners taking a break from Colonial Williamsburg or middle-aged members of a Harley-Davidson biker club. No credit cards or checks are accepted; it's strictly cash for your burgers, beer, shrimp and steaks (540 Water Street, ☎ 757-886-9964).

The **River Room** inside the Duke of York Motel serves breakfast and lunch in a diner-style atmosphere (☎ 757-898-3232).

Lodging

York River Inn B&B is on a high bluff overlooking the river in a new, but Colonial-styled home. It has three rooms with private baths and is furnished with Virginia antiques. Breakfast might include items like flan, clam pudding or crème brûlée (209 Ambler Street, ☎ 757-887-8800 or 800-884-7003, www.yorkriverinn.com, $$).

The Duke of York Motel is opposite the town beach and has an outdoor pool (508 Water Street, ☎ 757-898-3232, $$). The quaint one-bedroom **Moss Guest Cottage** is rented to vacationers (224 Nelson Street, ☎ 757-229-5606, http://hometown.aol.com/mosscottage1, $$).

Or, choose the modern **Courtyard Newport News Yorktown**, about seven miles outside Yorktown village (105 Cybernetics Way, ☎ 757-874-9000, www.courtyard.com, $$).

The Marl Inn B&B accepts well-behaved pets; no extra charge. This modern home in the historic district has three guest rooms with private baths and entrances (two are suites with laundry and kitchen facilities). The innkeepers provide bicycles to guests who want to cycle around town or into the nearby Yorktown Battlefield. The name "Marl" comes from the hard clay that was used as a building material by early Yorktown colonists. Children welcome (220 Church Street, ☎ 757-898-3859 or 800-799-6207, www.marl-innbandb.com, $$).

Information

York County Public Information Office, ☎ 757-890-3300, www.yorkcounty.gov.

Williamsburg

Creamy peanut soup made from a recipe brought to English colonies by African slaves. Hot cider steaming over an outdoor fire on a cold winter day. Clipped, staccato *rat-a-tat-tats* of a fife-and-drum corps marching. In these and so many other ways, Colonial Williamsburg is a feast for the senses.

A tree-lined gravel path leading into this re-created 18th-century town sets the stage nicely. In early summer, honeysuckle entwined around tree trucks makes the air heavy with its sweet scent. Around a white windmill, farmers dressed in breeches and short jackets tend rows of corn. There's a wheelwright barn where carriages are repaired. Up ahead is the Courthouse. Outside it are the public stocks, which visitors eagerly place head and hands into for an oft-repeated photo opportunity.

Around Town

The country's largest living history museum is located inside a real town of just 12,000 people, and is intended to appear as Virginia's colonial capital did in the 18th century.

Coastal Virginia

It's truly a remarkable arrangement in which costumed interpreters perpetuate a fantasy of time travel by stubbornly staying in character. Yet these are city-owned streets, and many homes on museum ground are private dwellings whose residents not only witness millions of visitors annually, but adhere to strict rules on renovation, upkeep and even holiday decorating, in which any materials they use must have been available in Colonial times.

We like to go in the off-season, either before or after the summer hordes have passed. I confess we usually don't purchase a ticket which, while not necessary to walk around the streets or visit stores and taverns, does allow entrance to the Governor's Palace, courthouse, artisan's shops and dozens of other buildings where costumed interpreters give tours and demonstrations of Colonial life.

I'll never forget a Christmas dinner at Christiana Campbell's, one of the authentic Colonial taverns. We dined by candlelight, the Colonial fare not gourmet by today's standards, but interesting and authentic nonetheless. We were invited to join in the Christmas caroling on the courthouse steps, and strolled down the street past elaborate door decorations made from odd assortments of cotton bolls, apples, lemons, and, of course, tiny pineapples (they were imported back then, and were not as big as today's varieties).

Attractions

Colonial Williamsburg is open every day of the year, 9am-5pm (9:30-4:30 from January 2 to mid-March). Admission tickets range from one day ($33 for adults, $16.50 for children ages six-17) to annual passes. Numerous vacation and holiday packages (including lodging and admission to other area attractions) are available.

Also part of Colonial Williamsburg are the **Abby Aldrich Rockefeller Folk Art Museum**, the **DeWitt Wallace Decorative Arts Gallery**, and **Carter's Grove** slave quarters and mansion, including the Winthrop Rockefeller Archaeology Museum (☎ 800-HISTORY, www.colonialwilliamsburg.com).

Even without Colonial Williamsburg, the twin theme parks of Busch Gardens and Water Country USA make Williamsburg an intensely popular family destination. **Water Country** is the mid-Atlantic's largest water theme park with 30 thrillingly wet rides and adventures, plus restaurants, entertainment and shopping, all with a 1950s and '60s surf theme. It's open daily, May through September; a single-day ticket is about $32 for adults and $25 for children ages three to six (☎ 800-

343-SWIM, www.watercountryusa.com). **Busch Gardens Williamsburg** is a European-themed park where six "villages" represent different countries, like Ireland, Germany and Italy. Each features food authentic to its region, as well as entertainment and shops. Of course, the real attraction is the spectacularly thrilling – or frightening – rides (depending on your tolerance for speed and heights.) Alpengeist is the world's tallest and fastest inverted roller coaster. Open daily at 10am, March through October; dates for opening and closing vary. Single-day tickets are about $43 for adults and $36 for children ages three to six (Route 60, east of Williamsburg, ☎ 800-772-8886, www. buschgardens.com).

Ready for more history? From Colonial Williamsburg, the **Colonial Parkway** can take you back in time to the first settlement at Jamestown, or forward to the ending of the Revolution at Yorktown. The 23-mile parkway, actually a national historical park, has no stoplights, few visible buildings – not even painted lines on the road surface.

There are two attractions at Jamestown: the actual site of the 1607 fort and a re-created one. **Historic Jamestowne** is a 1,500-acre national park preserving the ruins of the island settlement with active archeological digs. The site is open 8:30am-4:30pm daily, year-round, except Christmas and New Year's days. Admission is $6 for adults; children under age 17 free (☎ 757-898-2410, www.nps.gov/jame/). Two miles away is **Jamestown Settlement**, a state-operated living history museum that re-creates the settlement's early years with three replica ships, an Indian village, James Fort, and exhibit galleries. The settlement is open daily, year-round, 9am-5pm; closed Christmas and New Year's days. Admission is $10.75 for adults and $5.25 for children ages six-12 (☎ 888-593-4682, www.historyisfun.org).

The **Williamsburg Winery** gives guided tours with tastings and an explanation of the winemaking process. There's a museum, 50 acres of vineyards, a gift shop and the **Gabriel Archer Tavern** serving lunch and dinner. The winery is open Monday-Saturday, 10am-5:30pm; Sunday, 11am-5:30pm. Admission is charged (☎ 757-229-0999, www.williamsburgwineryltd.com).

Some of the restored **James River Plantations** (☎ 800-704-5423, www. jamesriverplantations.org) are open to the public in nearby Charles City County: **Shirley** (☎ 800-232-1613); **Berkeley** (☎ 888-466-6018, www.berkeleyplantation.com); **Evelynton** (☎ 800-473-5075; and **Sherwood Forest** (☎ 804-282-1441, www.sherwoodforest.org; note that the house may be toured by appointment only, but the grounds are open to the public). The grounds and gardens at **Westover** (☎ 804-829-2882) are open to the public as well. Admis-

Coastal Virginia

sion fees and times vary; call the various locations for complete information.

The College of William & Mary is the second oldest college in America, chartered in 1693. On campus is the **Muscarelle Museum of Art**, which features changing exhibits and is free to the public (☎ 757-221-2630, www.wm.edu/muscarelle).

Shopping

Entire bus tours are booked just for shopping in the Williamsburg area. There are more than 150 factory outlet stores, with **Prime One Outlet Mall** the largest concentration, and dozens of specialty shops in **Merchant's Square**. The vast **Williamsburg Pottery Factory** in Lightfoot, now covering nearly 1,000 acres, started it all in 1938. You can even watch the famous Williamsburg pottery being made (☎ 757-564-3326, www.williamsburgpottery.com).

Afterwards, you can see the production of soap and candles at the **Williamsburg Soap & Candle Company** (Route 60 West, ☎ 757-564-3354).

Dining

There are so many places to eat in Williamsburg, it would take too much space to list them all. Here are a few of our favorites:

The Colonial Taverns. Dining at one of Colonial Williamsburg's four authentic taverns means eating authentic Colonial food served by costumed waitstaff who explain the origins of strange-sounding foods like snippets (slim slices of toast you dip in your soup). This is Colonial English food, in general made from ingredients that would have been available at the time – the seasonal harvests of the fields, rivers and bays. Most have outdoor garden dining in season. For information on all four taverns, call ☎ 757-229-2141, or 800-HISTORY, www.colonialwilliamsburg.org.

Christiana Campbell's on Waller Street in Colonial Williamsburg made for an elegant, old-fashioned Christmas dinner for us one year. We were in good company – George Washington's diaries mention eating here. Serving dinner only; reservations suggested. **Chowning's Tavern** in Market Square is more casual, with no reservations needed and the playing of gambols (18th-century games and music) common. Open for lunch and dinner. **The King's Arms Tavern** was established in the tradition of the leading public houses of England to cater to gentlemen. It's open for lunch and dinner; reservations recommended for dinner. **Shields Tavern** is open for lunch, dinner and Sunday brunch; reservations recommended.

Can't wait to get back to the 21st century? **Cities Grille** has an eclectic menu with dishes named for American cities, a casual bistro atmosphere, and perhaps the best part – an extensive wine shop where you can choose your bottle for dinner (4511-C John Tyler Highway, ☎ 757-564-3955).

The **Trellis Restaurant** is just steps outside Colonial Williamsburg in Merchant's Square. The chef/owner has received national culinary awards, and uses fresh, seasonal ingredients, with many items grilled over an open fire. Desserts are fantastic (403 Duke of Gloucester Street, ☎ 757-229-8610, www.thetrellis.com).

The **Second Street Restaurant and Tavern** is a popular spot for diners and the sports bar crowd (140 Second Street, ☎ 757-220-2286, www.secondst.com).

You'll have to get in the car and drive to **The Whitehall**, but its impeccable European service, food and wine are well worth the trip. If they can satisfy a room full of 50 Germans and Austrians (our family reunion one year), then they are very good at what they do. The sauerbraten, schnitzel and spaetzle were, dare I say, as good as grandma's. The restaurant is housed in a late-1800s farmhouse, transformed into elegant dining rooms. A real treat is the wine cellar, which is visible through a glass floor panel in the dining room (1325 Jamestown Road, ☎ 757-229-4677, www.thewhitehall.com).

Lodging

Williamsburg accommodations could fill another book. There are more than 10,000 rooms available in town. We'll give you a diverse, representative selection, from modest to upscale, both within the historic district and outside it. For more, contact the Williamsburg Area Hotel/Motel Association (☎ 800-446-9244).

To get truly immersed in the Colonial experience, you can stay right in the Historic Area in one of the many **Colonial Houses** furnished with reproductions, yet offering modern comforts. The **Governor's Inn** offers economical family lodging ($), while the **Williamsburg Inn** is a world-class hotel resembling a country estate surrounded by a golf course ($$$$). The **Williamsburg Woodlands** is a casual retreat hotel on 44 wooded acres ($$), and the **Williamsburg Lodge** is a

Coastal Virginia

full-service resort hotel decorated with folk art ($$). For all of the above, ☎ 800-HISTORY, www.colonialwilliamsburg.org.

Kingsmill Resort has luxurious villa accommodations, spa, pool, golf course, tennis and marina. Provides free shuttle to attractions (1010 Kingsmill Road, ☎ 800-832-5665, www.kingsmill.com, $$$$)

To be close to the outlet shopping on Richmond Road (Route 60), check out the **Comfort Inn Outlet Center** (☎ 800-964-1774, $), and the **Quality Inn Outlet Mall** (☎ 800-524-1443, $).

The **Quality Inn Lord Paget** is a modestly priced motor lodge in a quiet, park-like setting. It's decorated in the Colonial style, and a separate building houses fully furnished suites with terraces looking out on the private duck pond (901 Capitol Landing Road, ☎ 800-444-4678, $$).

There are more than a dozen bed & breakfast inns in the Williamsburg area. An 1849 National Historic Landmark mansion, **Edgewood Plantation Inn,** has 10 fireplaces, antiques and canopy beds (4800 John Tyler Memorial Highway, Charles City, ☎ 800-296-3343, www. edgewood-plantation.com, $$$).

At the other extreme is the **Primrose Cottage B&B**, a four-room getaway decorated with antiques. You might have a hard time remembering which century you're in – you can play a harpsichord or get in a Jacuzzi! (706 Richmond Road, ☎ 800-522-1901, www.primrose-cottage.com, $$).

The **Fife and Drum Inn** is one of the most conveniently located private inns to the historic area (441 Prince George Street, ☎ 888-838-1783, www.fifeanddruminn.com, $$$).

 The Heritage Inn Motel accepts pets at no charge, but they request prior notice. Located in the heart of the historic district (1324 Richmond Road, ☎ 757-229-6220, $$).

Information

Williamsburg Area Convention & Visitors Bureau, ☎ 800-368-6511, www.visitwilliamsburg.com.

Colonial Williamsburg, ☎ 800-HISTORY, www.colonialwilliamsburg.org.

Smithfield

The view from the back porch of Windsor Castle sweeps down a green lawn, past red-painted barns, over fields planted with cotton, and settles on the winding passage of two creeks – the Pagan and Cypress. If the breeze picks up and blows your way, it will carry with it a heady tidewater blend of marsh and field. Arthur Smith found it all to his liking and settled here, his Windsor Castle estate covering 1,400 acres until the day a descendant, Arthur Smith IV, donated a small portion for the courthouse, and sold lots around it.

Thus was born Smithfield, a small town that for 250 years has seen fortunes rise and fall on the commodities of fishing, peanuts and pork – including the world-famous Smithfield Ham, coveted by English monarchs before the American Revolution.

Around Town

Downtown Smithfield is packed with quaint, familiar small town icons: the ice cream parlor, the candy store, the antique emporium and the ham shop (the last, actually, is exclusive to Smithfield, for which the world-famous Smithfield Ham is named). Fine two- and three-story homes feature ornate porches, scalloped eaves and slate-topped turrets that lend this old town an Old World feel. On summer Friday evenings, strains of French horns and violins arise from a free concert on "The Green."

After the Civil War, Smithfield became the center of a flourishing peanut industry. The **Historic District Walking Tour** describes 60 historic homes of Victorian, Colonial and Federal architecture, built by ship captains and merchants. Pick up the self-guided brochure, rent an audiotape to go with it, and watch an orientation video in the visitor center housed in the **Old Courthouse of 1750**, which was modeled after the Capital Building in Williamsburg. It's open daily 9am-5pm; free admission (130 Main Street, ☎ 800-365-9339)

The Battle of Smithfield was fought right here, on Main Street. Although a minor skirmish of the Civil War, it's been a great source of pride and storytelling for the town. While most of Smithfield's residents were attending church on Sunday, Jan. 31, 1864, a Union gunboat pulled up to the bottom of Church Street (where Smithfield Station now stands). Women and children were sent into a basement, and

175

Confederate troops fired canon straight down Main Street, hitting the gunboat. Before the ship was blown up, its gilded eagle emblem was grabbed from the bow as a trophy. It's displayed at the **Isle of Wight Museum**, a reminder that this was the one southern town that refused to surrender during the Union's Peninsula Campaign of 1862. Located at the corner of Main and Church streets, the museum also houses the history of the Smithfield ham, displaying a "pet ham" cured more than a century ago, Native American artifacts, and a 1900 country store. The museum is open Tuesday-Saturday, 10am-4pm and Sunday, 1-5pm; admission is free (☎ 757-357-7459).

Immediately outside Smithfield, the farm and forestland of surrounding Isle of Wight County show unmistakable symptoms of suburbia. Keep driving. Miles beyond the half-million-dollar homes, the county holds onto the past two centuries in such picturesque settlements as Foursquare, Moonlight, Comet and Rescue. The county seat, at a crossroads called Isle of Wight, is a cluster of modern brick buildings mixed with historic 18th-century county offices. The modern-looking county complex is built on land originally donated by Major Francis Boykin, who ran a profitable hostelry next door. Private residents raised $800,000 for the renovation of **Boykin's Tavern**, now open to visitors.

North, near the James River, watermen still bring their catch to the docks at **Battery Park**, as they have done for generations. Up the hill, a customhouse built in the 1780s still stands overlooking the James River. Two shillings per hogshead was the duty paid in Colonial times on the two- and three-masted schooners that docked and stocked here. In its heyday, three general stores kept pantries full. An oyster-packing house and two blacksmith shops provided work for laborers and tradesmen. Earlier this century, a cinder block service station with a jukebox inside sold nickel cold drinks and gas for a penny per gallon. The stores, shops and gas station are gone. Yet Battery Park, an enclave of neat, white clapboard homes and one of Isle of Wight's oldest settlements, still speaks of a long-ago time.

Recreation

Boating and **fishing** opportunities are abundant, with several marinas and boat ramps providing access to the rivers.

There are two **golf courses** in Isle of Wight County: **Cypress Creek** (☎ 757-365-4774) and **Smithfield Downs** (☎ 757-357-3101).

Attractions

Built in 1632, **Historic St. Luke's Shrine,** four miles south of Smithfield, is the oldest existing English church in the country and houses the oldest operable organ in the country. Open Tuesday-Sunday; closed in January (14477 Benns Church Blvd., ☎ 757-357-3367, www.historicstlukes.org).

Set high on bluffs overlooking the James River is **Fort Boykin Historic Park,** six miles west of Smithfield. Dating to 1623, when the original structure was built in the shape of a seven-pointed star, the fort was manned during every major campaign fought on American soil. Today it takes a bit of imagination to envision the outline of the fort, now covered with earth and vegetation. It's a great place for a picnic. Open daily 8am to dusk; free admission (7410 Ft. Boykin Trail, ☎ 757-357-5182).

Dining

In Smithfield's Historic District you can swivel on a bar stool at **Smithfield Confectionary and Ice Cream Parlor** (208 Main Street, ☎ 757-357-6166); choose homemade bread for your sandwich at **Smithfield Gourmet Bakery & Café** (218 Main Street, ☎ 757-357-0045); or try the local barbecue and Smithfield ham at **Twin's Ole Towne Inn** (220 Main Street, ☎ 757-357-3031).

For fine dining, you can eat where George Washington did at **Smithfield Inn & Tavern** (112 Main Street, ☎ 757-357-1752, www.smithfieldinn.com); or perch on the edge of the Pagan River at **Smithfield Station** (415 S. Church Street, ☎ 757-357-7700, www.smithfieldstation.com).

Outside the historic district, locals flock to **Angelo's Steak House** for Greek and American fare (1804 S. Church Street, ☎ 757-357-3104). For local flavor in Battery Park, there's **Battery Park Grill** (201 Battery Park Road, ☎ 757-357-1747); the **Courthouse Diner** in Isle of Wight (17167 Courthouse Highway, ☎ 757-357-6309); and **Captain Chuck-A-Mucks Sandbar & Grill** in Rescue (21088 Marina Road, ☎ 757-357-2342).

Coastal Virginia

Lodging

Ever dreamed of staying in a lighthouse? You can, in one of two suites at **Smithfield Station Waterfront Inn and Marina.** The main inn has 15 rooms and two suites. There's a marina, bike and canoe rentals, outdoor pool and restaurant (415 S. Church Street, ☎ 757-357-7700, www.smithfieldstation.com, $$).

Built in 1752 and located right in the Historic District, **Smithfield Inn & Tavern B&B** has five one-bedroom suites and a garden house (112 Main Street, ☎ 757-357-1752, www.smithfieldinn.com, $$).

Also right in town, **Isle of Wight Inn B&B** has eight rooms and four suites with fireplaces and Jacuzzis (1607 S. Church Street, ☎ 800-357-3245, $).

Porches on the James is just that – expansive guest porches overlooking the river with complimentary 5pm cocktail hour for guests (6347 Old Stage Hwy., ☎ 757-356-0602, www.porchesonthejames. com, $$).

 Outside town, **Four Square Plantation B&B** is on a plantation in the countryside. It has three guest rooms. The proprietors are dog owners themselves, and accept pets at no extra charge (13357 Four Square Road, ☎ 757-365-0749, $$).

Information

Smithfield & Isle of Wight Convention and Visitors Bureau, 130 Main Street, ☎ 800-365-9339, www.smithfield-virginia.com.

Events

The Olden Days Festival brings crafters, vendors, antique cars, strolling entertainers, carriage rides, and nighttime ghost walks to Main Street during Memorial Day weekend. (Contact the Smithfield & Isle of Wight Convention and Visitors Bureau, above.)

The **Pork, Peanut & Pine Festival** is held the third weekend in July at Chippokes State Park. Contact the park office at ☎ 757-294-3625.

Christmas in Smithfield is a month-long celebration with historic homes tours, tree lighting, boat illuminations and antiques show. Contact the Smithfield & Isle of Wight Convention and Visitors Bureau, above.

Virginia's Eastern Shore

The Eastern Shore is a place to relax and "get away from it all." Prior to the construction of the Chesapeake Bay Bridge Tunnel in 1964, this was an isolated locale, with a ferry the main link to Norfolk. With each passing year, more people discover this quiet gem. New retirement communities and golf courses are signs of things to come, but the Shore today remains by and large a close-knit, primarily agricultural – and increasingly aquacultural – area.

THE TOWNS
❋ Chincoteague
❋ Tangier Island
❋ Onancock
❋ Locustville
❋ Cape Charles & Kiptopeke
❋ The Barrier Islands

Getting Here

Access to Virginia's Eastern Shore is through Maryland from the north, or via the Chesapeake Bay Bridge Tunnel from Virginia Beach to the south ($10 toll each way). Route 13 runs the length of the DelMarVa Peninsula – everything's described as either "on 13" or "off 13."

The closest airport is **Norfolk International Airport** (☎ 757-857-3200, www.norfolkairport.com).

Regional Information

Eastern Shore Visitors Center and Tourism Commission, Route 13, Melfa, ☎ 757-787-2460, www.esvatourism.org.

The Virginia Tourism Corporation operates a **Virginia Highway Welcome Center** on US 13 south of the VA/MD border, ☎ 800-VISIT-VA, www.virginia.org.

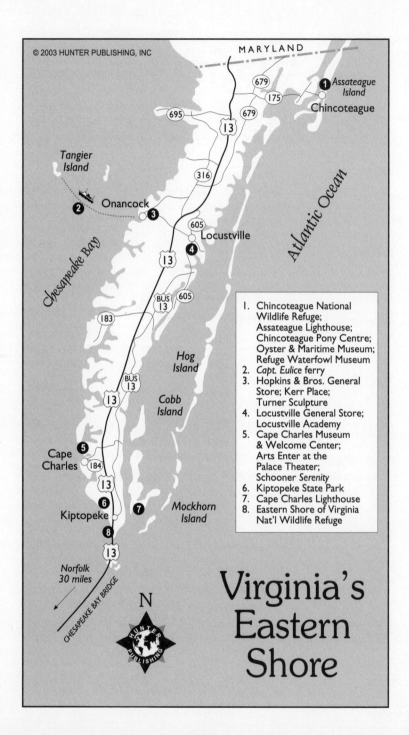

© 2003 HUNTER PUBLISHING, INC

MARYLAND

Assateague Island

Chincoteague

Tangier Island

Onancock

Atlantic Ocean

Chesapeake Bay

Locustville

Hog Island

Cobb Island

Cape Charles

Mockhorn Island

Kiptopeke

Norfolk 30 miles

CHESAPEAKE BAY BRIDGE

N

HUNTER PUBLISHING

1. Chincoteague National Wildlife Refuge; Assateague Lighthouse; Chincoteague Pony Centre; Oyster & Maritime Museum; Refuge Waterfowl Museum
2. *Capt. Eulice* ferry
3. Hopkins & Bros. General Store; Kerr Place; Turner Sculpture
4. Locustville General Store; Locustville Academy
5. Cape Charles Museum & Welcome Center; Arts Enter at the Palace Theater; Schooner *Serenity*
6. Kiptopeke State Park
7. Cape Charles Lighthouse
8. Eastern Shore of Virginia Nat'l Wildlife Refuge

Virginia's Eastern Shore

Chincoteague

The legend of Chincoteague's famed ponies holds that their ancestors swam onto this large barrier island from a shipwrecked Spanish galleon. It *is* legend – there are no *eyewitness* accounts – but the story has circulated as fact for the last century.

Historians can pinpoint specific shipwrecks on the shoals off Assateague Island, in which the boats were known to be carrying horses or ponies. Further scientific proof is found in skeletal remains of some Chincoteague ponies in which one vertebra is missing. This trait denotes not only a Spanish Barb breed of horse, but also the American Mustang, a descendant of the Spanish Barb.

And so they could be Spanish or they could be American. What's unquestioned is how popular the ponies are today. They are arguably the Shore's most famous and beloved residents, with a national reputation built on the storytelling of Marguerite Henry in her children's book *Misty of Chincoteague.*

Around Town

Throngs of visitors descend on this resort village each July for the annual **Pony Swim and Auction**. Business stands still for two days midweek as ponies are corralled on Assateague Island and herded across a narrow channel to Chincoteague Island. Many people take off work or close up shop to spend time at this carnival-like event. Buyers come from all over the country and bid on the trainable horses, many for use as children's mounts.

Proceeds from the auction benefit the Chincoteague Volunteer Fire Department, which owns the herd. The firemen hold a fair every weekend in July leading up to the swim, and for two weekends afterward.

Beach crowds and pony watching keeps Chincoteague hopping from Memorial Day through Labor Day. There are seafood restaurants at nearly every turn; if there's a wait at one establishment, you can get nearly identical fare at the next. Bike rentals and mopeds are a popular way to explore the island. Small boutiques carry everything from decoys to designer dresses.

After Labor Day, Chincoteague reverts to a sleepy coastal town. It's far from boring; this is our favorite time to visit. In early spring, late fall and

Virginia's Eastern Shore

throughout winter, a different kind of Chincoteague emerges. We hike, bike and bird-watch on the wildlife refuge, confident that cool temperatures will keep bugs to a minimum. The peak of waterfowl migration is in November and December, when tens of thousands of snow geese swim among the refuge's impoundments.

The refuge is a wonderful diversion in any season. A 3.2-mile Wildlife Loop circles the Snow Goose Pool. Refuge managers raise and lower the water in these pools in each season to provide suitable bird habitat. These practices are detailed in a brochure that describes numbered stops along the way, a convenient way to learn about barrier island ecology, its wildlife, birds and plant life. This gravel road loop is great for bikers, and from 3pm until dusk each day it opens up to vehicles.

For a more wilderness experience, you can hike along the beach for miles and miles. Specifically, it's 10 miles north to Maryland and the Assateague National Seashore. There – and only there – is backcountry camping allowed. Find a site and set up your tent among the dunes. There's nothing in the world like being lullabied to sleep by waves crashing on the beach.

Attractions

Chincoteague National Wildlife Refuge is at the end of Maddox Boulevard, and is actually on the island of Assateague. The **Assateague Lighthouse** is a red-and-white-striped landmark around which existed one of the island's largest communities. The last island resident moved off in the 1930s. Admission to the refuge is $5 per vehicle, good for three days. Other passes are available. The refuge is open year-round. Summer hours are 5am-10pm with the visitor center open 8am-5pm; winter hours vary. Pets are not allowed, even in the car (☎ 757-336-6122, http://chinco.fws.gov).

The **Chincoteague Pony Centre** offers daily riding lessons, pony rides and evening shows Monday-Saturday. Meet descendants of Misty and others in the stables. There's a continuous film, exhibits and carriage on display, and a gift shop. The center is open daily, 9am to 9pm; Sundays, 1-9pm. Closed after Thanksgiving weekend until Easter. Admission to the museum is $5; pony rides are an additional $5 (6417 Carriage Drive, ☎ 757-336-2776).

The Oyster & Maritime Museum is just before the entrance to the wildlife refuge. Exhibits preserve island history through the ongoing work of local artists and carvers, marine life and maritime artifacts from the oyster farming and the seafood industry. Open daily in summer, weekends in spring and fall, and closed in the winter (7125 Maddox Blvd., ☎ 757-336-6117).

The Refuge Waterfowl Museum preserves the history of everything to do with waterfowl: decoys, weapons, boats, a replica of a decoy shop, and carvings. A new 8,000-square-foot wing opened in 2002 dedicated to preserving Atlantic flyway water fowling history. Summer hours are 10am-5pm daily, except Wednesdays. Hours vary the rest of the year depending on demand, so give a call first. $3 adults, $1.50 children (7059 Maddox Blvd., just before the refuge entrance, ☎ 757-336-5800).

Wildlife Expeditions rents canoes and sea kayaks and takes visitors on guided sunrise, sunset and eco-tours (☎ 757-336-6811, http:// jcherrix.tripod.com).

Dining

Dining in Chincoteague means seafood eaten with a view of the water. **AJ's on the Creek** has casual elegance, its own herb gardens and a view of Eel Creek. Oysters, veal and hand-cut steaks are tops on the menu. Open for lunch and dinner daily (6585 Maddox Blvd., ☎ 757-336-5888).

An old waterman's home provides a setting for **Blackboard Bistro**; it's a casual little place where seafood is prepared with imagination. Call for hours (3837 Main Street, ☎ 757-336-6187).

Etta's Channel Side Restaurant, where crab cakes are the specialty, overlooks Assateague Channel and has views of the lighthouse. Lunch and dinner Friday-Sunday; dinner only Monday-Thursday. Closed January-March (7452 East Side D., ☎ 757-336-5644).

In the heart of downtown Chincoteague, you will find **Landmark Crab House**, open for dinner only, closed Mondays (☎ 757-336-3745 or ☎ 757-336-5552).

The candlelit porches of **Muller's Old Fashioned Ice Cream Parlour** complete the Victorian setting of this dessert spot. Ice cream dishes come as splits, malts and sundaes. Old Dominion Draft Root Beer is served and the house specialty is Belgian waffles with ice cream, fresh fruit and whipped cream. Built in 1875, the house was later home to Captain John B. Whealton while he supervised construction of the bridge and causeway linking Chincoteague to the mainland. Open daily, 11am-11pm (4034 Main Street, ☎ 757-336-5894).

Seafood lovers who don't mind making a mess head for **Steamers Seafood Restaurant**, where steamed entrées are served on tables decked in brown paper. Open daily for dinner (6251 Maddox Blvd., ☎ 757-336-6074).

Village Restaurant and Lounge on Eel Creek specializes in fresh oysters, steaks and veal. Open daily for dinner (7576 Maddox Blvd., ☎ 757-336-5120).

Lodging

Chincoteague has plenty of rooms with 20 motels and nearly 10 inns and B&Bs. We've chosen some that are on waterfront, some within walking distance of the refuge, and some just because they're so special. For a complete listing, with details and maps, visit www.chincoteaguechamber.com.

Cedar Gables is a waterfront refuge in a modern cedar-sided home on the waterfront. Screened-in pool with hot tub, dock outside for fishing and crabbing (Hopkins Lane, ☎ 888-491-2944, www.cedargable.com, $$$).

The **Channel Bass Inn** is an 1892 hotel turned B&B that serves afternoon tea (6228 Church Street, ☎ 800-249-0818, www.channelbassinn.com, $$). Toast sunsets from the waterfront sundeck at **The Year of the Horse Inn** (3583 Main Street, ☎ 800-680-0090, www.yearofthehorseinn.com, $$-$$$).

Two couples operate twin Victorian B&Bs, complete with gingerbread trim and wrap-around porches, both within walking distance of Chincoteague's shops and restaurants. The **Watson House Bed & Breakfast** is a fabulously restored late-1800s home (4240 Main Street, ☎ 800-336-6787, www.watsonhouse.com, $$). The owners built the **Inn at Poplar Corner** to accommodate the overflow. They also have rental cottages and a townhouse with a pool and a view of the Assateague Lighthouse (4248 Main Street, ☎ 800-336-6787, www.poplarcorner.com, $$).

A stay at the **Island Manor House** comes with a great bedtime story. In 1848 two young men pooled their money to build a large T-shaped house on Main Street. One was a doctor, the other the town's postmaster. The postmaster fell in love with a guest visiting from Baltimore, and they married. When her sister came to visit, the doctor fell in love with her, and they married. Trouble was, the sisters didn't like living together, so the house was split, and one couple moved next door. The current owners reunited the house with a large garden room (4160 Main Street, ☎ 800-852-1505, www.islandmanor.com, $$).

Two motels are just before the entrance to the wildlife refuge, which is within walking distance: **Driftwood Lodge** (7105 Maddox Blvd., ☎ 800-553-6117, $$), and the **Refuge Inn** (7058 Maddox Blvd., ☎ 888-257-0039, $$).

TIP

Pets are not allowed in the Chincoteague Wildlife Refuge, not even in the car. Nevertheless, several lodgings do accept them.

The **Garden and the Sea Inn & Restaurant** is a few miles from Chincoteague in New Church, but worth the drive if you have a pet and want to stay in a beautiful Victorian home on the Pocomoke River (☎ 800-824-0672, www.gardenandseainn.com, $$).

Motels accepting pets include **The Blue Heron Inn** (7020 Maddox Blvd., ☎ 800-615-6343, $); and the **Lighthouse Inn** (4218 Main Street, ☎ 757-336-5091, $$).

Camping

There are four private campgrounds on the island, some on the water. Visit www.chincoteaguechamber.com for details. They are: **Inlet View** (☎ 757-336-5126, www.happysnails.com/inletview); **Maddox Family Campground** (☎ 757-336-3111); **Pine Grove** (☎ 757-336-5200, www.pinegrovecampground.com); and **Tom's Cove Family Campground** (☎ 757-336-6498, www.tomscovepark.com).

Information

Chincoteague Chamber of Commerce, ☎ 757-336-6161, www.chincoteaguechamber.com.

> **★ DID YOU KNOW?**
>
> While the rest of Virginia's Eastern Shore voted to join the Confederacy in 1861, the people of Chincoteague Island voted 132 to 2 to stay with the Union to preserve sea trade with the North.

Events

Annual Pony Swim and Penning, held the last Wednesday and Thursday in July (☎ 757-787-2460).

Annual Seafood Festival, held the first Wednesday in May at Tom's Cove Park (☎ 757-787-2460).

Tangier Island

There's not a whole lot to do on Tangier Island, but that's its biggest appeal. Imagine spending an entire weekend on an island without cars, much less traffic. You can escape the telephone and e-mail, and there is no schedule and few decisions to make. Only a few places offer lodging and food, and there are only two ways to get here – by boat or small plane.

Oh, sure, Tangier Island has its distractions. You can tour the three-mile-long island by borrowed bike or rented golf cart, or cruise around it on a sightseeing trip. There are about a half-dozen gift shops, a 2½-mile beach to walk on and, if the watermen aren't too busy, they'll show you their crabbing operations. Explore some of the old graveyards – although many are in people's yards, so ask first. Far from city lights, the stargazing is magnificent.

There are three embarkation points to get to Tangier. Ferries depart Crisfield MD, Onancock on Virginia's Eastern Shore, or Reedville VA, on the "western shore." Daily excursions start in May and run through mid-October. A ferry operates from Crisfield year-round, but with just one trip a day, you have to stay overnight.

> **★ DID YOU KNOW?**
>
> During the War of 1812, about 1,200 British soldiers camped the island's beaches in preparation for the attack on Baltimore.

Getting Here

From Onancock

The *Capt. Eulice* passenger ferry departs for **Tangier Island** 10am daily Memorial Day weekend to mid-October. It's just a 12-mile trip, five of it on Onancock Creek, returning at 3:30pm. Fares are $20 per person round-trip, half-price for children ages six-12 (under six get in free). Pets allowed on a leash. No credit cards accepted. They also rent golf carts and bikes on the island. **Tangier-Onancock Cruises** (☎ 757-891-2240, www.chesapeakebaysampler.com/tangierisland).

From Crisfield, Maryland

The *Courtney Thomas* is owned and operated by Rudy and Beth Thomas, and named after their daughter. Captain Thomas is the fifth generation in his family to run the mail route from Crisfield to Tangier Island. He gives a narrative of Tangier during the trip. Day excursions run mid-May through mid-October. Year-round ferry service departs Crisfield daily at 12:30pm, leaving Tangier at 8am, requiring an overnight stay. $20 per person, round-trip; children free when accompanied by a parent. No credit cards accepted (☎ 410-968-2338).

From Reedville

Daily ferry departs from the Northern Neck on the western shore of the Chesapeake Bay, May-October (☎ 804-453-2628).

To fly into Tangier, contact **Accomack County Airport** in Melfa, Virginia (☎ 757-789-3719).

Around Town

If you depart from Onancock or Crisfield, your boat will likely be piloted by a native Tangier waterman, and when you arrive, it will be met by a friendly guide who gives 10-minute walking tours of the island. For $3, you can get a tour by golf cart. From Crisfield, it'll likely be captain Thomas, and from Onancock, captain Pruitt (you'll find these surnames, along with Crockett, all over the island). Wallace and Shirley Pruitt own the largest B&B on the island. Now retired, Wallace worked the Chesapeake Bay on tugboats. They, as well as other friendly natives you'll meet, have an accent notably different from mainland Virginians. It's said their dialect still retains remnants of Elizabethan English.

Tangier's surnames go way back. First discovered by Captain John Smith in 1608 and settled in 1686 by the large Crockett family who fished and farmed the three ridges that made up the "Tangier Islands." The 1800 census of Accomack County showed there were 79 people on the islands, most of them Crocketts or descendants of Crocketts. Joshua Thomas brought religion to the island in 1805 in the form of the Methodist church, which most people still belong to today.

Tangier Island remains much as it has been for centuries, a lifestyle reliant on the fishing industry, but increasingly, on tourism. Despite the convenience of the modern world, Mother Nature still rules island life to a large extent. Some winters the Chesapeake Bay freezes, making travel to the mainland impossible for a few days. In centuries past, people have been known to walk across the ice to get supplies, but today they can be flown in.

Attractions

A small museum in the back of **Sandy's Gift Shop** has artifacts of Tangier life, newspaper clippings, and the names of everyone who's ever lived or died here (Main Street, ☎ 757-891-2367).

RB's Island Nature Cruises offer eco-tours, charter fishing, family outings and trips to Smith Island aboard the *Elizabeth Thomas*, a 46-foot Chesapeake Bay deadrise. They'll fish out a crab pot for you to see the famous Chesapeake Bay Blue Crab, take you to see soft crab farms, pound net fishing, and the Tangier Light. Wildlife spottings could include pelicans, ospreys, heron, cormorants, eagles, stingrays and egrets. Buy tickets at the Tangier Mailboat Dock (☎ 757-891-2240).

> **★ DID YOU KNOW?**
>
> Some of the graves in people's yards here date back to the 1866 cholera epidemic. So many people were dying that graves were hastily dug in front yards, and often had no headstones.

Dining

Fisherman's Corner Restaurant is operated by four islanders who serve up generous portions of seafood and southern hospitality. Open daily, May-September, for lunch and early dinners, 11am-7pm; Sundays, 12:30-6pm (☎ 757-891-2900).

Hilda Crockett's Chesapeake House is actually two old houses operated now by Hilda's daughter, Betty, as a B&B and restaurant (Hilda passed away nearly 30 years ago). Dinner is served family-style from 11:30am to 6pm. Heaping platters of Virginia baked ham, crab cakes, clam fritters, hot corn puddings, and innumerable vegetables are brought to the tables that seat 12. Open daily from late April to mid-October (Main Street, ☎ 757-891-2331).

The Islander serves up steaming platters of seafood, chicken dinners, sandwiches and chowders daily, 9am-7pm, May through October. There's a screened-in deck in addition to the dining room (Chambers Lane, ☎ 757-891-2249).

The Waterfront Restaurant's name says it all. Located on the docks and open for lunch and afternoon snacks on outdoor picnic tables daily mid-May through October, 10am-4pm; Sundays, 1-4pm. They also rent bikes, and offer free food deliveries for overnight guests (☎ 757-891-2248).

Lodging

Hilda Crockett's Chesapeake House offers rooms in two old homes for $40 a night that includes family-style dinner and a full breakfast the next morning. Open late April to mid-October (Main Street, ☎ 757-891-2331, $).

In 1904, merchant Sidney Wallace opened an inn on the island to accommodate visitors. Nearly a century later, his grandson, Wallace Pruitt and his wife Shirley now operate **Shirley's Bay View Inn Bed and Breakfast.** You can stay in the main house, one of the oldest on the island, or in one of seven private cottages. Guests get both sunrise and sunset views on the manicured grounds from swings, hammocks and a double-decker gazebo. Coffee's ready at 7am; breakfast is served when guests are ready on "grandma's" century-old china. Children welcome (☎ 757-891-2396, www.tangierisland.net, $$).

At the **Sunset Inn Bed & Breakfast**, "Ms. Grace" Brown will be happy to acquaint you with what there is to do on the island. Her 10 cottages have views of the bay and are close to the beach where there's great surf fishing, swimming or just strolling and watching the spectacular sunrises and sunsets. Children under 12 stay free with an adult (☎ 757-891-2535, www.tangierislandsunset.com, $$).

> ⭐ TRAVEL TIP
>
> Pets are allowed on the ferry, and may be walked on the island while leashed, but none of the lodging establishments accepts pets.

Information

Eastern Shore Visitors Center & Tourism Commision, ☎ 757-787-2460, www.esvatourism.org.

Tangier-Onancock Cruises, ☎ 757-891-2240, www.chesapeake-baysampler.com/tangierisland.

> ⭐ TRAVEL TIP
>
> Tangier is a "dry island," meaning no alcohol is sold or served. You can bring your own, but keep it out of public sight.

Onancock

Around Town

Onancock bills itself as the "Gem of the Eastern Shore" and, thanks to a new generation of imaginative shop owners, it has achieved legitimate "must-see" status. As you pop in and out of fine antique and jewelry shops on Market Street, you might notice a theme take shape. **Tom Thumb Workshops**, ☎ 757-787-9596, features herbs and crafts. **Bizzotto's Gallery and Café**, ☎ 757-787-3103, combines good food, handicrafts and art. Dining table bases in **Truffles Bakery**, ☎ 757-787-8440, a café and antiques shop, are old treadle sewing machines.

Combining two or more businesses under one roof is one way that Onancock entrepreneurs survive the off-season. Karen Tweedie, owner of **The Spinning Wheel Bed and Breakfast**, ☎ 888-787-0337, and **Evergreen Antiques**, ☎ 757-787-1905, operates a mail-order jewelry business in the back room of her antiques store on North Street. That makes three businesses, but she's outdone by the Onancock Deli/Laundry with adjacent tanning salon and car wash.

"There aren't a whole lot of people coming through, so most businesses rely on a second income," said Tweedie, who "escaped" Washington DC a dozen years ago. She and most other business owners prefer things as they are: overhead is low, and nights are quiet and safe.

Onancock is a case study in how the Eastern Shore has developed in recent years. It is close to Hampton Roads and 190 miles from Washington DC, drawing couples and families from both regions on long weekend getaways. It reflects chic, urban tastes as much as those of traditional Shore life. That said, the charm still remains. "It's a quick ride, and it's like you're coming to a completely different place," said Tweedie.

Tourist season in Onancock runs May through October and that's when, down at the town wharf, a visitor can book a fishing charter or ferry trip to Tangier Island. While waiting for departure, take a seat on the "liar's bench," where old men have been known to tell a tall tale or two about fish they've caught. On this same wharf is **Hopkins & Bros. General Store**, one of the oldest on the East Coast. While it's maintained by the Association for the Preservation of Virginia Antiquities, it's still a working store and restaurant (☎ 757-787-3100).

Onancock's old-time fishing-village charm is mostly intact, even as restaurants, jam-packed antiques shops, fine art galleries and bed & breakfast inns have opened. Whether from-heres or come-heres, this is a town proud of its 300-year history. The 18th- and 19th-century homes are well-preserved, many with wrap-around porches and Victorian gingerbread, some in the Eastern Shore style of "big house, little house" with a colonnade and kitchen in-between.

Attractions

The Eastern Shore of Virginia Historical Society takes good care of **Kerr Place**, a 200-year-old home built in the Federal style by John Kerr. Detailed finishing and vibrant colors reflect Kerr's fine taste for his period. In the parlor stands a pianoforte, a musical instrument made in Vienna. On the second floor are interpretive exhibits, and on the first floor, a museum store with works by regional artists, crafters and authors. Outside are restored gardens. Open Tuesday-Saturday, 10am-4pm except holidays. Closed January and February. Admission is $4; children free (69 Market Street, ☎ 757-787-8012, www.kerrplace.org).

The *Capt. Eulice* **passenger ferry** departs for Tangier Island daily Memorial Day Weekend to mid-October. The island is just a 12-mile trip one-way (five miles of it on Onancock Creek), but it's a different world altogether. Cost is $20 per person round-trip; children six-12 ride for half-price, under six ride free. No credit cards accepted (Tangier-Onancock Cruises, ☎ 757-891-2240, http://tangierisland-va.com/eulice).

Pam Barefoot has made her **Blue Crab Bay Co.** specialty food products famous, starting as a cottage industry whose products were seen in the movie *Sleeping with the Enemy*, which starred Julia Roberts. If you haven't tried the Sting Ray Bloody Mary Mixer or Barnacles Snack Mix with the characteristic light blue crab labels, you're in for a treat. Go to their Web site, or visit the gift shop, four miles south of Onley on Route 13 in the Accomack Airport Industrial Park (☎ 800-221-2722, www.bluecrabbay.com).

Turner Sculpture on Route 13 in nearby Olney is famous nationwide for their wildlife sculptures in bronze and silver. Watch the foundry process and browse through the gallery (☎ 757-787-2818, www.esva.net/~turner).

Dining

The friendly Argentinean namesake of **Armando's** might be in the kitchen, cooking up his "New American" cuisine, or conversing with patrons on the patio. Professional service combined with specials like lobster ravioli, their homemade bread, and the fine wine list make for a memorable repast. Eat inside or on the garden patio. Thursday evenings feature a gourmet tapas menu; dinner is served Friday through Sunday, with a live jazz trio playing most Saturdays in the summer (10 North Street, ☎ 757-787-8044).

Step into **Bizzotto's Gallery and Café** and you might feel like you're in a Soho gallery instead of a small fishing village. The chef/owner, Miguel Bizzotto from Argentina, not only makes all the dishes, he makes the fine leather handbags displayed for sale. This storefront, with its pressed tin ceilings and original wood floors, was once a hat shop. The mirrored shelves where women admired their chapeaux are still on the walls. While waiting for your meal, browse the art craft items for sale: jewelry, pottery, and artwork. By the way, the food is awesome: creative salads and wraps for lunch, imaginative international dinner specials (41 Market Street, ☎ 757-787-3103).

Flounder's Restaurant is in a 19th-century Victorian home that still sports original wallpaper, lighting and wood floors. They have a rare thing on the shore – vegetarian specials – as well as seafood, beef, homemade desserts and the drink of the house, the Famous Blue Whale. Locals spread the word about the Sunday brunch buffet. Closed Mondays (145 Market Street, ☎ 757-787-2233).

Eastern Shore Steamboat Co. serves seafood from Hopkins Bros. store on the wharf. Eat lunch or dinner out on the dock or inside the historic 1842 general store (2 Market Street, ☎ 757-787-3100). If you're looking for a casual spot for lunch or dinner, **Peppers** serves specialty sandwiches and fresh salads daily (151 Market Street, ☎ 757-787-3457).

Stella's is a busy pizza and sandwich shop across from Armando's on North Street. Open for lunch and dinner, Tuesday-Saturday (☎ 757-789-7770).

Lodging

The 1810 plantation home known as **Montrose House Bed & Breakfast** was built in the Eastern Shore style known as "big house, little house, colonnade, kitchen." Antiques fill the four guest rooms (20494 Market Street, ☎ 757-787-8887, 757-787-7088 evenings, www.bbonline.com/va/montrose, $$).

Colonial Manor Inn Bed and Breakfast has a fully handicapped-accessible suite on the first floor with a ramped entrance. There are also ramps to the gazebo and sundeck, an outside intercom system, and a massage therapy studio (84 Market Street, ☎ 757-787-3521, www.colonialmanorinn.com, $$).

76 Market Street Bed and Breakfast is an 1840 Victorian at the same address as its name, with central air conditioning and featherbeds (☎ 888-751-7600, www.76marketst.com, $$).

Spinning Wheel Bed and Breakfast is an 1890s home, complete with rockers on the front porch (31 North Street, ☎ 888-787-0337 or 757-787-7311, www.1890spinningwheel.com, $$).

Information

Onancock Town Office, ☎ 757-787-3363.

Onancock Business & Civic Association, http://onancock.org.

For general area information, www.ChesapeakeBaysampler.com.

Events

The main event of the year is **Harborfest** in mid-August, and the **Christmas season** brings caroling, home tours and a parade. For information and dates, contact the Onancock Town Office, ☎ 757-787-3363, www.esvatourism.org.

★ TIP

Stop in at the **Corner Bakery** for homemade donuts and to taste the famous Eastern Shore sweet potato biscuits (36 Market Street, ☎ 757-787-4520).

Trip Journal

Locustville

One afternoon we decided to go exploring with Kirk Mariner's *Off 13* book, which is the bible for off-the-beaten-track spots on the Shore. This trip led us to the unlikely town of Locustville. Passing down the main street felt like stepping back more than a century. This small cluster of homes, a hotel and general store truly hasn't changed much since before the Civil War when Locustville was a stop on the stagecoach line from Maryland south to Eastville. Still standing are the original tavern, hotel, church, school and store.

A lot of old-time general stores say they're just like they were 100 years ago, but they're really not, not with those boutique-style gift items and upscale groceries. Except for the soda cooler, the **Locustville General Store** has remained pretty much the same since it opened in 1844. It exists not as a tourist stop, but to meet the needs of local people, which today are Mexican laborers who work the nearby tomato fields. When times are slow, the owner sits in the back near a pot-bellied stove. The original floors haven't been refinished; the owner merely polishes them with motor oil once a year. Modest grocery items and cigarettes line the shelves (☎ 757-787-3462).

Nearby, the **Locustville Academy** still stands in the 1859 building built to educate boys and girls headed for college. It's the lone survivor of about a dozen schools of higher learning built in the 1800s. There's a small museum inside, operated by the Society for the Preservation of Locustville Academy. It's open only during garden week in April and by appointment (☎ 757-787-4826).

A "come-here" has purchased and is renovating the Locustville Hotel (1820), and the **Wynne Tref Bed and Breakfast** has a private suite and serves breakfast (Open March-October, ☎ 757-787-2356, $$).

Locustville is located on the "seaside" of Route 13, near Onley. From the "T" intersection, turn down Burton's Shore Road, then left on Seagull Lane to reach Burton's Shore, once a popular place for sunbathing and picnics. The view is to Cedar Island where you can see the abandoned Coast Guard station.

Cape Charles – Kiptopeke

The Eastern Shore of Virginia boasts some of the best flat-water kayaking in the United States. Paddling among Atlantic barrier islands through tall grass marshes allows an intimate glimpse of the Shore's natural beauty. One of our more memorable kayak trips began in Cape Charles near the tip of the Eastern Shore. On this particular December Sunday morning, Main Street was quiet. Driving down tree-lined residential streets, past local churches, we saw residents dressed in their Sunday best hurrying to catch the start of services.

We left town from a public beach that, come summertime, would be crowded with sunbathers. As we paddled south, aided by a northeast wind, the shoreline morphed from the industrial forms of Cape Charles into high, red clay bluffs topped with loblolly pines. Near a set of gill nets, we surprised a deer swimming. Past Kiptopeke State Park, a sharp-eyed companion spied two bald eagles. Then, wonder of wonders, fins broke the surface. For 10 minutes or more, we bobbed and watched, enthralled by a half-dozen juvenile and adult dolphins that swam among our boats.

Already one of the Eastern Shore's larger towns, Cape Charles will only grow in prominence as the Shore develops. The local concrete plant is a steady employer and the rail-barge ferry serves Shore farmers by shipping their goods 26 miles across the mouth of the Bay to international port terminals in Norfolk. Anachronisms abound on the Eastern Shore, and this shipping terminal, the last of its kind in the United States, is but one.

Farming and loading boats is how this small port town has made its living since it was carefully laid out in the 1880s by the Pennsylvania Railroad. Tracks end at the town's protected harbor. It is still fascinating to watch cargo going from barge to railroad car and vice versa.

Around Town

Planners laid the town out on a grid. Eight streets run north-south and seven run east-west. The area contains more than 500 buildings, most built between 1885 and 1940, and many listed on the National Register of Historic Places. The nicest homes front the Bay. Diligent entrepreneurs have of late worked hard to restore them to their earlier Victorian charm, exemplified in tall windows, widow's watches and wrap-around porches. Several are now bed & breakfast inns. These, along with some antiques shops and cafés, are within walking distance of the town's marina.

Fishing is a major draw for Shore visitors, and Cape Charles is no different. In season, charters leave daily from the marina for sport fishing, pleasure boating and tall ship cruises.

Home-building is a growing industry on the Eastern Shore, fueled by lower property values and easy access to the water. Cape Charles officials have embraced the largest residential development yet, the 1,800-acre Bay Creek community, which surrounds the town like a horseshoe. Its two PGA championship golf courses designed by Arnold Palmer and Jack Nicklaus lure retirees and second-homers.

One of the town's best assets is a mile-long public beach right in downtown, with a boardwalk and gazebo where most events are centered. Since the town is on the western side of the Eastern Shore peninsula, it's possible to catch a beautiful sunset over the water. "Just like in Key West," says Felix Torrice, president of the Chamber of Commerce, which came up with the "Applaud the Sun Harbor" parties. The idea for the monthly sunset parties with food, beer, bands and boaters was taken from Florida's Key West.

Cape Charles wasn't the first to market the great Eastern Shore sunsets. South on Route 13 about eight miles, **Sunset Beach Resort** has been drawing travelers for decades, catching them right before they head over the Chesapeake Bay Bridge-Tunnel to the resort of Virginia Beach. The area is known as Kiptopeke. There's really no town, but there's plenty to do.

Kiptopeke State Park has camping, hiking trails, fishing and a beach for swimming and sunbathing in a harbor protected by sunken concrete-filled ships. This is the spot where the ferries to mainland Virginia docked before the bridge-tunnel opened in 1964 (☎ 757-331-2267).

The friendly guys at **Southeast Expeditions** (next door to Sunset Beach Resort) will hook you up with a kayak or kite-board (the newest water sport around), gear, and a guided trip or lessons if you need them (☎ 757-331-2660, www.sekayak.com).

Paddling access is either on the bay side from Sunset Beach or on the ocean side from the **Eastern Shore of Virginia National Wildlife Refuge,** straight across Route 13 from Southeast Expeditions. The 750-acre preserve at the tip of the Delmarva Peninsula is a haven for migrating birds during inclement weather. Each spring and fall brings hundreds of species on their north-south route. The visitor center has exhibits of waterfowl carvings and the migratory birds, including endangered species like the bald eagle and peregrine falcon. Outside, hiking trails lead through a butterfly field and to a World War II bunker turned elevated bird-watching platform. Admission is free. The refuge grounds are open year-round, from a half-hour before sunrise to a half-hour before sunset; the visitors center is open weekends only, 10am-2pm in January and February; daily, 10am-2pm, in March and December; daily, 9am-4pm, the rest of the year (☎ 757-331-2760, http://easternshore.fws.gov).

At this point, you are so close to the northern terminus of **The Chesapeake Bay Bridge-Tunnel** that you should explore one of the world's greatest engineering achievements. The 17.6 miles to Virginia Beach is the world's largest bridge-tunnel complex, and crossing it is an experience you'll never forget (particularly in rough weather). It's literally like driving out into the ocean – you can't see across the bay here at its widest point. The toll is steep: $10 each way, but if you stop at one of the two manmade islands and turn back, you have to pay only once. Also, if you return within 24 hours, the return trip is only $4. Information about the bridge-tunnel is available online at www.cbbt.com.

★ DID YOU KNOW?

Construction of the Chesapeake Bay Bridge Tunnel complex required building 12 miles of trestled roadway, two one-mile-long tunnels, two bridges, almost two miles of causeway, four man-made islands and 5½ miles of approach roads, for a total length of almost 23 miles. The first span opened in 1964. A second parallel bridge span was completed in 1999.

Eating at **The Sea Gull Fishing Pier and Restaurant,** on one of the islands 3.5 miles from Virginia Beach, really is like sitting in the middle of the Chesapeake Bay. You can shop in the gift shop, fish from the pier, bird-watch, or wait for one of the huge cargo barges or Navy ships to cruise over the tunnel. Once we were lucky enough to be crossing at the same time as an aircraft carrier. It was so massive and so close; we could wave to the sailors on the deck. Call ahead in high winds for any restrictions on rooftop cargo or bike racks. The bridge-tunnel has been known to close during hurricane warnings (☎ 757-331-2960).

Attractions

The **Cape Charles Museum and Welcome Center** is on the left as you enter town on Route 184. It opened in 1996 in a former building of Delmarva Power, circa 1947. Railroad artifacts and ship models are on display. Open afternoons, Friday-Sunday (☎ 757-331-1008). Downtown is the curiously named **Arts Enter at the Palace Theater** (say "Arts Enter" real fast and you'll get the gist). One of the Shore's active cultural groups, the Arts Enter gives dance, music and theater performances, as well as art exhibits and workshops in a restored theater

(305 Mason Avenue, ☎ 757-331-ARTS, www.capecharles.org/html/palace.html).

The **Cape Charles Town Harbor Marina** is recently renovated, with all new water, electricity, bulkhead and about 50 slips awaiting the pleasure boater (☎ 757-331-2357).

The **Low Sea Co.** sails its tall ship *Schooner Serenity* out of Cape Charles from April through November on sunset cruises and charters. Passengers can lend a hand setting the sail, or even take the helm. Or simply sit back and relax with a beverage. Reservations required (☎ 757-710-1233, www.schoonerserenity.com).

Dining

Eastern Shore restaurants often have shorter hours during the off-season, so call before you stop by. Those listed below include days open and meals served in summer.

A mile north of Cape Charles on four-lane Route 13, **Foggy Dog Pizza** has a whopping 30 toppings to choose from for your specialty pizzas, along with pastas, subs and salads. Open for lunch and dinner every day (☎ 757-331-2177).

South of town on Route 13 is **Shore Break Restaurant** with a menu of seafood, steak and daily specials for lunch and dinner. Closed Tuesdays (☎ 757-331-3900).

In downtown Cape Charles, **Garden Café and Gifts** serves seafood, prime rib and pastas daily for lunch and dinner (233 Mason Avenue, ☎ 757-331-1600).

A few doors down, **Harbor Grille** serves fresh local seafood as it comes into season. It has great soft shell crabs and a raw bar. Serving breakfast and lunch, Tuesday-Saturday; dinner, Thursday-Saturday (203 Mason Avenue, ☎ 757-331-3005).

Rebecca's serves down-home cooking in a 1930s grocery store turned arcade and dance hall that was once a Sears catalog store. It's named for the daughter of owner Eddie Bell, who is a former oysterman. Serving lunch and dinner; closed Mondays (7 Strawberry Street, Cape Charles, ☎ 757-331-3879).

Lodging

Cape Charles has a handful of motels, and a half-dozen B&Bs awaiting the traveler looking for a quiet stay in a port town. **Cape Charles House B&B** is a 1912 Colonial Revival with a wrap-around porch, and is filled with antiques and collectibles (645 Tazewell Avenue, ☎ 757-331-4920, www.capecharleshouse.com, $$).

Chesapeake Charm B&B is furnished with antiques and treasures made by the owners' four grandmothers (202 Madison Avenue, ☎ 757-331-2676, www.chesapeakecharmbnb.com, $$).

Sea Gate B&B has an enclosed breakfast porch decorated with artifacts collected during the owner's travels (9 Tazewell Avenue, ☎ 757-331-2206, www.bbhost.com/seagate, $$).

Wilson-Lee House is a 1906 Colonial Revival home furnished eclectically with period and contemporary styles (403 Tazewell Avenue, ☎ 757-331-1954, www.wilsonleehouse.com, $$).

Sterling House B&B is just three doors from the beach and the innkeepers will lend you umbrellas and bicycles. There's a hot tub on the back deck (9 Randolph Avenue, ☎ 757-331-2483, www.Sterling-Inn.com, $$).

About 10 minutes south of Cape Charles is **Nottingham Ridge**, an historic home on 100 acres with a private beach, offering four guest rooms (Nottingham Ridge Lane, ☎ 757-331-1010, www.nottinghamridge.com, $$).

 Also on Nottingham Ridge Lane and with a private beach is **Pickett's Harbor Bed & Breakfast**, which takes pets with a $25 charge (☎ 757-331-2212, www.bbonline.com/va/pickharb, $$).

 Near the entrance to the Chesapeake Bay Bridge-Tunnel, **Best Western Sunset Beach Resort** is a full-service hotel with 74 rooms, a pool, and a private beach. Pets accepted with a $10 charge (☎ 800-899-4786 or 757-331-1776, $$).

More rustic accommodations are found at **Cherrystone Camping Resort** in nearby Cheriton, offering 300 acres of Chesapeake Bay waterfront for camping or cabin rental. There are hot showers, a restaurant, four piers, boat rentals, fishing, mini-golf, playgrounds, and four pools (☎ 757-331-3063, www.cherrystoneva.com).

Information

Cape Charles/Northampton County Chamber of Commerce, ☎ 757-331-2304, www.ccncchamber.com.

Events

Cape Charles hosts July Fourth fireworks on the beach and the **Eastern Shore Blue Crab Music Festival** later in July (☎ 757-331-2304).

In October, there's **Schooner Feast** (☎ 757-331-1008), along with a **Harvest Festival** and a **Birding Festival** at Sunset Beach Resort near Kiptopeke (☎ 757-787-2460).

Trip Journal

The Barrier Islands

Along the seaside of Virginia's Eastern Shore is a chain of barrier islands, uninhabited except for wildlife. This wasn't always so. Since the mid-1800s, people have tried taming this coastal wilderness by building beach resorts, hunting and fishing clubs, and even entire communities. All have been lost to the ravages of sea and time.

On an overnight kayak trip to **Mockhorn Island** we discovered the well-preserved relics of a once posh turn-of-the-century hunting retreat. The Cushman family of New York City brought hunters to their own private game preserve. The kills of waterfowl were tremendous, this being before imposed limits, the outlawing of live decoys and killing of shorebirds. The 1902 lodge is still standing, as is an original 1852 house, although bamboo and ivy are taking over (Mrs. Cushman was fond of planting non-native species on the island). A large livestock barn was used for dances. Another barn served as a slaughterhouse. Rusty hooks and scalding tubs testify to the self-sufficiency forced on island inhabitants by their remote location.

The amount of effort used to transform this wild island into a hunter's playground is still visible – including a three-foot-tall concrete wall built around the farm to protect crops from salt-water intrusion. Everything had to be ferried over from the mainland; hence the club had its own small herd of cows and even grew feed for them. The Cushmans sold the island in 1948 to a government contractor who lavishly entertained generals that were flown in by helicopter for a weekend of hunting or fishing. Today, Mockhorn is a state wildlife refuge, with public access allowed.

Hog Island had a thriving community of about 250 people called Broadwater. Residents succumbed to a series of storms, and after the hurricane of 1933, gave up altogether, moving 17 houses by barge to the mainland town of **Willis Wharf**. The relocated community is now known as "Little Hog Island." Many islanders even moved their dead from the cemeteries to mainland graves. The last baby born on the island, now nearly 70, lives in Willis Wharf. (Many photographs of Hog Island and its inhabitants were taken by noted New York photographer Rudolph Eckemeyer and are in the Smithsonian Institution collection.)

For some 50 years, the resort on **Cobb Island** was one of America's most famous hunting and fishing resorts. Nathan Cobb owned and operated it, with help from his three sons. Arthur, the youngest, had a knack for accounting and a weakness for poker. Son Nathan Jr. lent his marksmanship on the island's many wildfowl hunts. Warren Cobb sailed and guided guests on hunts, fishing trips and egg- or shell-gathering expeditions. A railway stop on the Eastern Shore railroad serviced resort clientele. Carts and wagons brought guests and luggage into Oyster, Virginia, where a sloop carried all to Cobb's Island. Sportsmen reveled in the rugged life of hunting, and gentlemen enjoyed drinking, dances and games. Author Thomas Dixon visited in the 1890s, and several residents were photographed by Mathew Brady, the famous Civil War photographer.

In 2001, one of the last buildings on Cobb Island, a lifesaving station, was moved to the shore and restored by the Nature Conservancy. A century ago, the island was a magnet for the rich and famous, with a large resort hotel built by the Cobbs with their earnings from salvaging shipwrecks. Decoys carved by Nathan Cobb Jr. are exhibited in museums and worth thousands of dollars.

Assateague Island is best known for its wild Chincoteague ponies and its National Seashore, but until a 1962 storm wiped them out, there were about 50 dwellings here, a school and a store.

Severe storms, and perhaps more devastating, the gradually changing shoreline, doomed each of these communities and retreats. Locations of some buildings, and even lighthouses, are now under the sea, as the islands of sand shift continually. The lodge and buildings at Mockhorn are a notable exception, and probably represent the most intact historic buildings on any of the barrier islands.

Virginia's Eastern Shore

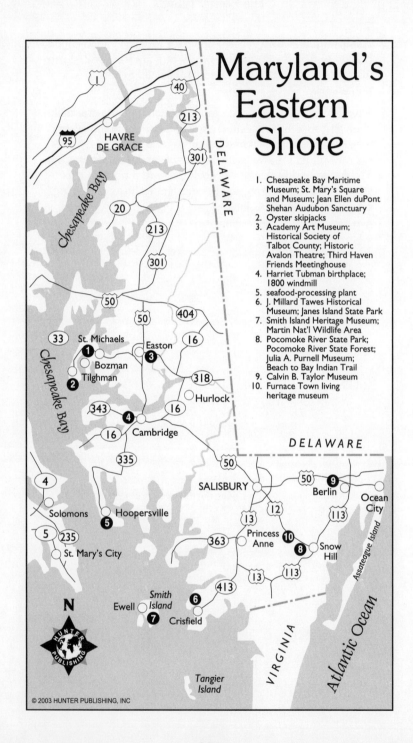

Maryland's Eastern Shore

1. Chesapeake Bay Maritime Museum; St. Mary's Square and Museum; Jean Ellen duPont Shehan Audubon Sanctuary
2. Oyster skipjacks
3. Academy Art Museum; Historical Society of Talbot County; Historic Avalon Theatre; Third Haven Friends Meetinghouse
4. Harriet Tubman birthplace; 1800 windmill
5. seafood-processing plant
6. J. Millard Tawes Historical Museum; Janes Island State Park
7. Smith Island Heritage Museum; Martin Nat'l Wildlife Area
8. Pocomoke River State Park; Pocomoke River State Forest; Julia A. Purnell Museum; Beach to Bay Indian Trail
9. Calvin B. Taylor Museum
10. Furnace Town living heritage museum

Maryland's Eastern Shore

Its Proximity to the major cities of Washington DC and Baltimore has caused Maryland's portion of the Eastern Shore to develop more rapidly than Virginia's. The largest towns are lively and crowded beach and bay getaways, with top-notch shopping and sailing. Smaller towns still retain their fishing village charm, where you can watch crab and oyster boats bringing in their catch, then sample some of it at a down-home restaurant.

THE TOWNS
▩ St. Michaels
▩ Tilghman Island
▩ Easton
▩ Crisfield
▩ Princess Anne
▩ Snow Hill
▩ Furnace Town

Getting Here

You can access the Eastern Shore two ways: over the **Bay Bridge Tunnel** from Annapolis, or from the north via routes **213** or **301** in Delaware.

There are several regional airports on the Eastern Shore: **Cambridge-Dorchester Airport** (☎ 410-228-4571), **Easton Municipal Airport** (☎ 410-770-8055, www.talbgov.org), and **Ocean City Municipal Airport** (☎ 410-213-2471).

Regional Information

State Welcome Centers are located on US 301 near Centreville, and on US 13 near the Virginia border.

St. Michaels

Around Town

It's obvious people come to St. Michaels to spend money. Boating and shopping seem to be the main distractions, and the quality of both are, quite simply, splendid. You could spend a couple of days browsing boutique after boutique housed in lovely, restored old houses from the 18th and 19th centuries. The main street, Talbot, is lined with well-cared-for Victorian and Colonial structures selling designer clothing, *lots* of antiques, and eclectic home furnishings.

I entered a cottage-like shop, the **"At Home"** store run by the adjacent Chesapeake Trading Co., and asked if I could just move in. They said, "Sure, if you pay the rent!" It was my dream house, with a light-filled, all-white, fully furnished bedroom, living and dining rooms, decorated in that "shabby chic" style of comfortable elegance. There is even a brick-paved courtyard where you can sit and have a coffee from the Chesapeake Trading Co. store, which also sells books, clothing and jewelry (102 S. Talbot Street, ☎ 410-745-9797, www.chesapeaketrading.com). A few doors down at **Flamingo Flats** (100 S. Talbot Street, ☎ 410-745-2053 or 800-HOT-8841), famous for its gourmet hot sauces and tasting bar, a local author was signing copies of his books. Keith Walters retired from NASA to live in the tiny nearby community of Bozman, to fish and write – about fishing. In the cozy **Town Hall Mall** of shops (☎ 410-745-0063), Phil Heim was making custom jewelry of gold, silver and gemstones. He'll even size a bracelet for you while you wait.

Amidst all the Saturday shopping frenzy, a bride and groom emerged from Christ Episcopal Church, a horse and carriage waiting for them at the curb. A block away, **Justine's Ice Cream Parlor**, on the corner of Talbot Street and Railroad Avenue, was busy with lickers coming and going – the door barely getting a chance to close (101 Talbot Street, ☎ 410-745-5416).

After the initial rush of shopper's delight, St. Michaels' retail offerings began to all look quite similar, and I wondered what else there was to do. A rumble from my stomach answered that question immediately.

At the end of Mulberry Street, we found a place to sit and eat on the water at **St. Michaels Crab and Steak House** (see *Dining*, page 209). Munching on the local favorite – fried oyster sandwiches – we passed the time watching yachts and pleasure cruisers look for a place to tie up in the crowded marina. A pair of middle-aged bikers maneuvered huge Harley cruisers onto the dock. A water taxi filled with a dozen sightseers passed by. Painted on the side: "25-minute scenic harbor tours: $6 adults, $3 kids." A young family rented bicycles from a long row of bright blue bikes, lined up close to the dock's edge, where piles of oysters once sat.

The restaurant, I learned, was built in the 1830s as an oyster-shucking shed. The iron anchors propped up in the landscaping outside once weighed down local oyster boats. I mused how this very spot where I sat was once the scene of the smelly, dirty work of unloading a waterman's daily catch. My eyes wandered over luxury cruisers and yachts costing several times more than most people's houses, tied to piers where not so long ago, salty, weatherworn workboats brought in their harvest.

St. Michaels, incorporated in 1804, prospered first as a shipbuilding center, then as a seafood processor of oysters and blue crabs. The 1829 opening of the Chesapeake and Delaware Canal added new seafood customers in Philadelphia and Wilmington to the existing ones in Baltimore and Annapolis. St. Michaels shipbuilders became known for small, shallow draft boats like the bugeye and the log canoe. The steamboat era at the end of the 19th century brought tourists and another means of shipping seafood. One of the larger packers was an African-American-owned business, Coulbourne and Jewett, located on the site now occupied by the Chesapeake Bay Maritime Museum (see below). As the oyster succumbed to over-harvesting and disease, tourism has turned out to be much more lucrative than seafood.

Streets once alive on weekends with watermen out on the town after a hard day's work are now the place to hob-nob with the rich and famous. Except for two bars, the streets pretty much close up at 6pm. That's not to say any of St. Michaels' charm has been lost; it's only enhanced by knowing what the town once was.

Attractions

Chesapeake Bay Maritime Museum is a great place to learn hands-on about the industries that built St. Michaels – shipbuilding, oystering and crabbing. It has a complex of nine exhibit buildings, the world's largest collection of traditional Bay boats, a working boatyard, and the 1879 Hooper Strait Lighthouse. Open daily, year-round; 9am-5pm in spring and fall, until 6pm in summer, closing at 4pm in winter. Closed Thanksgiving, Christmas and New Year's days. Admission is

Maryland's Eastern Shore

$8.50 adults, $4 for children ages four to 17 (Mill Street, ☎ 410-745-2916, www.cbmm.org).

St. Mary's Square between Mulberry and Chestnut streets is a feature of the original street plan made by James Braddock in 1778, who named the new town St. Michaels after the Episcopal parish nearby. He died before its fruition, but the plan was re-created in 1804-06. Today you can see the Mechanics' Bell, which was rung to mark the start and end of the workday for carpenters in nearby shipyards. **St. Mary's Square Museum** offers the experience of St. Michaels in the 1800s. The building, moved here in 1964, was built as a dwelling for a waterman in 1865 of huge timbers salvaged from a gristmill. Open weekends, May-October, or by appointment (☎ 410-745-9561 or 410-745-3984).

For a rustic, quiet change of pace, take a jaunt down to **Tilghman Island**, either by car, or a 24-mile round-trip bicycle trip. You can rent them at St. Michaels Marina at the end of Mulberry Street (☎ 410-745-2400, www.stmichaelsmarina.com). It's only $4 an hour or $16 for the whole day. It might sound like a long trip, but it's completely and utterly flat on wide, well-paved bike lanes down a narrow and rural neck of land. The neck is so narrow that at times you get glimpses of water on both sides, Harris Creek to your left, and the Chesapeake Bay to your right. See the section on *Tilghman Island*, pages 212-215, for more information.

Recreation

Tour de Shore can arrange everything for a biking trip: waterfront lodging, repairs, road support, and of course, the bicycles (114 Conner Street, ☎ 866-745-9011, www.biketds.com).

Captain Ed Farley of the skipjack ***H.M. Krentz*** takes sightseers out on trips when it's not oyster season. He picks up passengers at the Crab Claw Restaurant at Navy Point, at 10:30am April-October, but call him first for a reservation. Skipjacks are oyster-harvesting vessels powered by sail. The *Krentz* is one of the last such vessels built, in 1955. See the *Tilghman Island* section (pages 212-215) for more on skipjacks (☎ 410-745-6080, www.oystercatcher.com).

The Lucky Dog Catamaran Company will take you on a two-hour cruise aboard a 36-foot catamaran (St. Michaels Marina, Mulberry Street, ☎ 410-745-6203, www.luckydogcatamarancompany.com).

Patriot Cruises operates historic narrated cruises April-November out of the Chesapeake Bay Maritime Museum (☎ 410-745-3100, www.patriotcruises.com). **Dockside Express** gives historic and ghost tours by boat and foot (St. Michaels Harbor, ☎ 888-31-CRUISE, www.docksidexpress.com), and **Chesapeake Carriage Company** offers tours of St. Michaels by horse-drawn carriage (☎ 410-745-4011).

In the small community of Bozman, nine miles from St. Michaels, the **Jean Ellen duPont Shehan Audubon Sanctuary** occupies a 950-acre peninsula with eight miles of shoreline and 10 miles of trails. Call for hours (☎ 410-745-9283, www.audubonmddc.org/JEDSAS).

Dining

On the Water

At **St. Michaels Crab and Steak House**, you can eat inside the 1830s rustic tavern, or out on the patio under an umbrella-shaded picnic table. The building, one of St. Michaels' oldest, was originally an oyster-shucking shed. The menu says they'll prepare almost anything you request, "even if it's not on the menu." There's a raw bar, and if you order steamed crabs, they'll cover the table with brown paper, bring big, wooden mallets, and give you instructions on opening them (305 Mulberry Street, ☎ 410-745-3737, www.stmichaelscrabhouse. com).

Nearby is the **Town Dock Restaurant**, also with outdoor seating, offering seafood, steak and a vegetarian menu. A Friday seafood buffet and Sunday brunch are served (125 Mulberry Street, ☎ 800-884-0103, www. town-dock.com).

The Crab Claw Restaurant serves Maryland blue crabs every which way with harbor views (304 Mill Street at Navy Point, ☎ 410-745-2900, www.thecrabclaw.com).

On the Main Drag

208 Talbot (the name is the address) serves "innovative gourmet" dinners, Wednesday-Sunday (☎ 410-745-3838, www.208talbot.com).

Bistro St. Michaels strives to re-create a Parisian Bistro on the "left bank" of the Chesapeake (403 S. Talbot Street, ☎ 410-745-9111).

Chesapeake Cove Restaurant serves up seafood, prime rib and baby back ribs (204 S. Talbot, ☎ 410-745-3300).

Maryland's Eastern Shore

Madison's **West End** serves American gourmet with a Caribbean twist, original artwork and live music (106 N. Talbot Street, ☎ 410-745-0299).

Mezzalune Italian Ristorante is fine dining Italian-style (205 N. Talbot Street, ☎ 410-745-2911, www.mezzaluna.org).

Tavern on Talbot (409 S. Talbot Street, ☎ 410-745-9343) and **Poppi's Restaurant** are affordable, family places (207 N. Talbot Street, ☎ 410-745-3158).

Carpenter Street Saloon (113 S. Talbot Street, ☎ 410-745-5111) is actually two buildings, one a drinking establishment, the other a family restaurant; and **Characters Café** (200 S. Talbot Street, ☎ 410-745-6206) is a bar whimsically decorated with murals of cartoon characters. It offers a full menu of seafood, sandwiches and baskets, and live entertainment Friday and Saturday nights.

See also the Harbour Inn in *Lodging*, below.

Lodging

There are more than two dozen inns and bed & breakfasts, from Victorian tearooms to grand waterfront hotels. Here's just a sampling. For a full list, visit www.stmichaelsmd.org.

★ TIP

Most lodgings in the area offer substantial savings mid-week and off-season.

St. Michaels Harbour Inn & Marina is a waterfront suite hotel with outdoor pool and the **Harbour Lights** restaurant with views from a second floor dining room, creative cuisine of seafood, game and beef (101 N. Harbor Road; restaurant ☎ 410-745-5102; inn ☎ 410-745-9001; www.harbourinn.com, $$$$).

The Old Brick Inn has 12 rooms in an 1816 inn with fireplaces and an outdoor pool (401 S. Talbot Street, ☎ 401-745-3323, www.old-brickinn.com, $$$).

Barrett's Bed & Breakfast has a tea room serving tea, espresso, scones, and homemade pastries, daily 2-5pm (204 N. Talbot Street, ☎ 410-745-3322, www.barrettbb.com, $$$$).

Five Gables Inn & Spa has porches, fireplaces, an indoor pool, steam room and sauna (209 N. Talbot Street, ☎ 877-466-0100, www. fivegables.com, $$$$).

Dr. Dodson House Bed & Breakfast is a 1799 brick house where complimentary hors d'oeuvres and cocktails are served in the parlor (200 Cherry Street, ☎ 410-745-3691, www.drdodsonhouse.com, $$$).

The **Victoriana Inn** has harbor views and fireplaces, and is right next to the Maritime Museum (205 Cherry Street, ☎ 888-316-1282, www. victorianainn.com, $$$$).

The Parsonage Inn is an eight-room brick Victorian with brass beds, fireplaces and dining (210 N. Talbot Street, ☎ 410-745-5519 or 800-394-5519, www.Parsonage-Inn.com, $$).

The newly restored 1908 Victorian **George Brooks House B&B** is on seven acres where guests can enjoy an outdoor pool and hot tub, formal gardens and bicycles (Rolles Range Road and Route 33, ☎ 410-745-0999, www.georgebrookshouse.com, $$$).

 The Inn At Perry Cabin is one of the world's best country house hotels, and they actually welcome pets! Fine dining and a health facility are offered in this 1812 white Colonial mansion. There are 35 guest rooms and six suites, many with canopy beds, fireplaces and outdoor sitting areas overlooking the Miles River (308 Watkins Lane, ☎ 800-722-2949, www.perrycabin.com, $$$$).

 Kemp House Inn is an 1807 Georgian where General Robert E. Lee once stayed. Pets are welcome in the cottage (412 S. Talbot Street, ☎ 410-745-2243, www.kemphouseinn.com, $$).

> ★ DID YOU KNOW?
>
> Novelist **James Michener** lived in St. Michaels while researching and writing *Chesapeake*.

Information

St. Michaels Business Association, ☎ 800-808-7622, www.stmichaelsmd.org.

Talbot County Office of Tourism, 11 N. Washington Street, ☎ 410-770-8000, www.tourtalbot.org.

Maryland's Eastern Shore

Event

The **Antique & Classic Boat Festival** in mid-June brings more than 100 exceptional crafts for the judged show at the Chesapeake Bay Maritime Museum (☎ 410-745-2916).

Christmas in St. Michaels is a magical time, with a tour of decorated homes, a parade, and old-fashioned holiday traditions (☎ 410-745-0745, www.stmichaelsmd.org/christmas).

Tilghman Island

Around Town

For a glimpse of what St. Michaels used to be like, head south on Route 33 to Tilghman Island, a relaxed and truly authentic fishing village where most of the inhabitants still make their living from the Chesapeake Bay.

What makes Tilghman an island is a scant few dozen feet of water spanned by Knapps Narrow Bridge, a counterbalanced drawbridge that sets so low, chances of seeing it operate more than once during a visit are pretty good. It only takes a few minutes for the larger sailboats to pass by, and since there really isn't any reason to be in a hurry on the island, it proves a pleasant distraction.

Shopping on Tilghman isn't quite on par with St. Michaels, which is a nice change. There are a handful of quaint antiques and gift shops. An outfitter rents kayaks, while landlubbers can explore old cemeteries or the 57-acre wildlife preserve where bald eagles nest. There's a country store, the Island Market, and the Book Bank, a nautical-themed bookstore in the former bank building.

The island's biggest claim to fame is something worth seeking out. Down Gibsontown Road on Dogwood Harbor is the home of the last commercial fishing sailing fleet in North America. Between six and 10 skipjacks work out of Tilghman each winter. They're among the last in the world still in operation, and their crews carry out a tradition passed down through generations. Hundreds of skipjacks once cruised the bay, taking in enormous quantities of oysters. Between 1890 and 1910 it's estimated that a thousand skipjacks were built. Their large decks made them the oyster-dredging boat of choice, particularly since

Maryland's enactment in 1867 of a law restricting oyster-dredging to sail-powered vessels (a 1967 modification to the law allows the sailboat to be augmented by motorized "push" boats two days a week). Over-harvesting and two virulent oyster diseases all but decimated the Chesapeake oyster and the skipjack fleets by the last quarter of the 20th century.

But at least for now, you can still experience firsthand the work of an oysterman; help draw up the sails and dredge up some oysters. A good day, they'll tell you, is bringing in about 80 bushels (the limit is 150), working from sunrise to sunset, often in frigid temperatures, since the oyster season is November-March. To augment their income from oystering, the supply of which dwindles lower each year, several skipjacks take aboard the curious in the off-season, which happens to be the tourist on-season. They typically charge about $30 per person for a sightseeing cruise and oyster-dredging demonstration. They'll be glad to dredge up some bi-valves to show how it's done, and even open a few up for you.

To arrange a trip, contact captain Wade Murphy of the **Rebecca T. Ruark**, possibly the oldest skipjack on the bay, built in 1886 (☎ 410-886-2176, www.skipjack.org), or captain Ed Farley of the skipjack **H.M. Krentz**, one of the last skipjacks built, in 1955 (☎ 410-745-6080, www.oystercatcher.com). The *Rebecca* operates out of Dogwood Harbor, and the *Krentz* has started picking passengers up at The Crab Claw Restaurant in St. Michaels.

Maryland's Eastern Shore

> ★ HOW TO SAY IT
>
> Say "TILL-man." The 'gh' is silent.

Dining

The **Bay Hundred Restaurant** is just before you cross the bridge to Tilghman. Dine outside or in, on seafood, steaks, and Cajun and Creole fare (☎ 410-886-2126).

The Bridge Restaurant offers waterfront dining daily from noon to 10pm, and bar service until 1am (6136 Tilghman Road, ☎ 410-886-2330, www.bridge-restaurant.com).

Most of the dining establishments also have lodging, so look for them under *Lodging*, below.

Lodging

Just before crossing the bridge to Tilghman is **Knapp's Narrows Marina and Guest Quarters,** which caters to boaters, with transient dockage, a laundry and fishing charters. There's a restaurant, pool and cabana with observation deck (☎ 410-886-2720, www.knappsnarrowsmarina.com, $$).

Harrison's Country Inn, Chesapeake House Restaurant and Sport Fishing Center has everything the fisherman needs, including a hearty breakfast served extra early so you can board your charter fishing boat by 7am. When you return, dinner and a good night's sleep await. Pets are welcome with a $15 charge (21551 Chesapeake House Drive, ☎ 410-886-2121 or 410-886-2109, www.chesapeakehouse.com, $$).

Lazy Jack Inn B&B has Jacuzzis and fireplaces in an 1855 waterfront home with elegant rooms decorated with original artwork. The innkeeper, Captain Mike Richards, can arrange for a champagne sunset sail or lighthouse tour on *The Lady Patty*, his 1931 yacht (☎ 410-886-2215, 800-690-5080, www.lazyjackinn.com, $$$).

Tilghman Island Inn is a 20-room waterfront resort with gardens, views of the marsh and Chesapeake Bay sunsets. There's a spa where you can get a massage or herbal bath, and gourmet dining in the Bay Watch Room or the Gallery Dining Room, which showcases the work of regional artists. There's a pool, transient marina, charter fishing and boat rentals (Coopertown Road, ☎ 800-866-2141, www.tilghmanislandinn.com, $$$).

Black Walnut Point Bed & Breakfast Inn is on a private peninsula formed by the Choptank River and the Chesapeake Bay, with expansive views of both. For activity there's a pool, spa, tennis, fishing, boating, and hiking in a wildlife sanctuary, or just take a nap in a hammock. There's also a waterfront cottage (Black Walnut Road, ☎ 410-886-2452, http://tilghmanisland.com/blackwalnut, $$)

The **Chesapeake Wood Duck Inn** is an 1890 former boarding house from the steamboat era. Once there was even a bordello here, but today it's an elegant Victorian bed & breakfast furnished with antiques, heirlooms and art by local artist Maureen Brannon. The inn has six guest rooms and a cottage. Children 14 and older are welcome (Gibsontown Road at Dogwood Harbor, 800-956-2070, www.woodduckinn.com, $$$).

Norma's Guest House is actually two fully furnished guesthouses, each with a deck overlooking Dogwood Harbor (☎ 410-886-2395, www.tilghman.com/normas, $$).

Sinclair House was built in the 1920s as a fishing camp. The inn-keepers, Monica from Peru, and Jake, who served in West Africa with UNICEF, have interesting sea-faring stories to tell (5718 Black Walnut Point Road, ☎ 410-886-2147 or 888-859-2147, www.tilghmanis-land.com/sinclair, $$).

Information

For information about **Tilghman Island businesses**, including lodging, shopping, fishing and marinas, see www.tilghmanisland.com.

Talbot County Office of Tourism, 11 N. Washington Street, ☎ 410-770-8000, www.tourtalbot.org.

Events

The Tilghman Island Seafood Festival is in late June at Kronsberg Park with live music, parade, crab races, crab-picking contest and arts and crafts.

Tilghman Island Day in October is a rare opportunity to see watermen in their element, through workboat races, a boat-docking contest, exhibits, music, and, of course, plenty of seafood, including oysters served every which way.

Easton

Around Town

A commemorative jar in the window of **Hill's Pharmacy** in Easton bears the inscription "In recognition of dispensing one million prescriptions. Eli Lilly & Co. July 3, 1986." The family-owned pharmacy has been a local institution for nearly 75 years. We peered, eyes and hands pressed up to the glass, at this and other objects – old apothecary jars, pillboxes and medical instruments – bemoaning how we couldn't get inside and sit at the old-fashioned soda fountain others had told us

Maryland's Eastern Shore

about (it was past closing time). At that moment, a man came along and, with a set of keys, started opening the door. He gladly let us inside to see the soda fountain. The man was Mark Lappen, husband of Pamela Hill Lappen, who, along with her sister, are the third generation of pharmacists in the business their grandfather opened in 1928.

In an adjoining back room lit by a large skylight stands a long marble counter lined with stools where generations have had an ice cream soda or a sandwich. It's Maryland marble along the top, Italian marble on the front, for a total of 14 very heavy pieces of stone. Lappen should know – he moved it himself 20 years ago, piece-by-piece, from the front of the pharmacy to this larger room, which can accommodate more patrons with café tables and chairs. Out front, holes are still visible in one aisle where the stools used to be.

Lappen eagerly points to the spot where Bing Crosby stood and sang the first stanza of *White Christmas* to Pamela Lappen in the late 1970s. She had asked for his autograph on her copy of his famous Christmas record album, but he did her one better with a live rendition. He was staying just a half-block away, at the renowned **Tidewater Inn**.

These are the kinds of memories a family collects over 75 years in business. They now have three other, much newer, pharmacies, but this one remains the family's pride and joy. They've sold sundries to many notable Tidewater Inn guests over the years, including Tom Selleck and Adam West (who starred as Batman).

The rich and famous, as well as everyday sportsmen, have found the small town on the Eastern Shore a most genteel host for sport fishing and waterfowl hunting. In the last 25 years, the **Waterfowl Festival** has grown to bring upwards of 20,000 people to the town each November. The Duck and Goose Calling Contests bring competitors from all over the world.

When it's not hunting season, Easton is the busy seat of Talbot County government, a "weekday" town, as opposed to the weekend town of St. Michaels. Courthouse-related activity and shoppers keep the streets busy all day, but most businesses are locked up tight by 5pm. Unlike most Colonial towns that have built progressively newer and bigger courthouses, the original 1712 courthouse is still in use, albeit expanded over the years (☎ 410-770-8001). The historic downtown is full of antiques shops, boutiques, art galleries, coffee shops and interesting restaurants.

There's an indoor alley you can walk through to take a shortcut from Washington to Harrison streets. It's the only wooden sidewalk in Easton. Along the way are a deli, antiques shops and an art gallery.

Attractions

Academy Art Museum hosts changing exhibits of national and regional artists in an 1820s schoolhouse, merged with another 19th-century building. There are five galleries, art and dance studios, and a library. The museum is open Monday-Saturday, 10am-4pm; Wednesday until 9pm (106 South Street, ☎ 410-822-2787, www.art-academy.org).

Historical Society of Talbot County has three historic houses, a museum, antiques shop and award-winning Federal-style gardens. Pick up a self-guided walking tour brochure of town here. Admission is free. Open Tuesday-Friday, 11am-3pm; Saturday, 10am-4pm (25 S. Washington Street, ☎ 410-822-0773, www.hstc.org).

When it was built in 1921, the art deco **Historic Avalon Theatre** brought the latest in silent films and live vaudeville shows to Easton. Today, restored to its former glory, the marquee bills performing arts, community events and educational programs (40 E. Dover Street, ☎ 410-822-0345, www.avalontheatre.com). Each year the theater hosts **The Eastern Shore Chamber Music Festival** for two weeks in June (☎ 410-819-0380, www.bluecrab.org/escmf).

Local historians claim the **Third Haven Friends Meetinghouse** (1682) is the oldest religious building still in use in the country, and the earliest dated building in the state. There's a small museum and gardens you can walk through (405 S. Washington Street, ☎ 410-822-0293).

Easton shops close at 5pm sharp, even on weekends.

Maryland's Eastern Shore

Dining

Eagle Spirits Restaurant and Flagstix Bar & Grill in the Easton Club serve entrées from sandwiches to seafood in the elegant dining room, at the bar, or on the patio (28449 Clubhouse Drive, ☎ 410-820-4100, www.eastonclub.com). **Restaurant Columbia**, in a 1795 historic home, serves dinner with white linens, crystal and candlelight. Original artwork and fresh flowers complete the ambience (28 South Washington Street, ☎ 410-770-5172).

At **General Tanuki's,** cuisine from Pacific Rim countries is the specialty of the house, with Thai, Hawaiian, Filipino, Japanese, Vietnamese, and even some Californian samplings (25 Goldsborough Street, ☎ 410-819-0707). **Out of the Fire Café & Wine Bar** serves California and Mediterranean cuisine (22 Goldsborough Street, ☎ 410-770-4777, http://outofthefire.com).

Breakfast and lunch at **Hill's Soda Fountain** in Hill's Pharmacy cost under $5. Sit on a twirly stool at the marble counter or one of the café tables, and order a malt and a burger, just like they've been serving for 75 years (30 East Dover Street, ☎ 410-822-2666). **Coffee East** is a combination coffee shop, bakery, ice cream fountain, café, and wine and brew bar. It actually occupies two buildings in the historic district. High ceilings, large windows and wooden floors create an airy, hip and comfortable atmosphere for chatting over a cup or glass of your favorite beverage (5 Goldsborough Street, ☎ 410-819-6711).

Old Mill Market & Deli serves homemade soups and sandwiches (1021 N. Washington Street, ☎ 410-822-9613), **Mason's** sells gourmet food items and has a café (22 S. Harrison Street, ☎ 410-822-3204), and **Olde Towne Creamery** dishes up ice cream, smoothies, sundaes and Italian ice (9B Goldsborough Street, ☎ 410-820-5223).

The **Hunters Tavern Restaurant** is renowned for its classic regional American menu, serving lunch and dinner daily, and an exceptional Sunday brunch (101 E. Dover Street, ☎ 410-822-1300 or 800-237-8775, www.tidewaterinn.com).

See also The Tidewater Inn and The Inn at Easton, below.

Lodging

 The Tidewater Inn may be "only" just over 50 years old, but the tall ceilings, fireplaces, dark mahogany woodwork, and 18th-century reproduction furniture give off the air of a fine old hotel. There are 114 Federal-style guest rooms and an outdoor pool. The inn caters to hunters in the fall, as it has since being built in 1949. Hotel staff will arrange duck-hunting guide services, early morning hunt breakfasts, and kenneling of hunting dogs. Pets are not allowed in the rooms, but the inn has its own kennel, available to guests at no charge (101 E. Dover Street, ☎ 410-822-1300 or 800-237-8775, www.tidewaterinn.com, $$).

The Inn at Easton is in a Federal mansion that was built in stages in a period from 1790 to 1894. Modern comfort awaits guests inside, where antiques are paired with a vibrant paint scheme, and all rooms have been restored with private baths. The menu in the dining room changes every three weeks and utilizes fresh, local ingredients. The experience is of a fine European hotel and restaurant (28 S. Harrison Street, ☎ 410-822-4910 or 888-800-8091, www.theinnateaston.com, $$$).

The Bishop's House Bed & Breakfast is the 1880 home of former Maryland Governor Philip Frances Thomas and, later, the Episcopal bishop until 1955. There are five large rooms with private baths, and bicycle rentals available. Note: The house will be closed January-March, 2003 for renovations. Children 12 and over welcome (214 Goldsborough Street, ☎ 410-820-7290 or 800-223-7290, www.bishopshouse.com, $$).

Chaffinch House is a beautifully restored and colorfully decorated 1893 Queen Anne Victorian in the historic district. There are six rooms, period furnishings, hardwood floors and a wrap-around porch. Children under 12 are permitted with prior approval (132 S. Harrison Street, ☎ 410-822-5074 or 800-861-5074, www.chaffinchhouse.com, $$).

 Days Inn Easton allows pets with a nightly charge of $12 (7018 Ocean Gateway, ☎ 410-822-4600, 800-DAYS INN, $$).

John S. McDaniel House is an 1865 Victorian with six spacious guest rooms in the heart of the historic district. Full gourmet, multi-course breakfast served (always with a vegetarian option). Children are welcome (14 N. Aurora Street, ☎ 410-822-3704 or 877-822-5702, www.bnblist.com/md/mcdaniel, $$).

Information

Town of Easton, ☎ 410-822-0065, www.eastonmd.org.

Talbot County Office of Tourism, 11 N. Washington Street, ☎ 410-770-8000, www.tourtalbot.org.

Event

People from all around the country "flock" to the **Waterfowl Festival**, the second weekend in November, for a wildlife art sale of paintings, sculpture, decoys, photographs and crafts in 18 sites throughout the town. There are retriever, shooting and fly-fishing demonstrations, goose and duck calling contests and a decoy auction (☎ 410-822-4567, www.waterfowlfestival.org).

Trip Journal

Dorchester County

Driving south on Route 50 from Talbot County, you'll cross the Choptank River and enter into Dorchester County. Visitors are immediately greeted by a spectacular, giant white sail, grounded on the south shore. This is the home of the county's new visitor center. The expansive river views and the massive children's playground make the visitor center alone worth a pleasant pit stop.

Cambridge is a weekday town, busy because it's the county seat, but in 2002 a new Hyatt Regency opened on Route 50. It's a further indication that Dorchester County is well on its way to becoming a tourist destination, rather than a stop on the way to somewhere else.

This isn't your typical small town getaway, with Victorian inns and hip boutiques lining Main Street. Dorchester County is an enclave of unique historic and natural attractions, including the **birthplace of Harriet Tubman**, the largest number of nesting bald eagles on the East Coast (outside of Florida), and an **1800 windmill** that will make you think of Don Quixote and Holland.

In **Hurlock,** the ***Dorothy-Megan*** paddlewheel riverboat is berthed at the **Suicide Bridge Restaurant** for sightseeing and dinner cruises (☎ 410-943-4775). **Hoopersville** is a fishing village where you can watch watermen bringing in their catch, or tour a seafood-processing plant (**Mid-Atlantic Tour & Receptive Services,** ☎ 800-769-5912). **Old Salty's** is a good home-style restaurant there (☎ 410-377-3752).

For more information on this area, contact the **Dorchester County Office of Tourism,** ☎ 800-522-TOUR, www.tour-dorchester.org.

 TIP

Tune your car radio in to 1700 AM for visitor information, directions and events for the Harriet Tubman birthplace, the Underground Railroad driving tour, the Blackwater National Wildlife Refuge, and the Spocott Windmill.

Crisfield

Around Town

Crisfield is an unpretentious port town with a clear sense of identity. Here, it's all about seafood – the catching, packaging and consumption of it. Several seafood restaurants have views onto Somers Cove or the Chesapeake Bay. In season, charter fishing and sightseeing boats stay busy entering and leaving the harbor. A long fishing pier attracts anglers of all ages, while a museum and a handful of shops have nautical themes. And most refreshing, a good bit of the town's waterfront is still occupied by the industry that built it – seafood processing, aka "crab-picking" and "oyster-shucking." You can even take a tour of active seafood houses through the local museum.

Crisfield is a growing favorite among boaters and sportsmen. **Somers Cove Marina** (☎ 410-968-0925, www.somerscove.com) wins high marks with transient boaters for facilities and friendliness. There's a pool, laundry and shower facilities, a motel, tennis courts, a playground, as well as the local museum and visitor center on site. The 100 transient slips are within walking distance (very important for those who arrive by boat!), marine supplies, a grocery, and half a dozen restaurants.

Perched on the second floor deck of one of these restaurants, **Side-street Seafood Market**, we watched the *Capt. Steven Thomas* boarding passengers bound for a day-trip to Tangier Island. We ate a lunch of Maryland crab chowder (distinctly different from Virginia's version), a bucket of steamed clams and sweet tea. From our picnic table we had a bird's eye view of typical Crisfield scenery: families walking to the fishing pier with poles, buckets and coolers, shoppers going in and out of the bank and grocery, a few hot-rodders cruising down Main Street to where it dead-ends at the pier, then turning to cruise slowly back past us. Across the street, over the roofs of Main Street buildings, the rooftops of the busy seafood-processing houses were visible.

Crisfield became a major seafood exporter back in 1867 with the construction of the Eastern Shore Railroad. The largest one-day shipment of oysters from Crisfield was on December 19, 1920, when the railroad shipped 18 boxcars, or about 80,000 bushels. To say the town was built upon the seafood industry is quite literal – part of the town actually sits atop huge deposits of discarded oyster shells.

The oyster industry may have declined from its heyday, but the blue crab is still a mainstay for Chesapeake Bay watermen. One indication of just how important the little crustacean is to Crisfield is the street signs – they all bear the silhouette of a crab. Come to think of it, the signs on the restaurant's restrooms said "Jimmys" and "Sooks," the crab equivalent of "men" and "women."

Attractions

The **J. Millard Tawes Historical Museum** has hosted such unique displays as "Woolies," a collection of pictures made out of scraps of clothing and sails that 19th-century sailors sent home as handmade postcards. The museum also offers guided walking tours with access to seafood-packing houses. Tours meet in front of the museum at 10am, Monday-Saturday. The cost is just $2.50, a dollar for kids ages six-12, the same as admission to the museum, which is open 9am-5pm, Monday-Saturday (Ninth Street at Somers Cove Marina, ☎ 410-968-2501).

Access to **Smith Island** is by boat only. One way to get there is aboard the *Capt. Tyler*, a 65-foot modern sightseeing cruiser (☎ 410-425-2771, www.smithislandcruises.com). Trips leave daily at 12:30pm, returning around 5pm. It's about an hour's cruise each way, leaving you an afternoon to explore the village of **Ewell**, have lunch at the **Bayside Inn**, and visit the **Smith Island Center**, a heritage museum and visitor center. You can rent a golf cart or bicycle to explore further.

The northern half of the island is encompassed by the **Martin National Wildlife Area**. While the refuge is closed to the public to protect nesting habitats, there is a visitor center with exhibits. The island, settled in 1657, is inhabited by about 400 people, most of them descendants of original settlers. Most still derive their livelihood from the bay, and find no need for a town government, mayor or local taxes. Everyone contributes to maintaining community property, and if a problem arises, they call a meeting of citizens – perhaps democracy in its truest form. If you choose to stay overnight, there are a couple of bed & breakfasts: the **Ewell Tide Inn** (☎ 410-425-2141, 888-699-2141, www.smithisland.net) and **Inn of Silent Music** (☎ 410-425-3541, www.innofsilentmusic.com). The **Smith Island Center** (☎ 410-425-3351) is open daily, May-October, noon to 4pm.

Tangier Island is in Virginia waters, but it's only a 1¼-hour cruise from Crisfield aboard the *Capt. Steven Thomas*. In this small fishing community you'll find a way of life that hasn't changed much in centuries, a handful of shops and restaurants (see the *Tangier Island* section in the *Virginia's Eastern Shore* chapter). Cruises depart daily, mid-May through October, at 12:30pm, returning at 5:15pm (☎ 410-968-2338).

Recreation

Eco-Tours, given by an experienced waterman aboard the Chesapeake Bay workboat *Learn-it*, depart daily, at 10am and 1:30pm, from the Captains' Galley Restaurant (☎ 410-968-9870).

Rent kayaks and explore on your own. **Tangier Sound Outfitters** offers lessons, rentals, shuttle services, and gear for paddle-in camping (27582 Farm Market Road, Marion, ☎ 410-968-1803).

Janes Island State Park has more than 3,000 acres of beach, wetland and loblolly pine forests. There's camping, cabins and a conference center, as well as fishing, boat and kayak rentals, and plenty of wildlife viewing (☎ 410-968-1565, www.dnr.state.md.us).

Maryland's Eastern Shore

Dining

Captain's Galley and gift shop sits perched at the very edge of the water, serving seafood indoors and out (Main Street & City Dock, ☎ 410-968-3313). **Watermen's Inn** is owned by two culinary arts graduates; one is an expert in pastries, so the dessert buffet is outstanding (901 W. Main Street, ☎ 410-968-2119).

Side Street Seafood Market is just that, where you can watch oyster-shuckers during season (October-March), and soft-shell crabs being cleaned and packaged the rest of the year. Next door, at **J.C.W. Taxes,** you can see crab-pickers in action May-October. Get fresh seafood to go or sample it right here in the restaurant upstairs, with outdoor dining on picnic tables on the deck (204 S. Tenth Street, ☎ 410-968-2442, www.crisfield.com/sidestreet).

Peppy's, an Italian and seafood restaurant, is also up high to afford water views (821 W. Main Street, ☎ 410-968-2727). **The Circle Inn** caters to families and fishermen, opening at 5am for breakfast (4012 Crisfield Highway, ☎ 410-968-1969).

The Iguana Café shares a cottage with **Tropical Chesapeake**, an island-themed gift shop (712 Broadway, ☎ 410-968-3622). If you want a break from all the seafood, **Oriental Jade** serves Chinese fare (103 N. 4th & Pine streets, ☎ 410-968-3888).

Top off lunch or dinner with a walk along the **City Dock** and a cool treat on the **Ice Cream Gallery's** waterfront deck (☎ 410-968-0809).

Lodging

Bea's B&B was built in 1909 by the founder of the Handy Soft Shell Crab Company. There are stained-glass windows, pocket doors, a fireplace, and three guest rooms (10 S. Somerset Avenue, ☎ 410-968-0423, www.beasbandb.com, $$).

My Fair Lady Bed & Breakfast is a beautifully restored, elaborate Queen Ann Victorian with a three-story octagonal tower and wraparound porch (38 W. Main Street, ☎ 410-968-0352, www.myfairladybandb.com, $$).

 Gossamer Bed & Breakfast welcomes well-behaved children and pets with prior notice. The house was built in 1909 by Dr. R. Ransom Norris in the Mission/Arts and Crafts style. It's decorated with the innkeeper's love for the old and "odd," and the grounds have been designed to attract wildlife (211 S. Somerset Avenue, ☎ 410-968-3478, www.bbonline.com/md/gossamer, $).

If you want to stay on the water, or within walking distance of the marina, there are several motels. **Somers Cove Motel** is part of Somers Cove Marina (if driving from town, follow the blue signs). Rooms facing the front have expansive views of the marshes, rooms in the back overlook the marina and Somers Cove (700 Robert Norris Drive, ☎ 410-968-1900, $).

The Cove has nine rooms, all with whirlpool or Jacuzzi, and overlooks the marina (218 Broadway, ☎ 410-425-2771 or 410-968-2220, $$$); the **Paddlewheel Motel** at 701 W. Main Street has 14 rooms, some with hot tubs (☎ 410-968-2220, $$).

The Pines Motel has 40 rooms (some are efficiencies) and a pool; it's near the marina (☎ 410-968-0900, $).

Information

The **Crisfield Visitor's Center**, 3 Ninth Street (☎ 410-968-2501), at Somers Cove Marina, is open Monday-Friday, 9am-4:30pm, April-November. They are also open Saturday, 9am-2pm, from mid-April to mid-October. The city's official Web site is www.crisfield.org. Also check out the community Web site, www.crisfield.com, for more visitor information.

Somerset County Tourism is located in Princess Anne (☎ 800-521-9189, http://skipjack.net/le_shore/visitsomerset).

★ DID YOU KNOW?

The difference between Maryland and Virginia crab chowder is no trivial matter. Residents of both states claims theirs is the best. Maryland's has a tomato base with vegetables like green beans, peas and corn. Virginia's version has a white, creamy base, usually without vegetables, and normally with the moniker "she-crab" applied.

Maryland's Eastern Shore

Event

On Labor Day weekend the **Hard Crab Derby and Fair** features the Governor's Cup crab races, drawing fast crabs from all over. Thousands of crabs are then steamed for the seafood feast.

Trip Journal

Princess Anne

Thoroughly ensconced in the capital seat of Somerset County, the **Washington Hotel and Inn** is not only a landmark and institution in Princess Anne, but a family business four generations in the making. While the original portion of the structure dates to 1797, there's been an ordinary (a tavern with lodging) on this site since 1744.

Colleen Murphey's great-grandparents bought the hotel in 1937. Her grandmother, Mary Murphey, still runs the inn, even in her mid-eighties (we didn't get to meet her, though, for when we were there she had gone off to play bridge!). Colleen's father, Robert, ran the adjacent restaurant for 22 years. Now his 23-year-old daughter, a recent business graduate of The University of Maryland Eastern Shore right here in Princess Anne, has taken over the restaurant with gusto. She renamed it **Murphey's Pub**. Father and daughter renovated the dining rooms, selecting Colonial paint schemes and flooring, all while keeping open for the local lunchtime crowd.

"We couldn't close," says Colleen. "Families come back here generation after generation. The hotel has always been a focal point of the town." The "new" menu works off what Robert Murphey found successful, largely regional comfort foods: homemade soups, chicken and dumplings, stewed tomatoes, oysters, and perhaps muskrat, when in season.

You could certainly say the hospitality business is in this young woman's blood – and genes. Like her dad and his mother before him, Colleen grew up running around the corridors of the old inn, and they both have some great ghost stories to tell, which they relate with casual nonchalance. Such stories, like that of the Victorian lady who appears in the kitchen, make the hotel a favorite place for visitors on Halloween night, when the proprietors have been known to throw festive costume parties. Open for breakfast, lunch and dinner, Monday-Saturday (11784 Somerset Avenue, Princess Anne. Hotel, ☎ 410-651-2525; Murphey's Pub, ☎ 410-651-4155).

Snow Hill

In early August, just before harvest time, a dozen giant combines parade down Washington Street, then park along Green Street, dwarfing everything else around them. Here they await the blessings of local clergy for a good soybean and corn harvest. Nearly 500 people come to watch, bow their heads in respect to the area's farmers, then proceed with a down-home country fair of barnyard petting zoos, bluegrass and gospel music, bake sales and hayrides.

This unusual affair is Snow Hills' annual **Blessing of the Combines** (see *Events*, below), a symbolic gesture of support for those who earn their livelihoods from the land. That much hasn't changed in Snow Hill in hundreds of years. Agriculture is still a valuable sector of the economy, although the cash crops have evolved from tomatoes and tobacco to corn, soybeans and chickens.

Snow Hill was chartered in 1686, an agricultural settlement with an accessible trade route provided by the Pocomoke River, which flows through town. Other than paddling and nature watching on the river, the two things that bring people to Snow Hill today are the courthouse and antiques.

Around Town

Anyone who gets a speeding ticket, or needs a permit or a marriage license, has to come to Snow Hill, and they usually end up doing a little shopping, getting a hand-dipped cone at **Sweet Memories** or having lunch in **Bailey's Café**, an eatery with old-timey atmosphere. Unlike the passing fads that tourism can bring, this is the real ebb-and-flow of small town life.

While court business draws people who *have* to be here, a half-dozen inviting (and reasonably priced) antiques shops are what get people to stop on their way to the beaches of Ocean City or Assateague Island. They see the tantalizing items lining the sidewalks, park, get out and

Maryland's Eastern Shore

walk. Thus, a Snow Hill tourist is born. Slowly, ever so slowly, businesses have sprung up to meet these traveler's other needs, namely restaurants and bed & breakfasts, should they decide to extend their visit.

Barry Laws has seen tourism grow steadily, but by no means out of control, since he opened **Pocomoke River Canoe Co.** in 1982, outfitting recreationists with kayaks, canoes and guide services. Located in a barn-red restored lumber warehouse perched on the edge of the Pocomoke River drawbridge, it's probably the most visible landmark in town. His guides will take you up the freshwater river six or 12 miles and let you paddle back, or to the Nassawango Creek where Spanish moss drapes from bald cypress trees. They'll provide instruction if needed, box lunches, or arrange inn-to-inn trips (☎ 410-632-3971 or 800-258-0905, www.atbeach.com/amuse/md/canoe).

The river is the reason Snow Hill is mentioned in several outdoor guidebooks, and it has also received some press in large newspapers. But so far, it hasn't drawn so many people as to change the face of this small town very much at all.

The intimacy afforded by a small community is what brought businesswoman Helen Chambers here a few years ago. A transplant from Ocean City, she likes the fact that her son's 2002 graduating class had fewer than 100 students and that the streets close up by 10pm. In December 2001, she and a partner opened **I Remember This Antiques & Collectables** on the main street in North Washington. In the process, she filled two storefronts that had been empty, one a dry cleaner that went out of business, and the other a long, narrow building that she thought had most recently been an auto body shop. But since opening, she's had customers come in and tell her it used to be a three-lane bowling alley back in the 1930s. Next-door was a dance hall. With delight, she relates how people now well into old age tell how they used to meet their dates here. It sure makes the name of her shop most appropriate (302 N. Washington Street, ☎ 410-632-2222).

Attractions

About five miles south of Snow Hill, **Pocomoke River State Park** straddles the river, with Shad Landing on the south side, off Route 113, and Milburn Landing on the north side on Route 364. It actually takes nearly a half-hour to drive from one part of the park to the other! There are boat rentals, fishing, camping, hiking, and a swimming pool. The park is within the 14,750-acre **Pocomoke River State Forest**, which extends all the way to Pocomoke City. The forest has grand stands of loblolly pine and blackwater cypress swamps (☎ 410-632-2566, www.dnr.state.md.us/publiclands/eastern/pocomokeriver.html).

> **★ DID YOU KNOW?**
>
> Pocomoke means "black water."

The Julia A. Purnell Museum, established at first by a son to honor his mother's artwork, has grown to be known as "the attic of Worcester County." Exhibits interpret the lives of area residents in the 18th and 19th centuries. Of note are the memorabilia of African-American resident William Julius "Judy" Johnson, who earned recognition as the best third baseman during his baseball career from 1918-1939. The museum is open April-October, Tuesday-Saturday, 10am-4pm; Sunday, 1-4pm. Admission is $2 for adults and 50¢ for children ages five-12 (208 W. Market Street, ☎ 410-632-0515, www.purnellmuseum.com).

The Beach to Bay Indian Trail is a self-guided driving tour from Crisfield to Ocean City, following routes established by tribes of the Algonquin Nation, and also used by settlers. The detailed brochure is available in most visitor centers, and by calling the tourism numbers for either Worcester County (☎ 800-852-0335) or Somerset County (☎ 800-521-9189).

About 20 miles north of Snow Hill are **Ocean City** and access to **Assateague National Seashore's** undeveloped miles of white, sandy beaches, with camping, hiking, and up-close sightings of the famed Chincoteague ponies.

An alternative to Ocean City's festive but busy resort strip is **Berlin**, a quaint, small town that makes a nice, quiet base for exploring Assateague and the general area. The downtown has been recently restored with turn-of-the-century charm, and features antiques shops and boutiques to browse, and dozens of fine examples of Federal and Victorian architecture. For lodging, there's the **Atlantic Hotel** (☎ 800-814-7672, www.atlantichotel.com), a restored Victorian inn that just drips with yesteryear, and a handful of bed & breakfasts in historic homes. Take the self-guided walking tour of the historic district or visit the **Calvin B. Taylor Museum** of local history. Time your visit with one of the many festivals or fairs, like the Fiddlers Convention in September, Berlin's Victorian Christmas in December, or the Village Fair in June.

Maryland's Eastern Shore

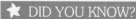

★ DID YOU KNOW?

In 1998, Berlin was the setting for the film *Runaway Bride*, starring Julia Roberts and Richard Gere.

Dining

The **Snow Hill Inn** serves gourmet selections of fresh local seafood and beef in a 1790 structure that once served as the local post office. Serving lunch Tuesday-Friday, dinner Tuesday-Saturday (104 E. Market Street, ☎ 410-632-2102).

David's (a Bistro!) serves lunch Tuesday-Friday, and dinner Tuesday-Saturday (208 Green Street, ☎ 410-632-2811, www.davidsabistro.com).

Bailey's Café has a Victorian pub-type atmosphere, serving breakfast and lunch Monday-Saturday and dinner Friday (104 W. Green Street, ☎ 410-632-3700).

The **Duck In Deli** is technically a convenience store, but also serves what they claim are the "best real beef hamburgers." Open daily, 6am-8pm (5610 Market Street, ☎ 410-632-0777).

Sweet Memories serves hand-dipped Hershey's ice cream, shakes and hot dogs (106 W. Green Street, ☎ 410-632-1000).

Lodging

The innkeeper at **The Mansion House** *loves* dogs; they're welcome with no extra charge. The 1835 waterfront home has four guest rooms (4436 Bayside Road, ☎ 410-632-3189, www.mansionhousebandb.com, $$$).

Chanceford Hall is a 1759 manor house furnished with antiques and books, and surrounded by lush gardens. Guests are greeted on arrival with wine and hors d'oeuvres (209 W. Federal St., ☎ 410-632-2900, www.chancefordhall.com, $$$).

The River House Inn offers lodgings in the 1860 Victorian country home, as well as two cottages, and a "little house" river hide-away. Dogs are welcome with a charge of $10 per day, per pet (201 E. Market Street, ☎ 410-632-2722, www.riverhouseinn.com, $$$).

Information

Town of Snow Hill, ☎ 410-632-2080, www.snowhillmd.com.

Worcester County Tourism, 113 Franklin Street, Unit 1, Snow Hill, ☎ 800-852-0335 or 410-632-3110, www.visitworcester.org.

Berlin Chamber of Commerce, PO Box 212, Berlin 21811, ☎ 410-641-4775, www.berlinmdcc.org.

Event

The **Blessing of the Combines** and street fair is held the first Saturday in August along Green Street (☎ 410-632-1334).

Trip Journal

Furnace Town

About five miles northwest of Snow Hill on Route 12 is a town where no one but a caretaker lives, but where the crafts and industry of the 19th century are alive and well. The **Furnace Town** living heritage museum is on the site of a town where 300 people lived and worked for a brief 20 years. It was a town of laborers and craftsmen, built in 1830 around the towering brick Nassawango Iron Furnace to smelt iron from ore dug up from the Maryland bogs. The furnace is the only remaining original structure. When the Maryland Iron Company went bankrupt in 1850, most of the residents left and the frame buildings rotted and fell to ruin.

Furnace Town Foundation has relocated more than a dozen 19th-century buildings, roughly similar to the originals, and hired people to carry on the skills of the era that made life in a small town possible. Artisans work on-site daily in the quaint buildings – broom makers, printers, weavers, gardeners – and they in turn pass down the skills to the younger generations. The youngest volunteers are only 14 years old.

Sixteen-year-old Stephen Lynch goes back and forth between the neighboring print shop and broom-making house, demonstrating the skills he learned here as a volunteer, and now a staff member. While we watched, he made us a "cat-teaser," a miniature broom-like toy for kitties. In the garden, a young girl is tending examples of what would have been grown to sustain the 19th-century village: vegetables, and cooking and medicinal herbs. There's also a company store, carpenter and blacksmith shops, and a smokehouse. At least two to four artisans are at work from 11:30am to 4:30pm on days the museum is open, and their handiwork is sold in the visitor center.

The ruins and foundations of the original structures, and a small museum in the Old Nazareth Church building tells the story of the town, from how they located bog ore (a blue, oily substance floating on swamp water), to the manufacture of iron tools and all kinds of other handy implements.

Furnace Town is in the middle of tranquil Pocomoke State Forest. The museum's land is shared with the Nature Conservancy, which maintains a couple of hiking trails that start from the parking lot. It is open daily, April-October, 11am-5pm. Admission is $4 for adults, $3.50 for seniors, and $2 for children ages two-18. For more information, ☎ 410-632-2032, www.furnacetown.com.

★ TRAVEL TIP

The **Chesapeake Celtic Festival** is held at Furnace Town the first weekend in October (www. celticfest.net).

Central Maryland

From hip Ellicott City, which is a stone's throw from Baltimore, to Emmitsburg, the revered home of the St. Elizabeth Ann Seton shrine, it's difficult to generalize about Central Maryland. Urban sprawl from Baltimore and DC certainly influence the once small towns near those cities, but mere minutes north are rolling farmlands and downright sleepy small towns.

THE TOWNS
✖ Emmitsburg
✖ Westminster
✖ Havre de Grace
✖ Ellicott City

Getting Here

The east coast's main transportation corridor, **I-95**, traverses the region, while interstates **83**, **70**, **295** and **97** spoke off from Baltimore in all directions.

Baltimore/Washington International Airport, BWIA (☎ 410-859-7111, www.bwiairport.com), serves Central Maryland, and there are two regional airports: **Frederick Municipal Airport** (☎ 301-662-8156, www.frederickaviation.com) and **Carroll County Regional Airport** (☎ 410-876-7200, www.poagefield.com).

Regional Information

State Welcome Centers are located on I-70 between Hagerstown and Frederick; on US 13 near the Virginia border; on US 15 just south of the Pennsylvania border; and on I-95 near Savage and Perryville.

Emmitsburg

The audio recording at the Mortuary Chapel of Elizabeth Ann Seton, the first American-born Catholic saint, makes this suggestion to visitors: "As you leave, say a prayer for the souls who have tried to emulate the life of Ann Seton." There's no need to wonder where those devotees repose. In neat rows, outside the chapel that was built by Seton's son William to honor her in death, stand hundreds of small, white headstones, all identical, with a simple engraved cross as ornamentation.

These are the grave markers of the devoted Sisters of Charity, and the dates etched into stone indicate nearly all died in their 70s, 80s and 90s. An inscription on the chapel tells us there are also many unmarked graves of children, widows and other unknown people who lived in St. Joseph's Valley in the early years of the Sisters of Charity. Encircling this graveyard is a high wall with Stations of the Cross carved out of stone.

Seton's shrine, a minor basilica of the Catholic Church, is spread across many acres in an area of Central Maryland settled by Catholics and Presbyterians. The Catholics were escaping persecution in Protestant English colonies, and the Presbyterians were drawn by the rich soil and abundant supply of water from three main streams. The widowed Ann Seton, a newly converted Catholic, came in 1809 with her five children to establish the Sisters of Charity of St. Joseph's, and open the nation's first free Catholic school, which became the foundation for today's parochial school system.

The Sisters didn't stay put in Emmitsburg; rather, they established orphanages and schools in key cities up and down the east coast, and as early as 1828 became pioneers into the western frontier, crossing the Allegheny Mountains and sailing down the Ohio River to St. Louis, where they opened a hospital, orphanage and school. Today there are six communities of the Sisters of Charity in the US and Canada.

The strength of Ann Seton's character to draw faithful followers to St. Joseph's, even after her death in 1821, is clearly evidenced by the many rows of grave markers. The shrine continues to draw the faithful, in the form of pilgrims and visitors, many of whom leave with a greater sense of inner peace. Public mass is offered Wednesday through Sunday.

★ SAINT ELIZABETH ANN SETON

Saint Elizabeth Ann Seton, born in New York City in 1774, wrote of her adopted Emmitsburg countryside: "The good news of the valley and mountains covers me with joy. Be assured my heart is there and always will be."

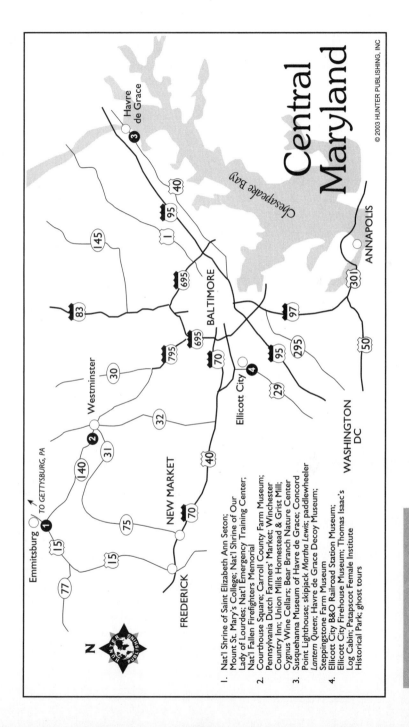

© 2003 HUNTER PUBLISHING, INC

Central Maryland

Chesapeake Bay

Havre de Grace ③

ANNAPOLIS

BALTIMORE

Westminster

Ellicott City ④

NEW MARKET

Emmitsburg ①

TO GETTYSBURG, PA

FREDERICK

WASHINGTON DC

N

1. Nat'l Shrine of Saint Elizabeth Ann Seton; Mount St. Mary's College; Nat'l Shrine of Our Lady of Lourdes; Nat'l Emergency Training Center; Nat'l Fallen Firefighters Memorial
2. Courthouse Square; Carroll County Farm Museum; Pennsylvania Dutch Farmers' Market; Winchester Country Inn; Union Mills Homestead & Grist Mill; Cygnus Wine Cellars; Bear Branch Nature Center
3. Susquehanna Museum of Havre de Grace; Concord Point Lighthouse; skipjack *Martha Lewis*; paddlewheeler *Lantern Queen*; Havre de Grace Decoy Museum; Steppingstone Farm Museum
4. Ellicott City B&O Railroad Station Museum; Ellicott City Firehouse Museum; Thomas Isaac's Log Cabin; Patapscot Female Institute Historical Park; ghost tours

Central Maryland

235

Around Town

Visitors to the town of Emmitsburg will find a quiet, but attractive Main Street of brick row houses with a handful of shops and taverns. The Federal, Georgian and Victorian architecture is well-preserved. The town is also home to Mount Saint Mary's College, the National Shrine of Our Lady of Lourdes, the National Emergency Training Center, and the Fallen Firefighters' Memorial. The **Emmitsburg Antique Mall** has more than 120 dealers (1 Chesapeake Avenue, ☎ 301-447-6471).

While the town was named for the Emmit family, it's disputed whether they were in fact the founders of the town. In any case, in 1757 Irishman Samuel Emmit purchased a tract of land and encouraged more settlers to come. In 1785, his son William laid out the town with numbered lots. Town folklore holds that the name Emmitsburg (it originally had two t's) came about during a drunken public meeting in Conrad Hochensmith's tavern. But the head of the Emmitsburg Historical Society, Michael Hillman, says the Emmits weren't the founders at all, that settlement of the area began prior to 1733, and that William and Samuel Emmit were not-so-savory landlords. One written account even claims that Samuel fell dead in the streets of Emmitsburg in 1817 on his way to start eviction proceedings against Mother Seton's Sisters of Charity (divine intervention, perhaps?). Visit **www.emmitsburg.net** for Hillman's many articles on the "true" history of Emmitsburg, some humorous, some not, many of which are also published in Hillman's column in the local newspaper.

Attractions

The **National Shrine of St. Elizabeth Ann Seton** consists of the original buildings of the Sisters of Charity community, a visitor center, Mortuary Chapel and cemetery. The Basilica was built in 1965 to venerate the remains of Ann Seton, the first American-born person to be canonized (in 1975). The visitor center has a museum, religious gift shop, and shows a 12-minute video on the half-hour. There's a self-guided walking tour of the 1750 Stone House where Seton established the religious community in 1809, the White House (1810), which served as the nation's first parochial school, and the cemetery where hundreds of sisters are buried. Hours are 10am to 4:30pm, Tuesday-Sunday. Closed the last two weeks in January (333 S. Seton Avenue, ☎ 301-447-6606, www.setonshrine.org).

Mount Saint Mary's College is the oldest private independent Catholic college in the country, established in 1808, and the second oldest seminary. The co-ed institution has about 1,400 undergraduates. The **National Shrine of Our Lady of Lourdes** behind the college is a replica of the famed Grotto of Lourdes in France where a peasant girl saw visions of the Virgin Mary. A million pilgrims visit the shrine each year, which is the oldest of its kind in America (☎ 301-447-6122, www.msmary.edu).

The **National Emergency Training Center** is where 15,000 emergency personnel receive training each year. It's the site of the National Fire Academy and Emergency Management Institute, and the **National Fallen Firefighters' Memorial,** dedicated in 1981. Each year the names of professional and volunteer firefighters who have lost their lives in service are added to the memorial (South Seton Avenue, www.usfa.fema.gov/dhtml/inside-usfa/ffmem.cfm).

Gettysburg, Pennsylvania is only 10 miles north of Emmitsburg, and many Union troops passed through Emmitsburg on their way there. In June 1863, 90,000 Union soldiers camped on the grounds of St. Joseph's and the Sisters of Charity feared a battle would occur right here. They prayed and promised to erect a statue of Notre Dame des Victoires if it did not. Their prayers were answered when the troops moved on to Gettysburg. But that became the bloodiest battle of all, albeit the turning point of the war. The sisters built their statue, which can be seen still today, near the cemetery at the Seton Shrine. To visit, contact the Gettysburg Convention and Visitors Bureau, ☎ 800-337-5015, www.gettysburg.com.

Dining

The **Carriage House Inn** serves fine food and spirits in an 1837 building listed on the National Register of Historic Places. It's been a

Central Maryland

warehouse, bus depot and broom factory, and first became a restaurant in 1943. President Bill Clinton and wife Hillary have dined there. The fare is seafood, steaks, veal, chicken and some vegetarian (200 S. Seton Avenue, ☎ 301-447-2366, www.carriagehouseinn.info).

The owners of **One More Tavern** may have feared there were too many taverns in town when they opened, but apparently there's always room for one more. In addition to cocktails, they serve sandwiches, subs, ribeye steaks, pizzas and typical munchies (135 Chesapeake Avenue, ☎ 301-447-6749).

Main Street Grill is located in the former Emmitsburg grocery store, and specializes in steaks, seafood, pasta and prime rib (304 East Main Street, ☎ 301-447-3116). **Ott House Pub & Restaurant** serves lunch and dinner in Center Square (☎ 301-447-2625), and the **Palm's Restaurant** is a small, locally popular family restaurant serving Maryland crab chowder, softshell crabs, prime rib and ribeye steaks (20 West Main St,. ☎ 301-447-3689).

Lodging

Stonehurst Inn Bed & Breakfast was built in the Catoctin Mountains in 1875 as a summer mansion. It was once owned by the first National Episcopal Bishop. There's a meditation chapel in the woods, a fishing pond, solarium, library, and wrap-around porches with wicker chaises (9436 Waynesboro Road, ☎ 800-497-8458, www.stonehurst-inn.com, $).

Antrim 1844 Country Inn is a four-star dining and bed & breakfast experience in Taneytown, about eight miles southeast of Emmitsburg via Route 140. The accolades "elegant" and "romantic" fit it to a T. The mansion has nine guest rooms, with another 13 suites and rooms in original, restored outbuildings, each with its own fireplace. The formal breakfasts feature Belgian waffles; butlers serve at the hors d'oeuvre parties; and their six-course dinners have been acclaimed in *The Baltimore Sun* (30 Trevanion Road, Taneytown, ☎ 410-756-6812 or 800-858-1844, www.antrim1844.com, $$$$).

Sleep Inn & Suites accepts pets, no extra charge, but you will be placed on the smoking floor. There are 79 rooms, 12 suites and one fireplace suite, an indoor pool and a fitness room (501 Silo Hill Parkway, ☎ 301-447-0044, $$).

Information

Emmitsburg doesn't have its own visitor center, but there's a **Maryland Welcome Center** just north of town on Route 15.

Emmitsburg Business & Professional Association, ☎ 301-447-3110, www.emmitsburg.net, provides local news, history, events, things to do and a business directory.

Tourism Council of Frederick County, ☎ 301-228-2888 or 800-999-3613, www.visitfrederick.org.

Westminster

Around Town

Beyond split rail fencing, sheep graze on rolling green pastures. Folks in 19th-century dress mill about farm buildings and homesteads. Small, casual groupings of fiddlers, banjo pickers, dobro and stand-up bass players are scattered about on the lawns, standing under trees or sitting at picnic tables. There are old men in starched white-collared shirts and cowboy hats, young men with ponytails, women in gingham dresses, boys in overalls. In the background, a lone guitar player sings a plaintive bluegrass ballad, amplified throughout the park. Abruptly, the relative quietude is broken by energetic shoes tapping on a piece of plywood – a couple spontaneously jumping up for some down-home clogging. Accompanying them are a pair of fiddle players who could be grandfather and grandson.

We have arrived in Westminster for the start of the annual **Fiddler's Convention** at the Carroll County Farm Museum. Each June brings the best musicians in the region to vie for cash in the bluegrass and "old-timey" competitions.

It's not quite noon and the fiddling is just getting warmed up, but the Knights of Columbus have been barbecuing for days. Big boulder-sized chunks of blackened meat sit on a metal, U-shaped pit barbecue grill that must be more than 10 feet long. Men and women work at two big slicing machines. The choices are pork, beef, ham or turkey with toppings of BBQ sauce, horseradish, mustard and mayonnaise. I heap the condiments onto a bun filled with pork and beef, and ask the men how long they've been cooking. One says "since Wednesday" (today

Central Maryland

239

is Sunday). The other laughs and says, "Oh we just threw them on this morning; waved our magic wand and they were done." We all laugh and I order two sodas to wash down the sandwiches.

We find a shady spot under a tree and sit down to eat and listen. The sun is shining, but there's no humidity on this beautiful Sunday afternoon and life just doesn't seem as if it could get any better.

Reluctantly, we eventually have to leave this little world, set apart from interstate traffic and suburbs. But what awaits in **downtown Westminster** is nearly as idyllic. Main Street is lined with furniture and carpet stores, cigar shops and cafés, antiques shops and fine old homes built by affluent businessmen in the 1800s. Founded in 1764 by William Winchester, this is the second-oldest town in Carroll County. Growth was slow in the beginning, until the new turnpike between Baltimore and Pittsburgh came through town, bringing traffic, commerce, and the county seat in 1837.

Courthouse Square has 10 historic sites, including the 1837 jail, the 1844 Ascension Church, and the 1838 courthouse, with its Greek Revival portico. You may take a self-guided walking tour of Courthouse Square, Main Street, and **Corbit's Charge,** which traces a Civil War skirmish between General J.E.B. Stuart and a Delaware cavalry. Although a minor conflict, it slowed Stuart's march to Gettysburg to warn General Robert E. Lee about major Union advances. The Civil War Driving Tour of Carroll County, "Roads to Gettysburg," is also available. A bit more lighthearted is the one-hour, self-guided Ghost Walk of Westminster, particularly fun in the evening. Brochures for all of these tours are available at the **Carroll County Visitor Center**, 210 E. Main Street (☎ 800-272-1933), where a guided walking tour starts every Sunday at 2pm.

Attractions

The 140-acre **Carroll County Farm Museum** is a living history museum and working farm where visitors can see domestic animals and life the way it was for a 19th-century farm family. See spinning, weaving, quilting, wood carving and blacksmithing. There's a general store where you can purchase items made on-site by the artisans, souvenirs and old-fashioned candy. The Farm Museum hosts a full calendar of exhibits and special events throughout the year, from Traditional Arts Week in April to festive holiday visits in December. In summer (July and August), the museum is open Tuesday-Friday, 10am-4pm; on weekends, noon-5pm. The rest of the year it is open weekends only. Admission is $3 for adults and $2 for children ages seven-18

(500 South Center Street, ☎ 410-848-7775 or 800-654-4645, http:// ccgov. carr.org/farm).

The **Carroll County Arts Council** has rotating exhibits of local and regional artists, changing every six weeks. Most are for sale. Open Monday-Saturday (15 E. Main Street, ☎ 410-848-7272, www.carr.org/ arts).

At **The Pennsylvania Dutch Farmers' Market,** Amish, Mennonites and local vendors display their products for sale. There's a bakery, fresh produce and flowers, cheese and meats for sale, as well. It's a half-mile east of downtown Westminster at Routes 140 and 97 South. Open year-round, Thursday-Saturday (☎ 410-876-8100).

Have afternoon tea and shop for gifts in the oldest structure in Carroll County, **The Winchester Country Inn,** built in 1760 by William Winchester, founder of Westminster. It's been completely restored and furnished with antiques. The inn discontinued the bed & breakfast in 2002, and now operates as a tea room and gift shop. **Gypsy's Tea Room** serves afternoon tea and desserts, Tuesday-Saturday, 11am-4pm (☎ 410-857-9818); **Inspirations** and **Westminster Gift Basket Co.** offer boutique items and gift baskets (☎ 410-857-0058).

Union Mills Homestead and Grist Mill is a 1797 inn and mill complex about five miles north of Westminster via Route 97. The Oliver Evans-designed mill with waterwheel is in operation, grinding rye, whole wheat, buckwheat and cornmeal for sale. Call for tour information and admission fees (3311 Littlestown Pike, Union Mills, ☎ 410-848-2288, www.carr.org/tourism).

Cygnus Wine Cellars is a small family winery about eight miles north of Westminster on Route 27. Open on weekends, noon-5pm and by appointment (3130 Long Lane, Manchester, ☎ 410-374-6395, www.cygnuswinecellars.com).

Farmers' Markets

Westminster has two – the **Carroll County Farmers' Market** on Saturdays, 8am-1pm, mid-June through early September at the Agriculture Center (702 Smith Avenue, ☎ 410-848-7748); and the **Downtown Westminster Farmers' Market** on Saturdays, 8am to noon, June through October in the Sherwood Square Parking Lot on Route 27 (☎ 410-848-4363).

Central Maryland

Recreation

Carroll County has 10 loop **bike tours** totaling more than 150 miles. The routes pass scenic stops and historic attractions, through farm and woodland, villages and backroads. The routes were compiled by local bicyclists from their favorite rides, ranging in d4ifficulty and length. Maps are available from the Carroll County Visitors Center.

The Carroll County Equestrian Council has put together a packet of detailed maps for **horseback riders** in five different natural areas where equestrian trails exist (225 N. Center Street, ☎ 410-386-2103).

Bear Branch Nature Center has observation and exhibit rooms, a planetarium, and hiking trails of the Hashawha Environmental Center surrounding it, including a handicapped-accessible trail. Open Wednesday through Saturday, 10am-5pm, and Sunday, noon-5pm (300 John Owings Road, ☎ 410-848-2517).

Dining

Baugher's Country Restaurant has pick-your-own strawberries, a fruit market, restaurant, and playground, all set on a hill at the west end of town, just off Highway 140. This is comfort food the way grandma makes it: fried chicken, succotash, apple fritters, delicious desserts, and apple cider pressed from their own apples. Kids can eat for as little as $2.50 (289 W. Main Street, ☎ 410-848-3600).

Fat Cat Café is located in a restored Victorian home (172 Main Street, ☎ 410-848-1181), and **Johanssons Brewing Company and Dining House** is a microbrewery and restaurant done in the style of a Victorian pub. There's even a red British phone booth in the bar (4 W. Main Street, ☎ 410-876-0101).

About eight miles north of Westminster is **Bradley's Fox Briar Inn.** It re-opened in 2002 with new owners, but the building goes all the way back to 1700, when it was an inn with a tollgate next-door. There's a pub for casual eating and fine dining in a separate room, with hardwood floors and a fireplace. The menu features seafood, prime rib and chicken entrées, as well as the ever-popular jumbo lump crab cakes. Kids' menu available. Open for lunch and dinner daily (4115 Littlestown Pike, Silver Run, ☎ 410-848-2316).

See also **The Westminster Inn** on the next page, and **Antrim 1844** on page 238.

Lodging

Once a schoolhouse, **The Westminster Inn** now offers 24 bed & breakfast guest rooms, casual dining in the Courtyard Café or Naughty Boy's Pub, the more formal Library and Botany dining rooms, or cocktails in the Teacher's Lounge. The cuisine is contemporary American. In the same building is the East End Athletic Club, which has an indoor track, swimming pool and other sports (5 South Center Street, ☎ 410-876-2893 or 410-857-4445, www.westminsterinn.com, $$).

The Westminster Inn also operates the **Bowling Brook Country Inn** a few miles north of Uniontown, and about 20 minutes west of Westminster. The mansion, with eight bed & breakfast rooms, is surrounded by 225 acres of farmland, which was a horse-racing training ground for five successive Preakness winners from 1878-1882 (Middleburg Road, Uniontown, ☎ 410-876-2893, $$).

At the **Yellow Turtle Inn** in nearby New Windsor, visitors are greeted by staff in Victorian clothing. You can arrange for a massage, a soak in a Victorian tub, tea and scones, or just sit on the wrap-around porch with a book. There's a pool and a carriage house filled with a costume collection. The inn has three guest rooms and two whirlpool suites (111 Springdale Avenue, New Windsor, ☎ 410-635-3000, www.bbonline.com/md/yellowturtle/, $$).

There's a **Best Western** in Westminster, with a hot tub, pool, Jacuzzi suites and efficiencies (451 WMC Drive, ☎ 410-857-1900 or 800-528-1234, www.bestwesternwestminster.com, $$).

 Days Inn Westminster allows pets in smoking rooms with a $15 per day extra charge (25 Cranberry Road, ☎ 410-857-0500 or 800-329-7466, $$).

 The Boston Inn at Route 140 and Route 97, allows dogs (no cats), with a $50 deposit. There are 120 rooms, an outdoor pool, and Jacuzzi suites (533 Baltimore Blvd., ☎ 410-848-9095 or 800-634-0846, www.boston-inn.com, $).

See also **Antrim 1844 Country Inn**, page 238; it's about 10 miles northwest of Westminster via Route 140.

Information

Carroll County Visitor Center, 210 E. Main Street, open Monday-Saturday, 9am to 5pm, and Sundays and holidays, 10am to 2pm (☎ 410-848-1388 or 800-272-1933, www.carr.org/tourism).

Havre de Grace

This port city is fortunate that the Marquis de Lafayette let out such a praising and beautiful exclamation upon first seeing the shore from the Susquehanna River. "Ah, le havre de grace," he remarked in 1782 on his way to meet General George Washington in Philadelphia. Translated from the French, that meant, "Ah, the harbor of mercy." You can almost hear the sigh of relief in his voice. It also reminded him of le Havre back home in France.

If not for his utterance, the town probably would have been given the name of an English burg or royal family member. Instead, Havre de Grace wound up with what is arguably the prettiest place name in all of Maryland. The city thanked him, it could be said, by naming a street after him.

If, however, the Marquis had tried sailing farther north up the river, he might have had something much less complimentary to say. Past Havre de Grace, the river was unnavigable and shallow with boulders, until the Susquehanna & Tidewater Canal was built in 1839.

★ HOW TO SAY IT

Simply say Havre de Grace as it's spelled – HAV-ray de GRACE – don't try any fancy French pronunciation.

Around Town

Today you can get a tour of the reconstructed lock at the southern terminus of the canal and the 1840 Locktender's House, which now houses the **Susquehanna Museum of Havre de Grace**. The canal served a vital role as boats carried timber, coal and agricultural products from Havre de Grace to points along the river 45 miles to Wrightsville, Pennsylvania, thus creating a navigable trade route between Baltimore and Philadelphia.

When chartered as a city in 1783, there were only seven houses in Havre de Grace. The Old Post Road (now US 40) spurred larger growth, serving as the stagecoach link between Baltimore and Philadelphia. In the 1789 Congressional vote to decide the nation's capital,

Havre de Grace lost to Washington DC by one single vote (cast by the Speaker of the House). It suffered the same fate as the capital during the War of 1812, when British troops attacked from a flotilla of 15 barges and burned the town to the ground. A single local militiaman, John O'Neill, attempted to defend the town with a cannon perched on a hill.

Today, Havre de Grace is a quiet little getaway (population 11,500), convenient to both Baltimore and Washington DC, and just five minutes off I-95. Tourism has replaced the bustle once created by the canal trade of the 1800s and the horse racing of the early 1900s.

Rent a bicycle at the corner of N. Union Avenue and Warren Street, or walk the self-guided tour of 35 historic spots in the city. Or take off on your own – there are more than 800 historic structures to see. Look for summer kitchens – small outbuildings with chimneys – scattered through the city. These were a necessary addition to any colonial household, given that hot summer temperatures and a hot kitchen would have made living conditions unbearable for the rest of the house (kitchens often caught fire, as well, so the practice protected the rest of the house).

Stroll the Promenade, a half-mile boardwalk along the Chesapeake Bay from one of the oldest operating lighthouses on the East Coast to the seven-acre Tydings Memorial Park, the site of various festivals and holiday celebrations throughout the year. Several historical museums within walking distance of the Promenade can satisfy anyone's yen for maritime history. Take a cruise on a restored skipjack or an original paddlewheeler, dine in a waterfront restaurant, then stay in an historic bed & breakfast. Whatever you decide to do, you'll find Lafayette's epithet still rings true.

Attractions

Susquehanna Museum of Havre de Grace at the 1840 Lockhouse. Tours are given May through October on weekends, 1-5pm. Admission is $2 adults, $1 seniors (Erie and Conesto Streets, ☎ 410-939-5780).

Next to the **Concord Point Lighthouse** (1827) is the cannon poor Mr. O'Neill fired so valiantly on the British. By the way, he was captured and nearly hung, but his young daughter, Matilda, rowed out to the British ship and successfully pleaded for his life. His reward: the job of lighthouse keeper. Lit almost continuously for the last 175 years, the lighthouse was among eight built by Havre de Grace native John

Central Maryland

Donahoo, as part of a navigational improvement effort. You can climb the 28 steps and the ladder to the top on weekends April-October, 1-5pm. Walk a half-mile on the boardwalk along the Chesapeake Bay to Tydings Park. Free admission (Concord and Lafayette Streets, ☎ 410-939-9040).

From Lighthouse Pier, the skipjack *Martha Lewis* departs for 90-minute sailing cruises on weekends, April through October. The working oyster dredge boat, built in 1955, is one of the last American vessels to fish under sail. It was restored in 1994 by a non-profit educational organization. Nostalgic cruises through the Susquehanna flats to the upper Chesapeake Bay depart on weekends at noon, 1:30 and 3pm. $10 adults, $5 children 10 and under. Wine and cheese cruises depart Wednesdays at 7pm from Hutchins Park and, in winter, on weekdays from November through March, you can even sign on and help with the oyster dredging. You have to pay for the privilege of working aboard one of the last working skipjacks: $100 per person, which includes meals (☎ 800-406-0766 or 410-939-4078, www.skipjackmarthalewis.org)/.

The *Lantern Queen,* an original turn-of-the-century paddle wheeler, operates public cruises from Hutchins Park on Thursday and Friday evenings (☎ 888-937-3740, www.lanternqueen.com).

Havre de Grace Maritime Museum preserves those busy days of commerce when the city was a major hub for waterborne traffic. Open weekends, May-September, 1-5pm. Free admission (100 Lafayette Street, ☎ 410-939-4800).

This is the self-proclaimed "Decoy Capital of the World," due largely to the **Havre de Grace Decoy Museum.** Here you can see the folk art form of both master craftsmen and backyard carvers on display. On most weekends, you'll find carvers giving demonstrations of their art. Open daily, 11am-4pm. Admission is $4 adults, $2 seniors and children over age eight (Market Street and Madison Mitchell Place, ☎ 410-939-3739).

Steppingstone Farm Museum is just outside the city in Susquehanna State Park. The museum demonstrates rural arts and crafts of the period 1880 to 1920, and preserves several historic farm buildings. Open weekends, May-October, 1-5pm. Admission is $2; children 12 and under free (461 Quaker Bottom Road, ☎ 410-939-2299).

Dining

At **MacGregor's Restaurant & Bar** all tables have a water view in this former 1924 bank building serving lunch, dinner and Sunday brunch. Seafood, of course, is the specialty, but they also serve pasta and steaks. There's an outside deck, gazebo bar, comedy club, and live music Friday and Saturday evenings (331 St. John Street, ☎ 410-939-3003, www.macgregorsrestaurant.com).

The location speaks for itself at the **Tidewater Grille,** perched at the end of Franklin Street overlooking the Susquehanna River. Dine inside or out on the decks (☎ 410-939-3313). **Price's Seafood Restaurant** shares the same view a block up on Water Street. Steamed hard and softshell crabs in season (☎ 410-939-2782).

The **Bayou Restaurant** is a friendly and locally popular restaurant serving seafood, homemade bread and pies (927 Pulaski Highway, ☎ 410-939-3565).

For lighter fare, there's gourmet coffee at **Java by the Bay** (118 N. Washington Street, ☎ 410-939-0227), **Fortunato Brothers Pizza** (103 N. Washington Street, ☎ 410-939-1401), and sweet treats, sandwiches and home-baked bagels at **Ice Dreams** (209 N. Washington Street, ☎ 410-939-1525).

Bay City Market & Lighthouse Deli (200 Congress Avenue, ☎ 410-939-3116) will be happy to pack a picnic lunch if you want to enjoy the outdoors. Try the steamed shrimp to go, BBQ chicken and ribs or a sandwich on homemade bread.

See also **The Crazy Swede**, below.

Lodging

The Crazy Swede Restaurant and Guest Suites has 10 suites in three historic buildings. All have private bath, phones, central air, refrigerators and many have sitting areas. The main building has four suites and houses the restaurant, where lodging guests receive a 20% discount on their meals. The restaurant serves fresh seafood and beef specialties for lunch and dinner daily, and a Sunday champagne brunch (400 N. Union Avenue, ☎ 410-939-5440, www.crazyswede-restaurant.com, $$).

The **Currier House Bed & Breakfast** overlooks the Susquehanna where it meets the Bay. Matthew Currier's original 1861 modest home has been enlarged several times over the years, with a wrap-around

Central Maryland

porch added. It is operated by the builder's great-granddaughter. Each of the four guest rooms has a private bath and is furnished with antiques and Currier family heirlooms (800 S. Market Street, ☎ 410-939-7886, 800-827-2889, www.currier-bb.com, $$).

Vandiver Inn Bed & Breakfast is a sprawling 1886 Victorian mansion with nine exquisitely decorated rooms, many with fireplaces. The adjacent Murphy and Kent Guesthouses offer another eight rooms. Four of the suites have Jacuzzi tubs, and all rooms are air-conditioned (301 S. Union Avenue, ☎ 410-939-5200 or 800-245-1655, www.vandiverinn.com, $$).

La Cle d'Or Guest House is the 1868 home of the Johns Hopkins family – yes, *the* Johns Hopkins of the famous Baltimore hospital. There are two suites appointed with antiques, chandeliers, and fabulous fabrics. Outside there's a Jacuzzi and a brick-walled "secret garden" (226 N. Union Avenue, ☎ 410-939-6562 or 888-554-8378, www.lacledorguesthouse.com, $$).

 Spencer Silver Mansion Bed & Breakfast has four guest rooms in the main house, and a carriage house that sleeps four, where guests with well-behaved pets can stay. Fresh fruit is served daily in rooms, and a full breakfast is served until 10:30am. The biggest decision you'll have to make is where to sit and relax: on the wrap-around porch, in the garden on the four-seat glider or Adirondack chairs, or on a hammock under a grape arbor (200 S. Union Avenue, ☎ 410-939-1097 or 800-780-1485, www.spencersilvermansion.com, $).

Information

The **Havre de Grace Tourism Commission**, 224 North Washington Street, ☎ 800-851-7756 or 410-939-3303, www.hdgtourism.com.

The Web site for the **City of Havre de Grace**, www.havredegracemd.com, provides information about the city's government and has a section for visitors that features a calendar of events, points of interest, and history of the town.

Event

The annual **Decoy & Wildlife Art Festival** is held the first weekend in May at the Decoy Museum and the middle and high schools (☎ 410-939-3730).

Ellicott City

Around Town

A full-grown man dressed in tights and a medieval cap blows huge bubbles outside a celestial-themed gift shop. Up Main Street a few doors, another man puts the finishing touches on an oil painting, working on an easel set up on the sidewalk in front of his studio. Meanwhile, a uniformed volunteer fireman raises the American flag outside the Firehouse Museum, a cute carriage house-turned-fire station perched on a triangle-shaped ledge high above the main street.

Is Ellicott City tragically hip or simply taking advantage of a great location between Baltimore and DC? That's for the individual to decide. Suffice to say, a word-of-mouth reputation draws thousands who seek that unusual buy, the rare or eclectic, the whimsical, the mystic, and the historic, all in the confines of an old small town.

Banners on the old-fashioned street lamps proclaim Ellicott City to be "pretty comfy," "pretty tasty," "pretty historic," and "pretty unique." Town promoters obviously had a tough time deciding on one phrase and sticking with it. Not surprising, since Ellicott City is all these, and more. The oldest railroad station in America and a 1780 log cabin share Main Street with head shops, art galleries, and gourmet eateries.

On Main Street you can get fresh fudge, antiques, home furnishings, or hippie beads. There are bakeries and coffee shops, and a brewpub where you can see shiny copper equipment brewing authentic German beer according to the Reinheitsgebot of 1516, the German Purity Law for beer and the oldest food law in existence.

All these are housed in historic and colorfully painted row houses, a scene that provides the raw material for artists like Steven Stannard. A transplant from big cities, the architect by day/artist by weekend finds inspiration for his luminous oil paintings in the buildings lining Main Street, built in another era. "I love to paint the architecture of Ellicott City," says Stannard, whose studio is on the second floor at 8120 Main. "It's not Ocean City – it can get sleepy at times, but my inspiration is right outside my door."

Visitors entering the **Ellicott City B&O Railroad Station Museum** are greeted by costumed guides and taken through a 19th-century living history experience tracing the development of the nation's first railroad, and life in Ellicott City from 1827 to 1868. Built by black

Central Maryland

laborers and Irish and German immigrants making 50¢ a day, the B&O (Baltimore & Ohio) celebrates its 175th anniversary in the summer of 2003. When the station was built for the transfer of freight, not passengers, in 1831, it was at the end of the line of 13 miles of track from Baltimore. Remnants of the "turn-table" used to turn the engines around can still be seen outside. Visitors can enter an 1885 Freight House, climb aboard a 1927 Caboose, and watch award-winning films. While they no longer stop, freight trains still pass the station regularly. Open Friday through Sunday afternoons; Mondays and Thursdays in summer only. Admission: $4 adults; $3 students and seniors; $2 for children 12 and under; kids under two admitted free (☎ 410-461-1944, www.ecbo.org).

★ DID YOU KNOW?

In 1972, Hurricane Agnes caused quite a bit of devastation in Ellicott City. At the Trolley Stop Restaurant, for instance, the high-water mark was above the first floor doorway. But some good came out of the storm, with the formation of **Historic Ellicott City, Inc.** (☎ 410-461-6908). Its mission: to revitalize the historic district and preserve historic structures, including the restoration of the Railway Station and Thomas Isaac's Log Cabin.

Attractions

Ellicott City Firehouse Museum is in a firehouse built in 1889 at a cost of $500; it's just big enough to house one piece of horse-drawn equipment. They chose one of the handiest spots in the city, perched on a triangular piece of land right above Main Street. It operated as the home of Volunteer Fire Company No. 1 until 1923, when the department needed bigger quarters for the new motorized engines, and the house was converted to city offices. Open Sunday, 1-4pm by appointment; admission is free (3829 Church Road, ☎ 410-313-2602).

Inside **Thomas Isaac's Log Cabin,** historians portray living history circa 1770-1820 for visitors to this way station on the National Road, which facilitated the fledgling nation's westward movement. The 1780 restored cabin and the oldest remaining structure in Ellicott City, was built as a settlers cabin, and originally located on Merryman Street.

Open Saturdays, 11am-4pm, and Sunday, noon-4pm (Main Street and Ellicott Mills Drive, ☎ 410-750-7881).

Patapsco Female Institute Historic Park is an unusual attraction, the stabilized ruins of one of the most famous girls' schools in the 19th century (1837-1891). This was a time when young women rarely had the opportunity for higher education. In this remote place the lucky few studied botany, history, language, music and art. The Greek Revival structure sits on the highest point in town, overlooking the Patapsco River Valley, just two blocks from the Ellicott City historic district. Open Sundays, 1-4pm, April through October, and for a variety of special events throughout the year. Tours are given at 1:30 and 3pm. Admission is $4 adults, $3 students and seniors; children five and under are free (3691 Sarah's Lane, ☎ 410-465-8500).

★ TIP

The Hauntings of Ellicott Mills Ghost Tours promise "true" tales of hauntings in the historic district. April through August on first Friday and Saturday evenings, 8:30pm. $8 adults, $6 for children under 12 and seniors. Reservations required (☎ 800-288-8747).

Dining

Cacao Lane is a casual dining establishment in an historic 160-year-old stone building. The menu has various continental and American influences – French, Italian, and regional seafood (8066 Main Street, ☎ 410-461-1378).

In a town full of antiques shops, it's only appropriate that the **Crab Shanty** has taken off with the antique motif. Diners are surrounded by objects that once adorned Victorian homes: wooden spindles, carved brackets from stairways and gingerbread porch trim. Three dozen leaded glass windows from a Masonic Temple in upstate New York, old post office boxes, oak beams from a razed barn, and pieces of treadle sewing machines complete the décor. Items such as a sled Bing Crosby rode in the film *Holiday Inn* while singing *White Christmas* are all designed to create a warm, nostalgic atmosphere. The menu includes seafood, veal, chicken and beef for lunch and dinner. Sunday brunch is also offered (3410 Plum Tree Drive, ☎ 410-465-9660, www.crab-shanty.com).

Central Maryland

Ellicott Mills Brewing Co. has been showered with accolades for its restaurant and brewpub where you can watch the beer-making process from behind a glass window. The fare combines American and German favorites – Buffalo chicken wings and kassler dippchen (smoked pork chops) are both on the menu. The Alpenhof brews, from Bohemian pilsner to the heavy, dark Doppelbock, are made with ingredients imported from Germany (8308 Main Street, ☎ 410-313-8141, www.ellicottmillsbrewing.com).

Tersiguel's French Country Restaurant is in the 19th-century home of Ellicott City's first mayor. The "rustic country fare" is reminiscent of the owners' homeland of Britanny, France. Tersiguel's features fine dining in six individual dining rooms perfect for that romantic dinner for two or a private party for up to 50 guests. In season, produce comes from their gardens, edible flowers from their greenhouse, and chèvre cheese from their goat dairy (8293 Main Street, ☎ 410-465-4004, www.tersiguels.com).

Also on Main Street are **La Palapa Grill and Cantina**, with authentic Mexican (8307 Main, ☎ 410-465-0070); **Tea on the Tiber** for tea and desserts (8081 Main, ☎ 410-480-8000); and **Silver Arrow Fudge Shop**, with 36 kinds, freshly made (8167 Main, ☎ 410-465-0119).

Il Giardino Ristorante is a fine Italian dining experience where the specialty of the house, cioppino, is a medley of clams, mussels, shrimp, crab, calamari and fish over pasta (8809 Baltimore National Pike, ☎ 410-461-1122).

The Trolley Stop is in an 1833 tavern once known as "The Bloody Bucket." We're not sure where that colorful name came from, but we do know that the trolley once stopped right outside the second-floor dining room, hence the current name. The number 9 trolley ran from 1927 to 1955; its route is now a nature trail. The fare, primarily soups, salads, sandwiches, pasta, steaks and seafood, is moderately priced (6 Oella Avenue, ☎ 410-465-8546).

See also **Alexandra's Restaurant** at Turf Valley Resort under *Lodging*, below.

Lodging

Sink into a down comforter or a deep claw-foot tub for a bubble bath at **The Wayside Inn**. The inn has four guest rooms, including two suites. The Ellicott Room is named for a mid-1800s rendering of Main Street that hangs on the wall (4344 Columbia Road, ☎ 410-461-4636, www.waysideinnmd.com, $$).

Turf Valley Resort and Conference Center is a golf and spa get-away with more than 220 rooms, suites and golf villas. **Alexandra's Restaurant** has fine dining overlooking the golf green and serves a delightful champagne Sunday brunch (2700 Turf Valley Road, ☎ 410-465-1500, 888-TEE-TURF, www.turfvalley.com, $$).

 Forest Motel has 25 rooms and a pool, and accepts pets at no extra charge (10021 Baltimore National Pike, ☎ 410-465-2090, $).

Information

Howard County Tourism Council's Visitor Information Center is adjacent to the Main Street post office in Ellicott City. It's open Monday-Friday, 10am-5pm, and weekends, noon-5pm (☎ 800-288-TRIP, www.VisitHowardCounty.com).

Event

The **Garlic Mustard Challenge** began to help rid the Patapsco River Valley of the invasive garlic mustard weed. There's a contest for the most creative dish using the plant. Held the second Saturday in May at Patapsco Valley State Park Avalon Area (☎ 410-480-0824).

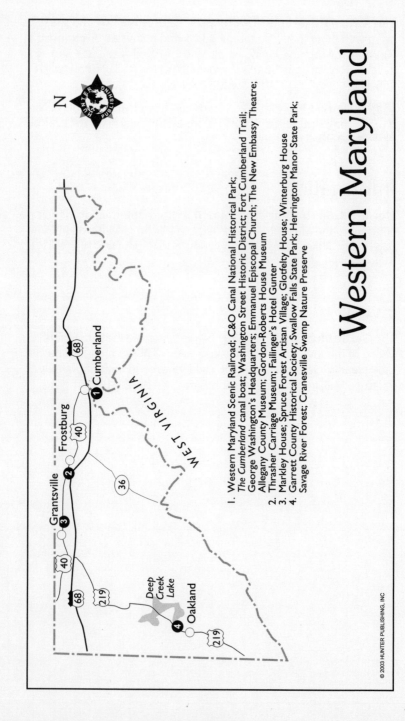

Western Maryland

1. Western Maryland Scenic Railroad; C&O Canal National Historical Park; *The Cumberland canal boat*; Washington Street Historic District; Fort Cumberland Trail; George Washington's Headquarters; Emmanuel Episcopal Church; The New Embassy Theatre; Allegany County Museum; Gordon-Roberts House Museum
2. Thrasher Carriage Museum; Failinger's Hotel Gunter
3. Markley House; Spruce Forest Artisan Village; Glotfelty House; Winterburg House
4. Garrett County Historical Society; Swallow Falls State Park; Herrington Manor State Park; Savage River Forest; Cranesville Swamp Nature Preserve

Western Maryland

I t's a thrilling trip on Interstate 68 into western Maryland, over the Eastern Continental Divide, over several mountains and
through the spectacular Sideling Hill gap,
where eons of geological history are displayed in a cliff of rock. West of the Divide,
you'll find a land where sparkling rivers flow
north instead of south, where vast state for-

THE TOWNS
▓ Cumberland
▓ Frostburg
▓ Grantsville
▓ Oakland & Deep Creek Lake

ests harbor multitudes of outdoor recreation, where the history of the
pioneer is a fairly recent memory, and where small towns are oases in a
land some might consider still quite wild.

Getting Here

I-68 passes through the region, providing easy access to the featured
towns of Cumberland, Frostburg and Grantsville. Oakland and the resort area of Deep Creek Lake are accessed via Route 219 south.

Western Maryland is served by the **Greater Cumberland Regional
Airport** (☎ 304-738-0002).

Regional Information

Allegany County Visitors Bureau, Western Maryland Railway Station, Cumberland, ☎ 800-425-2067, www.mdmountainside.com.

State Welcome Centers are located on I-68 near the West Virginia
border and at Hancock.

Cumberland

Around Town

A white Honda Civic pulls up to the C&O train station and out jumps a
young man. He quickly grabs a daypack, a small pair of sneakers and a

little boy from the back car seat. Dad looks at his watch, stuffs sneakers in the backpack and carries his stocking-footed boy across the parking lot, hurries up a flight of stairs and onto the train station platform. Dangling from the little boy's hand is a toy steam engine. It's 11:24 and the **Western Maryland Scenic Railroad** is about ready to leave the station.

Long-ago excitement of train travel is re-enacted daily in Cumberland, once the second largest city in Maryland, next to Baltimore. The National Road, our nation's first federally funded highway, started in this town, as did the Chesapeake & Ohio Canal, which hauled coal from the mountains of western Maryland to the east. At one time five railroads intersected here. The elaborate Queen Ann Station owned by the B&O Railroad had a dining room that seated 1,400 in which the Maryland governor held balls, and guests hobnobbed in game rooms and tennis courts. But when the heyday of railroading ended, so did the station. It was torn down in 1972.

Those days of wine and roses are long gone for Cumberland, but the railroad experience lives on aboard the Western Maryland Scenic, which departs from the fabulously restored **Historic Western Maryland Railway Station** for excursions, dinner trains and murder mystery trips. A 32-mile round-trip daily excursion through rugged mountains takes you to the small town of **Frostburg** for a 90-minute layover (see the *Frostburg* section, page 260). The train departs daily May through December, pulled by either a 1916 Baldwin steam locomotive or an early 20th-century diesel engine (and sometimes both!). Black smudges on engineers' faces are proof that the steam engine is indeed powered by coal. The train masters even wear the traditional striped denim overalls and caps (☎ 800-TRAIN-50, www.wmsr.com).

We usually travel on the cheap, but this time we went first class. The privilege of sitting in the Victorian dining car is well worth the extra money. Fresh flowers on the table, carved wood paneling, and lunch on a moving train make for a rare treat (it's offered on Sunday trips only). The journey begins and ends at the recently restored Historic Western Maryland Railway Station, built in 1913. Inside is the ticket office, the **Allegany County Visitor Center**, a restaurant and gift shop. On the ground level is the **C&O Canal National Historical Park Cumberland Visitor Center** where interactive exhibits tell the story of the canal (☎ 301-724-3655, www.canalplace.org).

Work is currently underway to "re-water" the last two miles of the canal so visitors can take boat rides and experience what canal travel was all about. You can see and board a replica of a canal boat, **_The Cumberland_**, at the Crescent Lawn Festival Grounds, a short walk from the

Railway Station; it's open for tours on weekends, 12:30-4:30pm, May-October.

Either before or after your train ride, take some time to explore downtown Cumberland. There are several great places to stroll, just steps away from the Railway Station.

Head to Washington Street, and turn left (west) across the tracks to explore the **Washington Street Historic District** on the **Fort Cumberland Trail**. While there's nothing really left of the 1755 fort, very detailed and informative markers along its boat-shaped outline where several blocks of large homes and a massive historic stone church now stand. The only building remaining that was associated with the fort is on Green Street. **George Washington's Headquarters** is a log cabin he used when he was a young aide to General Braddock.

Beneath **The Emmanuel Episcopal Church** are all that remains of the fort itself: its cellars, magazines and earthworks. The British Army used the fort during the French and Indian War, and it was commanded by George Washington for a number of years. The 1851 Gothic Revival towering stone church has an illustrious history itself. Louis Comfort Tiffany undertook its renovation in the early 20th century, creating three large stained-glass windows, carving the High Altar and designing the cross and candelabra. The congregation is still very active, with Sunday and weekday services (☎ 301-777-3364).

Next you'll pass the courthouse and its gargoyles, as well as large graceful homes with wrap-around porches. Stop midway on your self-guided tour at the **Gordon-Roberts House Museum**, where tea is served Victorian-style by a costumed docent as period music plays. The 1867 home was built for Josiah Hance Gordon, president of the C&O Canal. Open for tours and tea June through October: Tuesday-Saturday, 10am-5pm, Sunday, 1-5pm; the last tour is at 4pm (218 Washington Street, ☎ 301-777-8678, www.historyhouse.allconet.org).

Head back down Washington Street, back across the tracks, and the road changes names, becoming Baltimore Street, a three-block-long brick-paved pedestrian mall. Classical music is piped through kiosks and in the center are fountains, a waterfall and a stage for outdoor events. Grab a hot dog at **Curtis' Famous Coney Island** ("Famous Weiners since 1918"), or sit at an outdoor café table in front of one of several restaurants. Large department stores of the last century now house art galleries and trendy restaurants. Catch a film or play at **The New Embassy Theatre,** a 1931 Art Deco theater (49 Baltimore Street, ☎ 877-722-4692).

Don't forget to look up while peering in all the shop windows. Authentic examples of 19th- and early 20th-century architecture house these ground-floor shops and restaurants. On Thursdays and Saturdays the street is lined with fresh produce, flowers and baked goods for the **Farmer's Market**, 10am-2pm, June through mid-October (☎ 301-738-1093).

> ★ DID YOU KNOW?
>
> Washington slept here – three times. The young George Washington was a surveyor in Cumberland, then returned during the French and Indian War and the Whiskey Rebellion.

Attractions

Western Maryland Scenic Railroad: Reservations are recommended and, during October, are required. Recent ticket prices were $19 adults, $10 children ages 12 and under, $17 seniors. A first-class ticket (which includes lunch) costs $35 for adults, $15 children, $33 seniors. Departures are at 11:30am from Cumberland and return around 3:30pm, Wednesday-Sunday, May-September. Trips depart daily in October, with an additional 4:30pm excursion scheduled on some weekends. In November and December the train runs weekends only. Special events include train robberies, murder mysteries, dinner trains, a comedy express, and the Polar Express Christmas event, when kids are welcome to come in their pajamas for a bedtime story (☎ 800-TRAIN-50, www.wmsr.com).

The **Allegany County Museum** covers local industrial and transportation history of the area (210 S. Mechanic Street, ☎ 301-777-7200).

The Cumberland Theatre employs professional actors for its musicals and dramas (101 Johnson Street, ☎ 301-759-4990).

Dining

Choices for eating on the Baltimore Street pedestrian mall include the **Baltimore Street Grill**, known for great crab cakes (82 Baltimore Street, ☎ 301-724-1711); **Curtis' Coney Island Famous Weiners** (35 N. Liberty Street, ☎ 301-759-9707); and **The Oxford House**

Restaurant, which has an old-world atmosphere with a modern European menu (129 Baltimore Street, ☎ 301-777-7101).

Oscar's Food & Spirits has a "Georgetown" ambiance and an eclectic menu (1103 Oldtown Road, ☎ 301-724-7827, www.oscars.baweb.com).

A mile east of Cumberland at I-68, exit 46, are four unique restaurants, all in one spot. **Mason's Barn** has been serving home cooking for half a century (☎ 301-722-6155, www.edmasons.com); **Uncle Tucker's** is an 1819 brewhouse (☎ 301-777-7005); **Uncle Tucker's Pizza Cellar** serves wood-fired pizza and micro-brews (☎ 301-777-7232); and **JB's Steak Cellar** serves up steak and seafood (☎ 301-722-6060).

Lodging

The Inn at Walnut Bottom lends bikes to guests to ride the C&O Canal Towpath, after which you can arrange for a massage. The downtown inn has 12 rooms with antiques, telephones and televisions, and is within easy walking distance of the railway station and historic area. The inn operates a gallery with locally crafted art and crafts for sale. Children welcome (120 Green Street, ☎ 800-286-9718, www.iwbinfo.com, $$).

Terra Angelica has four rooms with fireplaces and cable television. It's located on nearly 250 acres where you can hike or fish in the stocked pond. Afternoon tea is served (14701 Smouse's Mill Road NE, ☎ 301-724-9110, www.terraangelica.com, $$).

 The Holiday Inn – Downtown is within walking distance of historic downtown and the railway station. Children 19 and under stay free; children 12 and under eat free with a paying adult at Harrigans Restaurant. Pets are accepted at no extra charge (100 S. George Street, ☎ 301-724-8800, www.cumberlandmdholidayinn.com, $).

Information

Allegany County Convention & Visitors Bureau, ☎ 800-425-2067, www.mdmountainside.com.

Events

C&O Canalfest takes place two days in mid-May at Canal Place with artisans, living history demonstrations, live entertainment and canal boat tours (☎ 301-724-3655, ext. 2).

During **Heritage Days**, the second weekend in June, Historic Downtown Cumberland and the Washington Street district are filled with more than 200 vendors, a carnival, antique car exhibits and children's activities (☎ 301-777-2787, www.alleganyartscouncil.com).

Frostburg

"I think that's a diesel engine whistle, honey," a mother says to her small son, obvious disappointment in her voice. They stand on a bridge over a single railroad track near Frostburg, eyes fixed on the bend where the big engine will come into view. Her son loves trains, she explains, and watching it pass beneath this narrow country road has become something of a daily ritual. "No, wait," she tilts her head to listen again. "I think it's the steam engine. Yes! It *is* the steam engine. Wonderful!"

It seems most locals and train enthusiasts waiting on the arrival of the **Western Maryland Scenic Railroad** know by sound alone the difference between a diesel and steam engine whistle. The scenic railroad uses both types, restored from early 20th-century use, but for some reason, nearly everyone thrills to see the coal-black steam engine chugging around the last curve, spewing steam and black smoke from its funnel-shaped spout.

The end of the line for the Western Maryland Scenic Railroad is a renovated depot in Frostburg. Dozens of passengers disembark for their 90-minute stop in this small city. But before shopping at trinket shops or heading to a café for a bite to eat, most watch the ingenious method used by railroads to turn their engines around at this dead-end stop. It's called a turntable, and it does look something like a giant record player (for those of you who remember *them!*).

In a nutshell, here's how it works: The engine is uncoupled from the passenger cars and proceeds a few hundred feet to the end of the tracks, an area surrounded by a circular moat and railing. A man in a booth engages a lever and, much like a lazy Susan, the turntable platform with the engine perched on top revolves ever so slowly, until the engine faces the opposite direction. Then another switch is thrown and the engine proceeds from whence it came, but diverted onto a parallel track. It passes the passenger cars and beyond them, switches back onto the main tracks, and proceeds in reverse until it's close enough to couple. When this daily scene is finished, passengers go about their sightseeing in the town that was established in 1812 as a stop on the National Pike.

> ★ TIP
>
> Tickets for the Western Maryland Scenic Railroad are purchased at the trip's start in Cumberland (☎ 800-TRAIN-50, www.wmsr.com). See the Cumberland section, page 258.

Around Town

It's a steep climb up a hill into downtown Frostburg, and many people prefer to stick around the depot itself during the layover. There's a row of shops in what used to be the Tunnel Hotel, built in 1850 as modest lodging for travelers. A tavern behind the hotel included a cave where the proprietor stored his alcohol. Today's shops – really a row of individual, rustic rooms with a porch running in front of them – each have a different theme: toys, candles, dolls, quilts, crafts, pottery, antiques and, of course, train souvenirs. The **Whistlestop Café** serves hamburgers, hot dogs, ice cream, and pork BBQ. Eat indoors or out on various decks and porches (Frostburg Shops By the Depot, ☎ 301-689-3676).

The Thrasher Carriage Museum is next to the depot and houses one of the best antique carriage collections in the country. More than 40 19th- and 20th-century horse-drawn carriages range from a 1914 milk wagon and a funeral wagon to the Vanderbilt Family Sleigh and President Roosevelt's inaugural carriage. They were all collected by local resident James Thrasher. Open Wednesday-Sunday, 10am-3pm, March-December; daily in October; January and February by appointment. Admission is $3 adults, $1 children 12 and up (19 Depot Street, ☎ 301-689-3380, www.thrashercarriage.com).

Up on Main Street you'll find more shops, restaurants and the **Failinger's Hotel Gunter,** a must-see landmark. The 1896 hotel was extensively renovated in 1987 by the Failinger family. There are 14 rooms for overnight guests and 19 long-term apartments, each room decorated in Victorian style and uniquely different. Mrs. Failinger really outdoes herself at Christmas, with several trees on every floor. Even if you don't stay here, they'll gladly let you walk up the grand carved oak stairway to a Victorian lobby, and go down in the basement to see their museum. At one time the train tracks went under the town, and coal cars came right under the hotel to deliver the fuel. You can also see a small jail used to house prisoners being transported over the Old Trail Road (Route 40) in the early 1900s. There's also a replica of a coal mine, several rooms of antiques and memorabilia found during the renovation, and a former game cock fighting arena, which doubled as a speakeasy during Prohibition (11 W. Main Street, ☎ 301-689-6511, www.hotelgunter.com).

Dining

The **Au Petit Paris French Restaurant** is one of finest restaurants in western Maryland, and has a great wine selection. The restaurant is decorated to resemble a Parisian café; the entrance hallway was once a city street that passed through the building (Main Street, ☎ 301-689-8946, www.aupetitparis.com).

The Acropolis serves authentic Greek fare with dishes from the childhood memory of owner Bill Diamond, a native of Greece (47 E. Main Street, ☎ 301-689-8277).

Gandalf's Restaurant & Pub serves exotic, organic and vegetarian fare from Ethiopian to Thai, along with micro-brews. Open for dinner Monday-Saturday (20-24 E. Main Street, ☎ 301-689-2010, www.gandalfs.org).

Princess Restaurant has been open since 1939 and is now operated by the family's third generation. The restaurant once served Harry Truman and his wife, Bess, in one of their casual diner booths, which bears a small plaque commemorating the visit (12 W. Main Street, ☎ 301-689-1680).

Tombstone Café, in a gothic-style stone building that housed tombstone manufacturers for more than a century, unabashedly proclaims it serves "food and drink to die for." Simple, yet eclectic gourmet food and coffee, and brunch served daily. Depending on the season, sit inside by the fire, or outside on the lawn (60 E. Main Street, ☎ 301-689-5254).

For a quick bite, **Kramer's Deli** offers gourmet sandwiches (105 E. Main Street, ☎ 301-689-5353).

Lodging

 Failingers Hotel Gunter is an 1896 hotel with 14 guest rooms, each decorated with a unique Victorian theme, and a museum in the basement (11 W. Main Street, ☎ 301-689-6511, www.hotelgunter.com, $).

The **Savage River Lodge** is in the heart of the vast 53,000-acre Savage River State Forest, just a few miles southwest of Frostburg. The 800-acre resort has 18 luxury cabins and a gourmet country restaurant. Some cabins can accommodate pets; there is a fee of $20 per night, which includes a gourmet pet treat, a game of Frisbee and a doggy Happy Hour on Saturday at 4pm in the meadow. You can hike, fish or get a massage – or hike, fish and *then* get a massage (1600 Mt. Aetna Road, ☎ 301-689-3200, www.savageriverlodge.com, $$$$).

 The Frostburg Inn is a motor lodge with 16 rooms. Pets can stay in the smoking rooms, with an additional fee of $5 per night. There's The Outback Lounge for dining and cocktails (147 E. Main Street, ☎ 301-689-3831, www.frostburginn.com, $).

Chain hotels in Frostburg include a **Hampton Inn** with an indoor pool and whirlpool (☎ 301-689-1998, $$), and a **Day's Inn & Suites** (☎ 301-689-2050, $$), both near Frostburg State University.

Information

Historic Frostburg, a Maryland Main Street Community, ☎ 301-689-6900, can provide information about lodging and dining, as well as history.

Allegany County Convention & Visitors Bureau, ☎ 800-425-2067, www.mdmountainside.com.

Grantsville

Around Town

We were initially told not to expect much from Grantsville. We're glad we ignored that advice. We found it a relaxing respite off Interstate 68, good for a stop-off or an overnight, mostly due to the existence of a private effort that dates back nearly a half-century. It's called the **Penn Alps Restaurant and Craft Shop** and its adjacent **Spruce Forest Artisan Village**, which offers visitors a glimpse of folkways and hand-made crafts.

If you spend the day browsing Spruce Forest's historic log cabins, where local artisans work in open-view, then spend the night at the nearby **Elliott House**, a delightful Victorian B&B, you're left feeling as if time has slipped back a century or two. The laid-back pace of the 19th century soothes 21st-century nerves. The rhythm of the loom or potter's wheel slows down your pace. The aromas of citrus, eucalyptus and coconut envelop your senses. It is a time to appreciate the meticulous handwork of how things were made before mass-production.

The dozen historic log and frame structures have all been relocated to this spot from within about a 20-mile radius. The late Alta Schrock, a Mennonite and native of the Allegheny Mountains, moved them here to create a market for local cottage industries and to preserve the hand-crafts, music, history and values of old.

Bird carver Gary Yoder works in the oldest building, the **Markley House**, which was built in 1775 in Pennsylvania and moved to Spruce Forest Village in 1985. After 30 years of carving, Gary has built up his skill to the point where it's hard to tell his intricately carved wooden feathers from the real thing. Nearly all his work is done for custom orders, fetching between $2,000 and $10,000 per bird. He doesn't sell anything here in his studio, but it's a great opportunity to see one of the country's master bird carvers at work.

If it's summer, a weekend or a holiday, you'll likely see weaver Ann Jones working at the loom in the **Glotfelty House**, which was constructed in 1776 near Pocahontas, Pennsylvania The rest of the year she's a public school teacher. For 27 years she's done her weaving here, making beautifully textured scarves, throws, pillows and other items. She searches the globe (via mail-order) for tantalizing yarns made of silk, cashmere, wool, interesting blends and plain old cotton and linen.

In the **Winterburg House**, built in 1820 as a stagecoach stop for the National Pike in Grantsville, you can see a potter at work. The aroma of fragrant herbs and oils greets you at the walkway to **Fernwood Soap**, where all natural and botanical soaps and lotions are made. On cold days there's a campfire outside with benches to sit and warm yourself.

As the sign at the entrance says: "We invite you to cross over to an old-time world of folkways, festivals, crafts and fine foods." There's also an historic gristmill on the property. Altogether, it's quite a little complex of preserved Maryland history.

The Spruce Forest Artisan Village is just east of downtown Grantsville. It's free of charge, open Monday-Saturday, 10am-5pm, May through October. But even in the off-season, you might find a couple of artisans at work as some of them work in their wood-heated studio cabins year-round (☎ 301-895-3332, www.spruceforest.org).

Dining

After exploring Spruce Forest Artisan Village, walk over to the **Penn Alps Restaurant**, where you can dine on country food inside. If it's a nice day, order "to go" and walk down to picnic tables set under tall, shady trees along the Casselman River. Your backdrop is the 1813 stone-arch Casselman Bridge, over which the National Pike's original route crossed. The Penn Alps Restaurant has been enlarged six times over the years, but the core of it is the last log hospitality house on the National Pike still serving travelers (125 Casselman Road, ☎ 301-895-5985, www.pennalps.com).

Hilltop Inn Restaurant & Lounge has daily specials of steak, seafood and Italian fare with a Friday fish fry and Saturday buffet (12336 National Pike, ☎ 301-895-5168).

Eastern Shore crabs in western Maryland? They're caught fresh daily in the rivers around St. Michaels and Hooper Island and rushed by truck to **Hen House Inc.,** four miles east of Grantsville on the National Pike (☎ 301-689-5001).

See also the Casselman Inn and Holiday Inn under *Lodging*, below.

Lodging

The Casselman Inn was built in 1824 to serve travelers on the National Road. You can stay in one of the rooms in the rustic hotel, or in the modern motor inn behind it. The restaurant in the first floor of the hotel has two dining rooms with fireplaces, and a sitting room filled with rockers. Your nose will lead you to the basement where there's a bakery with goods for sale as well as an antiques shop. There's a Sunday morning buffet, all you can eat for under $5. Open for breakfast, lunch and dinner Monday-Saturday (Main Street, ☎ 301-895-5055, $).

Adjacent to the Penn Alps, the **Elliott House Victorian Inn** has a storybook entrance through a pink archway into the restored 1870 home. It has four rooms in the main house and three river-view cottages with private decks. All have private baths. Fly-fish for trout right from the backyard, or arrange for a massage in your room (146 Casselman Road, ☎ 800-272-4090, www.elliotthouse.com, $$).

 The Holiday Inn is newly renovated, kids stay free and so do pets (reserved for rooms on the third and fourth floors, however). There's a fitness center, arcade, restaurant, and guest laundry (Route 219 North, ☎ 301-895-5993, $).

 Walnut Ridge B&B takes dogs only (no cats) in their cabin, but not in the main house. Add a $10 charge and be sure to have a copy of up-to-date vaccinations. Inside the main house are two guest rooms and a suite, with either a fireplace or a kitchen. There's even a player piano in the parlor. Outside there's a hot tub, gazebo, gardens and porch swings (92 Main Street, ☎ 888-419-2568, www.walnutridge.net, $$).

Information

Greater Grantsville Business Association, ☎ 301-895-3332, www.grantsvillemd.com.

Garrett County Chamber of Commerce, ☎ 301-387-4386, www.garrettchamber.com.

Events

The **Spruce Forest Artisan Village** hosts a summer music series Saturdays at 7:30pm, June-September, ranging from chamber music to Celtic, a bluegrass concert series and a summer festival and quilt show (www.musicatpennalps.org).

Oakland &
Deep Creek Lake

Around the Area

Fishing, sightseeing and hiking take visitors far afield in Garrett County, Maryland's mountainous western county. But historic Oakland, where Garrett County life revolves around small shops and services, keeps drawing them back.

We spent an afternoon browsing shops on Second Street in Oakland's historic district. Set off the main highway, the district is easily overlooked by hasty travelers looking for jet-ski rentals on nearby Deep Creek Lake. To miss this would be a shame. From old-fashioned street lamps flutter bright-colored banners declaring this "A Great Small Town." All the proof you need is found at the soda fountain on the corner of Second and Alder streets.

We weren't in the purchasing mood, but the town's book store, men's shop (in business since 1939), and handful of antiques shops and boutiques were stroll-worthy. The **Garrett County Historical Society Museum** houses a Victorian surrey, an 1873 hotel gazebo, and an extensive genealogical library. We were drawn to the museum by an array of local history books displayed in the window that tell the story of loggers, railroads and ghosts. The museum volunteer kept us enthralled with tales of Henry Ford and his Detroit buddies, who vacationed in the surrounding state parks. (Open May-December, Monday-Saturday, 11am-4pm; free admission; ☎ 301-334-3226.)

Then we headed out into Garrett County for some adventure in the mountains and waters north of Oakland where some truly unique sights await.

At Deep Creek Lake, when the Heise family opened the **Will o' the Wisp Motel**, they made only $14 during their first month. That was February, 1950. Looking for new ways of attracting winter visitors, they opened a ski resort. Their efforts solidly planted this area in the "four season" resort category.

Deep Creek Lake's 65 miles of shoreline today are packed with vacation homes, resorts and condos. Still, the area retains much of that 1950s family atmosphere and charm. There's lots of shopping, from local crafts to antiques, fishing and boating on the lake, rafting the "Upper Yough" (short for Youghiogheny River; the short form is pronounced "Yock" and the full name is "YOCK-a-gany"), golf, skiing, biking or horseback riding.

About 10 miles north of Oakland via Herrington Manor Road, are two state parks. The first thing you notice about **Swallow Falls State Park** (☎ 301-334-9180 or 301-387-6938) is the deafening roar of the Youghiogheny River. The next thing you notice is the marked stillness when you leave the river and enter a virgin stand of hemlock, a rarity in this part of the country. The park encompasses two falls – the park's namesake, and the even more spectacular, 63-foot high Muddy Creek Falls, one of the highest in Maryland. Henry Ford, Harvey Firestone and Thomas Edison used to camp at the base of the falls on their early SUV excursions in Model Ts. Hiking trails lead from the park to the very edge of the falls (dogs are allowed only on the trail on the opposite side of the river from the park). There's camping, picnicking and nature programs. Nearby **Herrington Manor State Park** has cabin rentals, a 53-acre lake and wooded trails (☎ 301-334-9180).

Savage River Forest is the state's largest forest, with 53,000 acres, about 10,000 of it designated "wildlands." There's primitive camping, hunting, fishing, snowmobiling, canoeing, mountain biking and hiking in this northern hardwood forest (☎ 301-895-5759).

 TIP

No alcohol is served or sold in Garrett County on Sundays.

Dining

In Oakland, **Englander's** is an old-fashioned grill and soda fountain that also sells antiques – 4,000 square feet of them, to be exact (corner of Second and Alder streets, ☎ 301-533-0000).

The **Cornish Manor Restaurant & French Bakery** is in an 1868 Victorian home with a fireplace in every room. Open for lunch and dinner, Tuesday-Saturday. Reservations required (Memorial Drive, just off Route 219 in Oakland, ☎ 301-334-6499).

On Deep Creek Lake, choices range from the hip and sometimes rowdy **Uno Chicago Grill**, with its "Honi-Honi Bar" (open daily 11am to the wee hours of the morning, ☎ 301-387-4UNO), to the quiet and refined **Four Seasons** at Will o' the Wisp, where Muzak plays in the background, and the menu is extensive and quite sophisticated. Open for breakfast, lunch and dinner daily (Route 219, ☎ 301-387-5503, Ext. 2201).

Between meals, try the **Copper Kettle Popcorn Factory** (☎ 301-387-5655) on the lake and, next to it, **Lakeside Creamery** (20282 Garrett Highway, ☎ 301-387-2580), where you can grab a cone or sundae and sit by the water (open summer only).

Lodging

Within walking distance of Oakland's historic downtown, there's the **Oak Mar Motel & Restaurant** (☎ 301-334-3965, $); and the **Town Motel** (243 N. 3rd Street, ☎ 301-334-3955, $).

At Deep Creek Lake, there's the **Will O' the Wisp** motel and condominiums (☎ 301-387-5503, www.willothewisp.com, $$); the **Carmel Cove B&B**, a former monastery with 10 luxury rooms (☎ 301-387-0067, www.carmelcoveinn.com, $$$); and many vacation rental homes. **Lake Pointe Inn B&B** is a late 1800s renovated lodge just feet from the lake and across the street from the ski and golf resort (☎ 800-523-LAKE, www.deepcreekinns.com, $$$$).

 All of the following accept pets: **Wisp Mountain Resort Hotel** (290 Marsh Hill Road, Deep Creek Lake, in McHenry, ☎ 800-462-9477, www.WispResort.com, $$$$); **Comfort Inn** at Deep Creek Lake (2407 Deep Creek Drive, ☎ 301-387-4200, $$); **Savage River Lodge** (1600 Mt. Aetna Road, Frostburg, ☎ 301-689-3200, www.savageriverlodge.com, $$$$); and **Swallow Falls Inn** (1691 Swallow Falls Road, Oakland, ☎ 301-387-9348, www.swallowfallsinn.com, $$).

 TIP

There are many places to stay in Garrett County; call the Chamber of Commerce and request the *Official Four Season Vacation Guide for the Deep Creek Lake Area* (☎ 301-387-4386, www.garrettchamber.com).

Information

Garrett County Chamber of Commerce, ☎ 301-387-4386, www.garrettchamber.com.

> **TIP**
>
> Contact the Maryland Department of Natural Resources to request the *Maryland State Forests and Parks* brochure, which has a thorough listing of the services offered in the more than 50 parks and forests in the state, ☎ 800-830-3974, www. dnr. state.md.us.

Trip Journal

The Sub-Arctic Swamp

The small lettering on Maryland's state map read, "Sub-Arctic Swamp." Even if we were avowed sun-worshippers, I knew we'd find a way to visit this natural area. The term was just so intriguing, and fun to say. What we weren't expecting as we entered the Nature Conservancy's **Cranesville Swamp Nature Preserve** on a hot summer day, was the cool, dense shade of a small tamarack forest, the country's southernmost stand of the only conifer to lose its needles in winter.

Mature tamaracks are the only conifer that turn color – a fiery, burnt orange – and lose their needles in fall. So dense an overstory does the interlocking branches create that virtually nothing grows beneath a mature stand. It's a scene straight out of my childhood in Upstate New York, where a tamarack forest was a wonderful place where I could run unhindered beneath a canopy of the trees, the dense shade leaving the ground free of troublesome clinging bushes. Needles fell in such numbers, it created a smooth carpet of long, amber quills.

There was a small pocket of tamaracks between the hills behind my grandfather's house. We kids found it a great hideout from the summer heat (and summer chores). Once we found the skeleton of a cow, partially hidden by the needles (the land had once been a dairy farm). We took the skull home, much to our mother's chagrin, and the find forever marked the tamarack forest as a mystical place. Grandpa loved the tamaracks as much as we did, for he named the dirt road leading to his new house Tamarack Hill.

My maternal grandfather was equally fond of this tree. A school principal, he tried his hand at writing nature and adventure articles. His article entitled *The Beauty of Tamaracks*, published posthumously in *The Conservationist* (Vol. 40, No. 3, November-December 1985), explained how the trees are typical of northern bogs and swamplands, having followed close behind the retreating glaciers, taking up residence in "moss-fringed kettles and tarns left by the ice.... But it is the beauty of the tamaracks, their ethereal grace and delicacy that fills me with delight. Twice my spirits have been lifted by the radiance of their golden glory, unexpectedly and by pure chance."

Of those two "incidents," one was on a Maine tidal river, the other 1,000 miles north on a Canadian river tundra. So imagine my surprise at seeing a stand of this northern tree here – south of the Mason-Dixon line!

This pocket of northern boreal forest dates to the last Ice Age. Although the glacial ice sheet did not reach this far south, it did push a cool climate and permanently wet conditions into the region. The glacier retreated north, but in a few high mountain valleys, frost pockets were trapped. The Cranesville Swamp, along with a handful of areas in West Virginia, are relics of a northern forest bog that remains 10,000 years after the last Ice Age.

Several well-marked trails traverse the small preserve and pass through distinctly different plant communities – from dry heath to conifer forest to wetland, where a boardwalk crosses the peat bog's carnivorous plants and sphagnum moss.

Living and traveling in the mid-Atlantic, we certainly don't get to see tamaracks very often. It's good to know there are a few nearby.

Cranesville Swamp Nature Preserve is located off Lake Ford Road near Cranesville, West Virginia. There are no facilities, just a board showing a map of the trails.

TIP

Cranesville Swamp Nature Preserve is not easy to find, so it's best to get the brochure with directions and trail map ahead of time. It's available from the Garrett County Chamber of Commerce (☎ 301-387-4386, www.garrettchamber.com).

Southern Maryland

S and cliffs and harbors are the dominant features of communities on the Chesapeake Bay side of this peninsula, while Potomac River wildlife refuges line the west side, where b ald eagles nest, just a short drive from the nation's capital. In between are small towns set amid acres and acres of golden soybean and corn.

THE TOWNS
▨ Chesapeake Beach & North Beach
▨ St. Mary's City
▨ Solomons Island

Getting Here

Route 301 is the north-south route through southern Maryland.

Southern Maryland is served by **Baltimore/Washington International Airport/BWIA** (☎ 410-859-7111, www.bwiairport.com).

Regional Information

A **State Welcome Center** is located on US 301 at Newburg, near the Virginia border.

Chesapeake Beach & North Beach

T he farms of Maryland are growing houses – McMansions some call them – huge new homes on small lots, laid out on grids. They sprout throughout northern Virginia and into central Maryland. Down on the peninsula of southern Maryland, the pace of suburban sprawl slows a little, but there's no doubt that it's coming. On the approach to

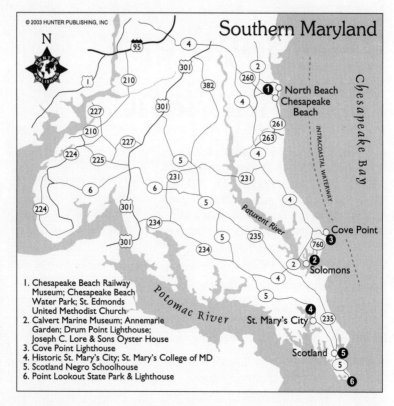

© 2003 HUNTER PUBLISHING, INC

N

Southern Maryland

1. Chesapeake Beach Railway
   Museum; Chesapeake Beach
   Water Park; St. Edmonds
   United Methodist Church
2. Calvert Marine Museum; Annemarie
   Garden; Drum Point Lighthouse;
   Joseph C. Lore & Sons Oyster House
3. Cove Point Lighthouse
4. Historic St. Mary's City; St. Mary's College of MD
5. Scotland Negro Schoolhouse
6. Point Lookout State Park & Lighthouse

Chesapeake Beach, tobacco fields are being turned into housing developments, commercial fishing centers into sport fishing getaways.

Around Town

As if anticipating the oncoming tide of homes and people, the town hangs a huge banner on the approach road, SR 260, that reads: "Chesapeake Beach – Welcome Home." Who could blame their enthusiasm? The homebuilding that started in the 1980s has revived what some would have called a ghost town.

Chesapeake Beach, 32 miles east of metro DC, marketed its proximity to the nation's capital long before the new homes started sprouting up. Back at the end of the 19th century, a Colorado entrepreneur named Otto Mears poured his own and his investors' money into building a railroad from DC to the beach and creating a resort. Arrow-straight SR 260 follows the former railroad bed.

On summer weekends, thousands of city-dwellers rode the rails to the beach to escape the humid city. Once here, they played in the water and sand, rode a roller coaster that was built on stilts right over the water, and walked the 1,600-foot boardwalk over the water. The boardwalk had a dance pavilion, carousel, and booths for vendors. A mile-long pier extended into the Chesapeake Bay to receive steamboat passengers from Baltimore. The resort was built to rival New York's Coney Island and New Jersey's Atlantic City.

North Beach sprang up north of the resort, linked by a trolley, with housing for those who wanted to rent summer cottages and for those who worked at the resort.

The heyday was relatively short-lived, however. The railroad went bankrupt in 1935, due in part to the Great Depression. But also the advent of the automobile and the building of the Bay Bridge over to the Eastern Shore meant city-dwellers could get to the more desirable ocean beaches under their own steam, rather than packed into hot train cars. Gone are the hotels, the roller coaster and the carousel – although that last amusement ride found a new home in a park in Camp Springs, Maryland. What really killed the amusement park in the 1970s was the outlawing of what had kept it thriving after World War II – slot machine gambling.

Today North Beach has a nice boardwalk, a bathing beach with a fishing pier, and some quaint boutiques and antiques shops, but it's still primarily residential. Chesapeake Beach also has a scenic boardwalk, a water park, restaurants and marinas, and is home to Maryland's largest sportfishing fleet.

One gem from the resort era remains. The **Chesapeake Beach Railway Museum** (see *Attractions*, next page, for additional information) tells the whole boom-and-bust story through exhibits, old photographs, and a short film. Outside the miraculously preserved railway station stands *Delores,* the railway's last remaining train car. Curator Harriet Stout believes the station escaped destruction, dilapidation and damaging remodeling because the amusement park used it as a storage facility for slot machines for decades, and in the process, kept it secure from vandalism and fairly intact. Ironically, while the station remains, all traces of the amusement park are gone, replaced by a housing development called Chesapeake Station.

The depot's greatest saviors were probably the owners of the Rod 'N' Reel restaurant next door (more about them on page 277). Early on, shortly after the amusement park closed, they saw it as a benefit to their restaurant and the community to have a museum on-site, and offered it to the Calvert County Historical Society for a 99-year lease of $1 a year. It opened in 1979.

The museum offers tourist-type brochures on the area, including other railway museums throughout the mid-Atlantic. "Within 100 miles of Baltimore, there's more railroad history than anywhere else in the country," says Stout.

Attractions

Chesapeake Beach is the charter boat capital of Maryland. Some of the outfitters are: **Breezy Point Charter Boat Association** (☎ 410-760-8242), **Chesapeake Beach Fishing Charters** (☎ 301-855-4665), or **Rod 'N Reel Charter Captain** (☎ 301-855-8450).

Chesapeake Beach Railway Museum is near the boardwalk in Chesapeake Beach. Open 1-4pm daily, May-September. Open weekends 1-4pm in April and October, by reservation at other times. It's handicapped-accessible and admission is free (☎ 410-257-3892).

Chesapeake Beach Water Park has a children's pool, slides, tubes, and giant floating creatures. Open Memorial Day to the first day of school, 11am-8pm. Admission is $14 for adults, $12 for children under 12; county residents receive a discount (☎ 410-257-1404).

St. Edmonds United Methodist Church was originally built of logs in 1865 to serve the African-American community as a school and church. The original burned and the present structure was built in 1893 (3000 Dalrymaple Road, Chesapeake Beach, ☎ 410-535-2506).

★ LOCAL HISTORY

It's believed the wooden horses on the Chesapeake Beach Carousel were carved by Gustav A. Dentzel of Philadelphia. The carousel was sold in 1974 to a resident historian in Prince George's County who saw an advertisement offering it for sale. It's now at Watkins Regional Park in Upper Marlboro (☎ 301-218-6700). The carousel operates 10am-7pm, daily except Monday in summer, weekends only in September; a ride is $1.

Dining

In Chesapeake Beach, **Rod 'N' Reel** restaurant is all about seafood. There's a Friday night seafood buffet and outdoor dining at the Boardwalk Café (☎ 410-257-2735, 301-855-8351 or 877-763-6733, www.rodnreelinc.com). Also at the Rod 'N' Reel dock is **Smokey Joe's Grill**, offering ribs and chicken (☎ 410-257-2427).

Abner's Crab House is a Chesapeake Beach favorite of local watermen, with a tiki and raw bar (3748 Harbor Place, ☎ 410-257-3689). **Chaney's on the Chesapeake** has a waterfront tiki bar, beach volleyball and horseshoes (8323 Bayside Road, ☎ 310-855-2323), and **Vic's Italia by the Bay** serves homemade ravioli, lasagna and wood-fired pizza (3800 Harbor Road, ☎ 410-257-1601).

The menu at **Lagoons Island Grille** combines the tastes of the Caribbean, Southwest and Cajun. Live music on weekends (8416 Bayside Road, ☎ 410-257-7091).

There are two Chinese restaurants: **Little Panda** (7863 Bayside Road, ☎ 410-257-2545), and **Peking, Inc** (3801 Chesapeake Beach Road, ☎ 410-257-3333).

Chesapeake Beach has two coffee shops. **Bayhill Accents** has tables inside and out on the deck, and sells gourmet food products and antiques (7544 Bayside Road, ☎ 410-257-2349). **One of a Kind Gallery and Espresso Bar** features an art gallery, framery, gift shop, and bakery in addition to the coffee bar (3725 E. Chesapeake Beach Road, ☎ 410-257-7580, www.artspresso.com).

In North Beach, there's the **Coffee, Tea and Whimsey** coffee shop (9122 Bay Avenue, ☎ 410-286-0000); a **Tastee Freez** (8831 Chesapeake Avenue, ☎ 301-855-0585); **Neptune's Seafood Pub** (8800 Chesapeake Avenue, ☎ 410-257-7899); and **Thursday's Bar and Grill** at the end of the boardwalk, serving steaks and seafood (9200 Bay Avenue, ☎ 410-286-8695).

Lodging

Bay Views is a waterfront bed & breakfast with a "whimsical, tropical flair." There's a third-floor waterfront suite and a smaller room overlooking the garden. Children 12 and older welcome (9131 Atlantic Avenue, North Beach, ☎ 410-257-1000, www.bayviewsbb.com, $$).

Serenity Acres Bed and Breakfast is a five-acre mini-estate about 10 miles south of Chesapeake Beach. Four rooms with private bath, and children are welcome (4270 Hardesty Rd, Huntingtown, ☎ 410-535-3744, www.bbonline.com/md/serenity, $$).

Breezy Point Beach & Campground is open May-October (Breezy Point Road, Chesapeake Beach (☎ 410-535-0259). **Breezy Point Cabins** is open April-November and has boat slips and a fishing pier (5230 Breezy Point Road, Chesapeake Beach, ☎ 410-535-4356, $).

There are no hotels in either Chesapeake Beach or North Beach. The nearest is the **Holiday Inn Express** in Prince Frederick (☎ 410-535-6800 or 800-565-8815, $$), where there are also a couple of B&Bs. However, the owners of Rod 'N' Reel restaurant have plans to build the **Chesapeake Beach Hotel and Spa** adjacent to the restaurant, right on the beach. Plans at the time of this writing were to be open for business sometime in 2003.

Information

Town of Chesapeake Beach, ☎ 410-257-2230 or 301-855-8398, www.chesapeake-beach.md.us.

Town of North Beach, ☎ 301-855-6681, www.ci.north-beach.md.us/index.html or www.nbeachmd.com.

North Beach Welcome Center, 9023 Bay Avenue, ☎ 301-812-1046.

Calvert County Tourism, ☎ 800-331-9771, www.co.cal.md.us.

Events

The **Antique Car Show** the third Sunday in May brings scores of classic car buffs to the Chesapeake Beach Railway Museum (☎ 410-257-3892).

The nicest homes are open to the public during the **North Beach House & Garden Tour** the first Sunday in June (☎ 410-257-6127). The **North Beach Bayfest** offers fun on the beach the fourth weekend in August (☎ 301-855-6681).

St. Mary's City

Around Town

It was a beautiful summer evening driving down the southernmost tip of St. Mary's County. We'd come on back roads past farm fields with their acres of gold-tinged corn, past glistening rivers, past small, snug inlets. We were thoroughly relaxed by the time we hit this rural peninsula, but in need of a town, or at least a hamlet. A place we could get out, walk around, maybe have a cold drink and a bite to eat.

We stopped to ask a couple walking their dogs along Point Lookout Road near St. Mary's College. St. Mary's River formed a storybook backdrop, surrounded by trees in full green leaf, with nary a building in sight. "Where's the town?" we asked. Did we somehow miss it?

Well, turns out there really isn't a town of St. Mary's in the way we think of towns nowadays, at least not since the turn of the century – the *17th* century, that is. **Historic St. Mary's City** is an active archeological dig and 800-acre living history museum. Like Jamestown in Virginia, St. Mary's City was the Maryland Colony's first 17th-century capital, from 1634 to 1695. But when the capital was moved to Annapolis in 1695, the city was abandoned, and soon virtually all trace of the "Metropolis of Maryland" was gone. Even at its height, the term "city" was pushing it a little. The 200 year-round residents were spread out on large plantations. Still, as the center of commerce, government and the courts for the colony, St. Mary's was the most populous place in all of Maryland for a time. It had the first printing press in the Colonial South and was the first to practice separation of church and state.

A new exhibit in the Visitors Center opened in 2002 tells the story of the Maryland Colony's first 60 years through objects recovered in the archeological excavations. Elsewhere in "the city," costumed guides help interpret archeological sites. You can see a re-creation of the ship, the *Maryland Dove*, one of two vessels that brought the first settlers from the Isle of Wight in England in 1634. They purchased land from the Wicomico Indians and started farming. Tour Godiah Spray's tobacco plantation, the re-created State House of 1676, and a Woodland Indian Hamlet. Stroll the miles of trails and rest by the St. Mary's River – it's a landscape that truly hasn't changed all that much in more than 350 years.

Southern Maryland

Historic St. Mary's City is open March-November, Wednesday-Sunday, 10am-5pm. Call for hours in the off-season. Admission is $7.50 adults, $6 seniors and students, $3.50 ages six-12 (Route 5, 800-762-1634, www.stmaryscity.org).

The Shop at Farthing's Ordinary is a gift shop adjacent to the State House (☎ 240-895-2088).

Attractions

If you continue past Historic St. Mary's City on Point Lookout Road (Route 5) to the tip of the peninsula, you will find some dining and lodging, and eventually come to **Point Lookout State Park** and **Point Lookout Lighthouse.** The historic 1830 lighthouse was purchased by the state from the US Navy in May 2002. State funding is in place to save and restore this unusual lighthouse, which will become part of the adjacent state park. The light is another of the eight lighthouses built by John Donahoo in the 1820s and '30s. It's not your typical, cylindrical tower lighthouse, but rather an iron tower perched on top of a square brick house. To track the progress of the renovations begun in July 2002, and keep updated on when it might be open to the public, visit www.ptlookoutlighthouse.com. There you can even sign up for the *Point Lookout Lighthouse News* e-mail list.

Even before the light was built in 1830, Point Lookout served as a position to watch for British ships during both the Revolution and the War of 1812. During the Civil War, there was a Union hospital and prisoner of war camp, where more than 52,000 Confederate troops were held. Today, Point Lookout State Park occupies this tranquil natural setting, offering camping, fishing, swimming and boating. A monument honors the 3,000 Confederate soldiers who died in prison. Fort Lincoln is an earthen fort built by the prisoners, and there's also a Civil War museum. The park is open year-round, 8am to sunset. The Civil War museum is open 10am-6pm, closed in winter (Route 5, Scotland, ☎ 301-872-5688, www.dnr.state.md.us/publiclands/southern/point-lookout.html).

St. Mary's College of Maryland is a state-supported liberal arts college with a beautiful campus on the St. Mary's River and about 1,700 full and part-time men and women students. It's adjacent to Historic St. Mary's City, which augments the college's programs of colonial history, archaeology, and museum studies, and boasts a rich history of its own. The college was founded in 1840 as a "living monument" to the first settlers of St. Mary's City who had vigorously practiced religious tolerance. Despite the religious-sounding name, it is non-sectarian (admissions, ☎ 800-492-7181; information, ☎ 240-895-2000; www. smcm.edu).

The **Boyden Art Gallery** on the St. Mary's College campus is open free to the public Monday-Saturday, 11am-3pm, featuring a permanent collection and changing exhibits. Located on the second floor of Montgomery Hall (☎ 240-895-4246). Each year the college hosts a free outdoor concert series and, for the past 30 years, the **Governor's Cup Yacht Race**, the Chesapeake Bay's longest overnight race, in early August. It starts in Annapolis Harbor and finishes the next day on the shores of St. Mary's River with an all-day party (☎ 240-895-3058).

Scotland Negro Schoolhouse is on land donated by a Quaker family for a public school for blacks in 1878. The building you see was a white elementary school that was moved from Carriage Lane Road in 1879 (Route 5, Scotland, ☎ 301-872-5655).

Dining

Ridge, a few miles south of St. Mary's City on Route 5, has restaurants, a marina and a yacht club. **Spinnakers Restaurant at Point Lookout Marina** serves gourmet, innovative fare in a casual setting. There's fresh seafood, of course, plus farm-raised game in the fall, with a waterfront setting, open mid-February-December. Much of the art and photographs displayed are for sale (Wynne Road, ☎ 301-872-4340, www.spinnakersrestaurant.com). **Courtney's Restaurant & Seafood** serves just that, along with steak and sandwiches (Wynne Road, ☎ 301-872-4403). **Scheible's Crab Pot Restaurant** (see Scheible's Motel, below) has waterfront dining and carry-out, open May-November (☎ 301-872-0028).

See also the Brome-Howard Inn under *Lodging*, below.

Lodging

The closest place to stay near Historic St. Mary's City is **The Brome-Howard Inn,** an 1840 farmhouse surrounded by woods with a beach (they lend guests bicycles to explore). Here, a guest enjoys candlelit dinners, fireplaces and views. There are five large bedrooms, two dining rooms, a parlor and library, all furnished with family heirlooms. Open for dining Thursday-Sunday, outdoors in season (18281 Rosecroft Road, Route 5, ☎ 301-866-0656, www.bromehowardinn.com, $$).

In Ridge, **Bard's Field of Trinity Manor Bed & Breakfast** is a 1798 waterfront home with a large porch, two fireplaces, three guest rooms, and access to boating, fishing and bird watching (15671 Pratt Road, ☎ 301-872-5989, www.travelguides.com/inns/full/MD/23861.html, $). **Longpoint Cottage**, also on the water, has two bedrooms, a wood-burning stove and a private beach and pier (Wynne Road, ☎ 301-872-0057, www.birdwave.com, $$).

 Scheible's Motel is a modest and inexpensive motel used primarily by those crabbing or fishing from their 500-foot dock, or going out on a fishing charter. The motel has eight rooms and accepts small pets only, no extra charge **Scheible's Fishing Center** boasts everything you need for a great fishing vacation (Wynne Road, Ridge, ☎ 301-872-5185, www.webgraphic.com/scheibles, $).

Continuing farther south just a couple of miles is the community known as Scotland (you'll also find California and Hollywood in St. Mary's County). Here there's **The Hale House Bed & Breakfast's** three rooms with private entrances and baths, panoramic river views, a pool, pier and a golf tee (open April-November, ☎ 301-872-4558, $$), and **St. Michael's Manor Bed & Breakfast** (1805) with four rooms furnished with antiques, water views, a vineyard, boating and swimming. Open mid-February through December (50200 St. Michael's Manor Way, off Route 5, ☎ 301-872-4025, www.stmichaels-manor.com, $$).

 Wide Bay Cottage has two bedrooms, a kitchen, and Chesapeake Bay views on a 95-acre farm; weekly rentals only (Route 5, Scotland, ☎ 301-884-3254, $$).

Information

Historic St. Mary's City, ☎ 800-SMC-1634, www.stmaryscity.org.

St. Mary's County Department of Economic & Community Development, ☎ 301-475-4411, www.co.saint-marys.md.us/tourism.

TIP

If you arrive when the visitor center is closed, the grounds of Historic St. Mary's City are open every day from dawn to dusk, so you can stroll at your leisure, no charge. Pets are allowed to walk with you on a leash, but are not permitted inside the exhibits.

Events

The **Historic St. Mary's City Farmers Market** is held on Fridays from late June through mid-September, 3:30-7pm, at Historic St. Mary's Church.

St. Mary's College hosts a free outdoor **River Concert Series** in June and July with the Chesapeake Orchestra (☎ 240-895-4107, www.smcm.edu).

Solomons Island

A s Bill and I finished our travels for this book, a longing for that perfect spot to end a long weekend took hold. Our goal was simple: To sit somewhere on the water, have a drink and toast our good fortune. There's a little bit of history here: I had in my mind the image of a perfect afternoon we had spent 10 years ago on the very first trip we took as a couple. Back then, we had logged a long day of driving the Outer Banks, ending with a ferry to the mainland and the tiny waterfront town of Beaufort, NC. We found a long dock on the water, lined with restaurants and shops. I have a picture I took of Bill – unshaven and suntanned, wearing a neon pink Bob Marley tank top, a bottle of Corona in his hand. Looking back, it seemed so carefree (back before we started writing about the places we visited, and travel became a little like work!).

Anyway, that's what I had in mind when I spotted Solomons Island on the map, a small fishhook-shaped piece of land, but neither of us had a clue what it would really be like until we parked the car and started walking around. Framed by the Patuxent River and the Chesapeake Bay, the island is separated from the mainland by a scant 23 feet. Along "Main Street," a boardwalk along the Patuxent River, we walked

Southern Maryland

slowly, letting a breeze cleanse and refresh after the stuffiness of an air-conditioned Jeep.

★ LOCAL HISTORY

The boardwalk, known as **Riverwalk**, features historic markers about the Governor Thomas Johnson Bridge that looms before you. It was named for the first governor of Maryland and opened in 1977. Another marker draws attention to the river's nickname, "Watery Grave." But it's not as morbid as it sounds. An S49 submarine lies at the bottom in 126 feet of water, intentionally blown up and sunk during military testing.

Around Town

It was a late Sunday afternoon in June; the sun had just started its slow summertime descent on the river. Up and down the boardwalk walked families with strollers, couples with ice cream cones, fishermen with tackle boxes. We too got cones from the stand perched right on the boardwalk and made a mental note, maybe for our next visit, that you can rent a skiff for an hour or a day. Across Solomons Island Road, surf and gift shops bustled, and seafood restaurants starting livening up with an evening dining crowd.

It was getting to be time for that perfect restaurant to appear. We had our dog with us – was it beyond hope that a restaurant with patio seating would admit animals? Timidly, I approached **Solomons Pier**, mostly expecting a curt "no" in reply. I walked out onto the pier that extended into the river and found an outdoor bar, umbrella tables and a pair of guitarists singing in the style of Jimmy Buffett. It was exactly what I had envisioned. The waiter's response to the dog question was "No problem." I couldn't believe it!

We grabbed a table close to the water's edge, ordered Margaritas and the house specialty, a "Beach Bucket" of fried clams, crab balls and shrimp. Out on the water, sailboats, personal watercraft and motorboats cruised the Patuxent River. A middle-aged customer, obviously enjoying the band and a few Coronas with his wife, blurted out spontaneously, "Are we in paradise yet?" This bearded fellow in sunglasses, a Jimmy Buffett T-shirt and flip-flops voiced my own feelings of the moment.

Billy Breslin and his brother Tommy called out for requests, and delivered on every one that came back. Someone wanted "something" by Gordon Lightfoot, so they sang *If You Could Read My Mind, Love.* Someone else asked for Buffett and they crooned *Come Monday.* Then there was Pure Prairie League's *Amy; Wild Night* by Van Morrison; followed by an unusual surprise rendition of the Rolling Stones' *Dead Flowers.* They also threw in some originals, humorous tunes on growing up in rural Maryland.

I like to think we could never have found a place or planned an experience any closer to that one 10 years ago. Solomons Island turned out to be the perfect ending to a hard day's work touring Maryland small towns. And it became the last town profiled in this book of travels. We hope you've enjoyed them as much as we have.

Attractions

The **Calvert Marine Museum** does a fabulous job preserving and portraying the history of maritime life on the Chesapeake Bay in general and the history of the circa 1870 fishing village of Solomons in particular. There's a restored lighthouse, a re-created salt marsh, river otter habitat, woodcarving shop, extensive museum exhibits and touch tanks, and you can even take a one-hour cruise aboard an historic oyster workboat.

The **Drum Point Lighthouse**, one of only three of the original 45 screwpile lights left on the Chesapeake Bay, was built in 1883 at Drum Point to mark the entrance to the river. Climb through the hatch and explore the restored interior. The museum is open daily, 10am-5pm. Admission is $5 adults, $4 seniors and children five-12. The **Wm. B. Tennison**, originally built as a sail-powered, log-hulled vessel in 1899, was converted to power and served as an oyster buyboat until 1978. One-hour cruises around Solomons Harbor and the Patuxent River depart from the museum dock at 2pm, Wednesday-Sunday, May-October, with additional weekend cruises in July and August. The cost is $6 adults, $3 children five-12 (14200 Solomons Island Road, ☎ 410-326-6691, www.calvertmarinemuseum.com).

From the Calvert Marine Museum, you can take a shuttle to the **Cove Point Lighthouse**, which they claim to be the oldest continuously operating lighthouse in Maryland. The 40-foot brick lighthouse was built in 1828 by John Donahoo, and has its original lantern, made in Paris in 1897. Open daily, June-August, with several tours daily; weekends and holidays only in May and September. Admission is $3 and is obtained through the museum (☎ 410-326-6691, www.calvertmarine-museum.com).

A half-mile from the museum you can see an actual seafood packing house. At **Joseph C. Lore & Sons Oyster House,** opened in 1934, learn about the boom and bust of the area's commercial seafood industry through exhibits of the tools of the trade and wooden boat building demonstrations. Open daily, June-August, 10am-5pm; weekends and holidays only in May and September. Admission is free (14430 Solomons Island Road, ☎ 410-326-2878, ☎ 410-326-2042, www.calvertmarinemuseum.com).

Annmarie Garden on St. John is a public sculpture garden on St. Johns Creek. Museum-quality artwork combines with nature's own for a quiet spot to reflect. Special events are held throughout the year. Pets are allowed, but not during special events. Open daily, 10am-4pm. Free admission (Dowell Road, ☎ 410-326-4640, www.annmarie-garden.org).

> ★ TIP
>
> The **Chesapeake Biological Lab** near the tip of Solomons Island has a Visitor Center where you can find out about their research on the ecology and status of the bay. Open April-December, Tuesday-Sunday, 10am-4pm (1 Williams Street, ☎ 410-326-7443, www.cbl.umces.edu).

Dining

For its small size, Solomons Island has a remarkable number of places to eat – about 20. **Solomons Pier Restaurant** can easily claim the best view around – you're surrounded by water on three sides on a pier extending into the Patuxent River. There are great sunsets out on the deck and live music most weekend evenings. Open daily for lunch and dinner, and Sunday brunch (14575 Solomons Island Road, ☎ 410-326-2424).

On the other side of the road there's a string of waterfront restaurants, all with views. For seafood there's the **Lighthouse Inn** (☎ 410-326-2444, www.lighthouse-inn.com); **Catamarans Seafood and Steaks** (☎ 410-326-8399, www.catamaransrestaurant.com); and **The Wharf Restaurant & Lounge** (☎ 410-326-3261). For authentic Italian, there's **DiGiovanni's Dock of the Bay** (☎ 410-394-6400). The

Tiki Bar (☎ 410-326-4075) on Charles Street is a popular hangout for cocktails and evening entertainment with its open-air Polynesian atmosphere.

Across the bridge on the mainland, waterfront restaurants include **The Dry Dock Restaurant** (☎ 410-326-4817); **Captain's Table** (☎ 410-326-2772); **The Naughty Gull Restaurant & Pub** (☎ 410-326-4855, www.naughtygullpub.com); and **Stoney's Kingfishers Captain's Grill** for breakfast and lunch (☎ 410-326-1036).

If you're not looking for a waterfront seafood restaurant per se, there's **Boomerangs Original Ribs** (☎ 410-326-6050); **Bowen's Inn** for steak, pasta and all-you-can-eat tacos on Thursday nights (☎ 410-326-9880); innovative cuisine and espresso at **The C.D. Café** (☎ 410-326-3877); and the New Orleans-style fare at **Harbor Sounds Restaurant** (☎ 410-326-9522, www.harborsounds.com).

Lodging

Back Creek Inn Bed & Breakfast is an 1880 waterfront inn with a private pier and seven suites furnished with antiques (Alexander Lane and Calvert Street, ☎ 410-326-2022, www.bbonline.com/md/backcreek, $$). Next door is **By-The-Bay Bed and Breakfast,** another Victorian with two rooms, a suite and a dock (14374 Calvert Street, ☎ 410-326-3428, www.chesapeake.net/~bythebaybandb, $$). Nearby is **Kathi's Cottage** with two rooms and a deepwater pier (250 C Street, ☎ 410-394-1939, www.kathiscottage.com, $$).

Down near the tip of the island is **Solomons Victorian Inn** overlooking Solomons Harbor, with eight guest rooms, some with whirlpool tubs and water views (125 Charles Street, ☎ 410-326-4811, www.solomonsvictorianinn.com, $$).

 TIP

Note that most of the B&Bs listed above indicate they accept children ages 12 and over only.

 Locust Inn Rooms welcomes children and small pets. Facing the Patuxent River, the inn has eight rooms and a pool (14478 Solomons Island Road South, ☎ 410-326-9817, $).

Motels include the watermen's favorite, **Bowen's Inn** with a bar, restaurant and dock (14630 Solomons Island Road South, ☎ 410-326-

9880, $). **Comfort Inn Solomons** has 60 rooms on the waterfront with marina, restaurant, pool and hot tub (Lore Road, ☎ 410-326-6303, $$), and **Island Manor Motel** has 10 rooms and is located behind the Tiki Bar and 77 Charles Street restaurant (☎ 410-326-3700, $).

Holiday Inn Select Solomons is a nine-acre waterfront complex with 326 rooms, a health club, pool, tennis, marina, and The Maryland Way Restaurant (155 Holiday Drive, ☎ 800-356-2009, http://solomonsmd.hiselect.com, $$).

Information

You'll practically drive right into the parking lot for **Solomons Island Information Center** as you exit Route 4, just before the Governor Thomas Johnson Bridge. Open daily, 9am-5pm (☎ 410-326-6027).

Solomons Business Association, ☎ 888-580-3856 or 410-326-1950, http://sba.solomons.md.us/.

Calvert County Tourism, ☎ 800-331-9771, www.co.cal.md.us/.

Index

Index